DAWN CUMMING

In Search of
✤Annalena✤

A Life of Tragedy and Triumph
in Renaissance Florence

Matador
9 Priory Business Park,
Wistow Road, Kibworth Beauchamp,
Leicestershire. LE8 0RX
Tel: 0116 279 2299
Email: books@troubador.co.uk
Web: www.troubador.co.uk/matador
Twitter: @matadorbooks

ISBN 978 1800460 799

British Library Cataloguing in Publication Data.
A catalogue record for this book is available from the British Library.

Printed and bound in the UK by TJ Books Limited, Padstow, Cornwall
Typeset in 11pt Minion Pro by Troubador Publishing Ltd, Leicester, UK

Matador is an imprint of Troubador Publishing Ltd

In memory of my dear Mum and Dad

and

given with love to my husband Richard,
my children Natalie and Mark, son-in-law Nic, daughter-in-law Tamie
and my grandchildren Finley, Delilah, Arabella and Neivah

Contents

List of illustrations

All photographs and diagrams are the author's own. Specific permissions are included below.

List of illustrations

Acknowledgements

This book is the result of many years in the making, since from its conception it remained dormant in my mind only to be reignited in more recent times. The beautiful city of Florence holds a special place in my heart and will forever do so. I am grateful that my 'love affair' with this city served to ensure that my initial desire to write the fascinating story of Annalena Malatesta would never leave me.

I am very grateful to the many people that have assisted me during the course of writing this book. I would particularly like to thank Ilaria Ciseri, Director of the Bargello Museum and Luisa Palli as well as Barbara Pini of the Museo del Cenacolo di San Salvi and Dr Rosamund Garrett formerly of the Courtauld Institute. I wish to express my appreciation for the assistance given by Professor Victor Coonin and Emeritus Professor Nerida Newbigin. I should also like to thank Alyson Price, archivist at the British Institute of Florence and extend my gratitude to Francesco Gurrieri in Florence and to Alberto Barelli at Sorci castle.

I am grateful also to the staff at the Pensione/Hotel Annalena for their hospitality over the years and for keeping the spirit of Annalena alive. I would also like to express my thanks to all of those other individuals who took the time to share their enthusiasm and knowledge which helped to contribute to the content of this book.

Finally, I would like to take this opportunity to thank my family and friends for their patience. At long last they will see the 'fruits of my labours' and hopefully may appreciate the appropriateness of the saying 'Good things come to those who wait'. I am truly indebted to my husband Richard since he has indeed been my soulmate on this journey. He has supported, assisted and encouraged me all the way. Without his help Annalena's story would never have been told.

Glossary

Tertiary   a religious woman of the 'third order' who has not taken the full
                  vows of a nun

Quattrocento   fifteenth century

Abbreviations

ASF   Archivio di Stato, Florence
BNCF   Biblioteca Nazionale Centrale, Firenze
V&A   Victoria and Albert Museum, London

Notes

In fifteenth century Florence, the new year began on March 25th, which means that from January 1st until March 25th, Florentine dates were a year behind modern ones. In this chronology and in the text of this book, I use the modern calendar.

Monastero – in the *quattrocento* the word was used to describe both male and female religious members; the word *convento* applied to males only.

A variety of names have been documented to describe the convent that Annalena founded. I use these interchangeably in the text and they include: '*Annalena convent*', '*Monastero di San Vincenzo*', '*Monastero di Annalena*', '*Monastero di San Vincenzo d'Annalena*', '*San Vincenzo di Annalena*', '*Monastero di San Vincenzo (detto Annalena)*' and '*San Vincenzo*'.

I use the terms 'companions', 'sisters', 'daughters', 'nuns' and 'Annalena women' interchangeably in the text to denote the tertiary nuns of the Annalena convent.

St. Mary Magdalen and St. Mary Magdalene may be used interchangeably. I have chosen to use the latter in the text.

Selected chronology

1389	Birth of Antonino Pierozzi (Archbishop of Florence), later St. Antoninus
1417	Pope Martin V elected
1420	Annalena Malatesta born
1433	*September*. Cosimo de' Medici and his brother Lorenzo exiled from Florence by the Albizzi faction, led by Rinaldo degli Albizzi
1434	*September 29th*. Cosimo de' Medici recalled to Florence
1436	*March 25th*. Consecration of the new cathedral of Florence; Santa Maria del Fiore
1437	*June 19th*. Baldaccio d'Anghiari made a Florentine citizen and given a house behind the present church of San Firenze (Palazzo Anguillara)
1438	*December 16th*. Baldaccio d'Anghiari buys a house in Via Romana that would later form the nucleus of Annalena's convent
1439	Ecumenical conference in Florence was held between the leaders of the Byzantine and Roman churches
	February 5th. Baldaccio d'Anghiari dowry arrangements for wedding
	February 7th. Annalena and Baldaccio's marriage contract signed in Contessa Elisabetta da Battifolle's house in Santa Felicita, Florence

1440	*June 29th.* Battle of Anghiari
1441	*May.* Guidantonio born to Annalena and Baldaccio d'Anghiari
	September 6th. Baldaccio d'Anghiari murdered
1445	*February 4th.* Annalena regains possession of her house that was originally purchased by Baldaccio in 1438
1447	Pope Eugenius IV dies
1448	*September 1st.* Death of Contessa Elisabetta da Battifolle
1449	Lorenzo de' Medici (the Magnificent) born
1450	Annalena travels to Rome in this Jubilee year under the protection of Cosimo de' Medici and obtains a brief from Nicholas V.
	September 16th. Guidantonio (son of Annalena and Baldaccio d'Anghiari) dies of plague after pilgrimage to Rome
	December 12th. Annalena is licensed by Pope Nicholas V to receive a cloistered community of Dominican tertiaries in her home
1453	*August 4th.* Annalena with twelve others take the cloth in the Dominican church of Santa Maria Novella in Florence. Annalena and her group officially became tertiary nuns
1454	Annalena formally establishes her convent
1455	*June 9th.* Pope Callisto III grants Annalena permission for a public Oratory to be built in her own home
1457	*November 22nd.* Neri Capponi dies (age 69)
1464	*August 1st.* Cosimo de' Medici dies
1475	*September 8th.* New Annalena church is consecrated by Francesco Soderini
1478	*April 26th.* Conspiracy of the Pazzi. Giuliano de' Medici, Lorenzo's younger brother, is assassinated; Lorenzo survives
1490	Savonarola begins his sermons on the apocalypse in the Monastery of San Marco, Florence
1491	*March 3rd.* Annalena Malatesta dies (aged 71)
	Following the death of Annalena, Maria Malatesta (Annalena's niece) becomes prioress of the Annalena Convent
1492	*April 8th.* Lorenzo de' Medici (the Magnificent) dies
1494	French invade Florence
1503	Caterina Sforza's son hidden in the Annalena Convent
1511	*January 11th.* Fire virtually destroys the Annalena Convent

Selected chronology

1545	Military fortifications built by Duke Cosimo I; this results in damage to facade of the San Vincenzo d'Annalena church
1563	Council of Trent
1571	Demolition of fortifications of Duke Cosimo I; the area associated with the Annalena convent complex is then left abandoned for many years
1573	Annalena and her two nieces re-interred in new tombs
1621	*March 2nd*. Nuns of Annalena convent acquire Ospedale di San Pier Novello dei Ridolfi
1701	Restoration of the church of San Vincenzo d'Annalena executed by A. M. Ferri. Interior renovated but antique layout of church survives
1786	Annalena convent remains active until this date and then changes into a *Conservatorio* for widows
1790	Marquis Tommaso Corsi buys land to build the first romantic garden in Florence (still known today as the Corsi Annalena garden)
1807	Luigi Gargani buys land that had belonged to the Annalena convent
1808	Napoleonic suppression of convents in Florence
1817	Goldoni Theatre opens on the site of the Annalena convent
1820	The *Casa d'Annalena* is purchased by General Macdonald of the French army who renovates it and then lives there with his wife, Napoleon's sister, Caroline Bonaparte
1919	Part of the palazzo is converted by the Calastri-Rossoni family and it takes the name of 'Pensione Annalena'
2019	Centenary of the establishment of the Hotel Annalena
2020	600th anniversary of the birth of Annalena Malatesta

From tears of sadness may you then go on to find tears of joy.

Dalle lacrime di tristezza puoi continuare poi a trovare lacrime di gioa.

BOOK 1

Introduction

I should have written this book many years ago when I first became interested in the life of Annalena Malatesta. In all honesty, I cannot remember exactly when this was, but suffice it to say that it was a very long time ago. My husband and I had fallen in love with Tuscany from our very first visit and in particular with the beautiful city of Florence. It is no exaggeration to say that it was as though the blindfolded cupid from Sandro Botticelli's great masterpiece, the *Primavera*, had struck us with his arrow since we were both instantly smitten and have been returning there ever since. In those early days we often chose to stay in the lovely Tuscan countryside and visited Florence on day trips. We would arrive early in the morning so that we could make the most of our time there, and more than often we would park our car on the steep road leading up to the beautiful part of Florence known as Bellosguardo which lies just outside the ancient city gate known as the Porta Romana, on the southern side of the city. We would then walk back down and enter the city through that very same gate.

The road leading from the Porta Romana into the centre of Florence is called the Via Romana and this was a road that we would come to know well. The Via Romana is located in a part of Florence which is known as the *Oltrarno* or literally 'across the Arno', the area to the south of the river Arno. In those early days tourists rarely found their way over to this part of the city. If they did, then they were usually lost or had chosen to stay at cheaper lodgings far from the city centre. In ancient times the Via Romana was the old pilgrim road leading to Rome and throngs of pilgrims would once have trodden along its path. In those days the route was lined with several hostels which served to cater for those pilgrims who would have exited the city from the Porta Romana (so called because of its position at the beginning of the route from Florence to Rome). Indeed, the Via Romana, from the piazza San Felice to the piazza della Calza, was known as the '*Strada degli Ospedali*' or 'street of hospitals' and it is still possible today to see the remains of some of these old hospitals and hostels that were once a feature of this part of the city. With its smattering of quaint artisan workshops and interesting historic dwellings, some of which still bear ancient, weathered coats of arms above their portals, this area still retains a charm that is fast becoming lost in other parts of the city. Over the years we have become rather fond of this part of Florence and I would even go so far as to say that I, in particular, have a great affinity with this area.

One place specifically that had always attracted my attention was the Pensione Annalena (now known as the Hotel Annalena; see **Figure 1**) which is located just opposite one of the entrance gates to the world-famous Boboli Gardens, only a few steps away from the magnificent Pitti Palace. I have no idea why I felt especially drawn to this building but for some strange reason I was. I rather liked the pensione's neoclassical facade which faces on to the Via Romana and the fact that the bulk of the palazzo building itself appeared to be set in a garden (quite a rare find in Florence). Each time I passed by I couldn't help but notice the stone plaque with the name '*Casa di Annalena*' ('House of Annalena') see **Figure 2**. This is next to the entrance door of the palazzo building, whose address is number 34, Via Romana. Additionally, slightly further along, above the entrance to a neighbouring *vivaio* (nursery garden) the words: *HORTI ANNALENAE* or the 'Gardens of Annalena' can be seen incised within a lintel.

I was soon to discover that the name Annalena actually extended well beyond the pensione and its neighbouring garden, since this area is still sometimes called the *Zona d'Annalena* or the Annalena area. Even the aforementioned entrance into the Boboli Gardens is known as the *Ingresso d'Annalena*, see **Figures 3 and 4**, alternatively known as the *Cancello di Annalena*, *Porta di Annalena* or Annalena Gate. Within the Boboli Gardens itself there is a grotto named the *Grotta d'Annalena* (also known as the *Grotta di Adamo ed Eva*), as well as a building nearby known as the *Palazzina d'Annalena*. Adjacent to the *vivaio* is yet another garden which incorporates the name Annalena within its title, since it is known as the Corsi Annalena garden.

I was intrigued... who was Annalena? Clearly, whoever she was, she must have been someone of great importance to the Florentines to have left her mark upon the urban fabric of the city, even today. I just had to find out more about the woman whose name still lives on in the city of Florence.

CHAPTER 1:

First encounters with Annalena

Back in the early days when we first visited Florence I vaguely recall seeing an information panel that had once stood close to the Pensione Annalena, which gave mention to someone called Annalena Malatesta and her associations with the building. The panel no longer seems to exist today and so it is possible that I am simply imagining this. Whatever the case, in a nutshell, Annalena Malatesta was a young Renaissance noblewoman who had suffered great tragedy in her life. Following the murder of her husband and the terrible loss of her son, the grief-stricken young Annalena chose to dedicate herself to God. She transformed her home into a convent, which incorporated the site of the present-day Hotel Annalena and its adjacent nursery and gardens.

I remember at the time feeling great sympathy for Annalena since her story was indeed such a tragic one. I just couldn't imagine how she could have carried on living, let alone found faith in God. From that moment on, her heartbreaking story was forever etched in my mind and I can remember scribbling down her name in my notebook with the intention of discovering more about her at a later date. It would, however, be a great many years later before I would seriously think about pursuing the story of Annalena further.

We have of course visited Florence many times since then and often for extended periods. However, despite my fascination with the story of Annalena Malatesta and the convent that she founded in the fifteenth century, we had never actually stayed at the Pensione Annalena. Do not misunderstand me, I had often suggested to my husband Richard that we should give it a try, but he was never that keen. I think the word *pensione* rather put him off and I have to admit that I too had my reservations. The word generally conjures up images of lodgings that are usually small and family run, perhaps even pokey and lacking in the facilities that a larger hotel might offer.

Although the Pensione Annalena had not been our hotel of choice in those early days, in my heart I still had a deep yearning to experience what it would be like to stay in that old historic palazzo. It was as though Annalena, like some siren, was luring me to this particular place, so eventually many years later we decided to give it a try. Needless to say, the Pensione Annalena soon became one of our favourite places to stay in Florence and we have returned there many times since. The actual building known as the *Casa di Annalena* itself has many a story to tell but none so fascinating as that of Annalena and her convent. Of course over the centuries the building has been modified and today it accommodates not only a hotel but also residential apartments, an architect's studio and a restorer's workshop. Despite all of the changes that have occurred one can still get a sense that this building has witnessed an interesting past from the minute you step inside from the street. Upon entering its dimly lit vestibule the visitor will notice a long corridor immediately ahead of them and may be forgiven for thinking they have entered into a church. Indeed, this building once incorporated part of the ancient Annalena convent church and I will discuss this at length in later chapters. At the end of the corridor some glass doors give access to the aforementioned *vivaio*, but the visitor must refrain from exploring this outside space since this is private property and doesn't actually belong to the pensione. Suffice it to say that this garden also has a secret past since it was upon this ground that part of the Annalena convent complex existed in the fifteenth century.

The actual Pensione Annalena itself can be found on the second floor of the building and can be reached by climbing a substantial stone staircase located on the right-hand side upon entering the building. Some large glass doors emblazoned with the words *Dallapiccola Annalena* welcome the visitor into an antechamber lined with four large, rather garish paintings depicting the seasons. The initial thought is that this must simply refer to the *'piccola'* (little) Annalena Malatesta, however, it probably alludes to the Italian composer and pianist called Luigi Dallapiccola who lived in the palazzo until his death in 1975. I was struck by the clever conflation of words which admirably describes the associations of the building with two of its most famous personages from the past. One then passes from the antechamber into the hotel reception area itself. In reality, this is a lofty-ceilinged lounge area which also serves as a sitting room and breakfast room. During our early visits, this public space had the atmosphere of a bygone era with its simple, elegant green velvet seats, sofas, objets d'art and a few pieces of antique furniture. Of course such decor may not have been to everyone's taste but I rather liked the charm of it all. Whilst contemporary hotel interiors with their minimalist furniture and decor can indeed be smart and elegant, they can also be rather impersonal at times.

Passing from the hotel reception to some of the bedrooms, guests may notice what appears to be a marble bust of a young girl resting on top of a rather lovely inlaid wooden cabinet. This I have been told is an imaginative artistic impression of the young Annalena Malatesta. Nearby is a sculpture of a crouching man which is by the sculptor Olinto Calastri who lived and had a studio at the pensione during the 1920s. Calastri was the son-in-law of one of the original managers of the pensione. Whereas most hotel guests might enquire about the opening times of museums or the best places to dine, the staff at the Hotel Annalena very quickly became accustomed to my frequent questioning about the history of the building and its associations with Annalena Malatesta. Of course, I asked them if they knew who had made the bust representing the young Annalena. They believed, although they weren't certain, that it too had been sculpted by Olinto Calastri. Naturally, I have gazed upon this bust many times and I have given careful attention to the way the sculptor had chosen to represent the young Renaissance noblewoman. The young girl's hair appears short but may be piled up at the back beneath her close-fitting cap and she wears a dress that is of antique style. Her head and eyes are slightly lowered and she appears suitably modest and beautiful as apparently Annalena is said to have been in real life. I have often wondered if the sculptor had worked from any reference source.

Over the course of several years of staying at the hotel we became quite friendly with a member of the staff called Ettore. When he first learned that

I was an art historian and that I was hoping to write a book about Annalena Malatesta he made sure that we were given room number 9, the 'writer's room' as he called it, whenever it was available. It just so happens that the Pensione Annalena has long been a magnet for writers over the years and several great authors, including the Italian poet and Nobel Prize winner Eugenio Montale and Carlo Levi, had found inspiration within its walls. Eugenio Montale had resided in room 9 during the 1930s with his glamorous American lover and muse, Irma Brandeis. Montale even composed a poem entitled '*Interno–Esterno*' ('Inside–Outside'), which describes one of the moments he spent with his lover in the pensione. Now, I must confess the love affair between the great writer and his glamorous muse had caught my imagination hugely and indeed I would have been intrigued to find out more had I not had Annalena at the top of my agenda. With such a literary heritage behind room 9, I hoped that I too might find great inspiration within its walls.

It has to be said that whenever we booked to stay at the pensione I hoped that the writer's room would be available for us. It had become a sort of talisman for me and it was as though no other room in the pensione could infuse my soul with the words and inspiration that I needed for writing my book. Fortunately, more times than not we were able to stay in room 9, and it became almost like a second home for us whilst we were in Florence. The room itself is fairly large by Florentine standards, and this sense of space is achieved mainly by its lofty ceiling. A rather ordinary candelabra light hangs suspended from the centre of the ceiling and adds to that feeling of space. The furnishings are simple and include a bed, desk, rickety wardrobe and a fridge that has seen better days. The bed, with its red and gold headboard and richly patterned bedcover, adds an element of charm and character to the room and saves it from appearing merely functional. A further accent of interest can be found in the rather lovely fireplace tucked within a recess. The fire would undoubtedly have been a fully functioning one at one time. Some tall French windows open out on to a terrace or balcony space and this is an absolute delight particularly in the cooler months when the dreaded *zanzare* or mosquitoes are at bay. It is here, overlooking both the adjacent Corsi Annalena garden and the neighbouring *vivaio*, that I have often sat collecting my thoughts about Annalena, scribbling notes or simply enjoying the warm sunshine and listening to the birdsong that fills the air. For us, the major appeal of the Pensione Annalena, besides its obvious associations with Annalena Malatesta, is its location, since it sits just on the fringes of the historic centre. It is far enough away from the 'madding crowds' but close enough to all of the major artistic and architectural sites. On a daily basis Florence strains to cope with the army of tourists that descend upon its streets. But here at the Pensione Annalena standing within its own little oasis of green it is still possible to capture a welcome breath of fresh air in an otherwise suffocating city.

Of course, from our very first stay at the pensione my interest in the life of Annalena Malatesta became even more heightened and it was from this point that I first began to seriously undertake research into her life. The pensione had a small brochure available for guests which gave a brief history of the palazzo and its associations with Annalena. From this I was surprised and excited to learn that Annalena had connections with the Medici family since it claimed that during her early life she had been adopted by Cosimo de' Medici (Cosimo il Vecchio de' Medici; 1389–1464). When I first read this, I was truly amazed since in all of the years that I had studied the history and art of the Italian Renaissance I had never encountered any mention of Cosimo de' Medici and his links with Annalena Malatesta.

Cosimo was a member of the House of Medici, the great banking family and political dynasty who came to rule over the city of Florence beginning in the fifteenth century. Italy in the fifteenth century was not a unified country but a collection of city states, each having their own character and government. Florence was one of the major city states. Florence was ostensibly a Republic but in practice after his return from exile in 1434 Cosimo became the 'de facto' ruler of the city and one of the richest men in Europe. Even if the visitor to Florence has never heard of the Medici family then they soon will, since this name is synonymous with Florence and their presence can be felt everywhere in the city. Such associations between the subject of my book and the great Medici family were indeed quite a revelation. With her noble status and connections Annalena must have brushed shoulders with some of the most important and wealthiest families in Renaissance Italy.

Interestingly, it was also written in the pensione brochure that much of the history of Annalena and her palazzo had been handed down by the Renaissance politician and writer Niccolo Machiavelli in his *Istorie Fiorentine* or *Florentine Histories*, which was written in the early sixteenth century. Most of us will be familiar with the term 'Machiavellian' meaning 'cunning', 'scheming' and 'unscrupulous' and may know that this term derives from Machiavelli's best known work, *The Prince*. He wrote this as a handbook for aspiring rulers and it remains one of the most famous and widely read Western treatises on politics. Machiavelli's lesser known work *Florentine Histories* does 'exactly as it says on the tin' since it tells the history of the city of Florence from its origin until 1492. It was commissioned by Pope Leo X in 1520 and it is Machiavelli's longest work and comprises eight books. It is within volume six that we find a brief mention of Annalena at the end of an entry relating to the murder of her husband Baldaccio d'Anghiari in 1441. Naturally, this would be a logical starting point for me to begin my research. I wanted to read for myself what Machiavelli had actually written about Annalena.

The assassination of Annalena's husband, as we will discover in a later chapter, was hugely entwined with Florentine politics and took place during the years of Cosimo de' Medici's ascendancy to power in Florence. The fact that Machiavelli actually recorded the episode suggests that it was considered to be significant in the history of the city. However, all that Machiavelli had written about Annalena was that she was left a widow at a young age and that following the loss of both her husband and her son she removed herself from the world to found a convent in the company of like-minded women. I was disappointed to say the least that Machiavelli hadn't included any biographical details about Annalena or any additional information about the convent that she founded. I suppose we should be grateful to him that he even mentioned her in his work since it is essentially a political history of Florence with no real mention at all of any artistic or social events. Sadly, it seemed that the life of Annalena was overshadowed by the more sensational story surrounding the murder of her husband. As I would discover, Machiavelli's take on the event would become almost a template for many other later accounts which would be written about Annalena.

The majority of sources that have been written about Annalena tend to be brief in content or are loosely based on fact. I was astonished to discover that no one had actually written a scholarly book wholly dedicated to her life and legacy. I soon came to understand why this should have been the case. From the outset, I would find that my task would not be an easy one, since very little is known with any certainty about Annalena's life. Few contemporary sources survive and many of the secondary sources are conflicting in nature. Furthermore, sadly, nothing really survives of the actual physical structure of the convent that she founded in the fifteenth century and there are scant contemporary sources that have survived related to this.

The Annalena convent, like so many other Florentine convents and monasteries that were established during the late medieval and Renaissance periods, were suppressed by the French in 1808. As a result the purpose and appearance of these convents and their sites, including that of the Annalena convent, were altered significantly over the years. Many ex-convents from the period were restructured as art centres, schools, museums, army/police headquarters and even prisons. At the time of the suppression many of their contents including precious manuscripts and artistic treasures were dispersed and either found their way on to the open market to be sold or were acquired by museums and galleries. Additionally, tragically, many original manuscripts that had belonged to the Annalena convent perished during a fire which virtually destroyed the whole convent complex during the sixteenth century. Furthermore, the only file in the Annalena archives that contained *quattrocento* (fifteenth century) documents related to the early years of the Annalena convent was damaged in the terrible floods that occurred in Florence in 1966 and is sadly not available for consultation. Also no records of any personal writings by Annalena exist to help understand her better.

In my capacity as a researcher I have therefore had to use those primary and secondary sources that are available, in order to create a plausible reconstruction of Annalena's life and her convent during the fifteenth century. The subject of Italian Renaissance convents and religious women of the early modern period has attracted a great deal of attention in recent years and there have been some excellent studies made in this field. This is one body of sources that I have made extensive use of to gain a better understanding of the subject and to further my knowledge about the convent that Annalena founded in Florence.

Additionally, I have had to rely heavily upon a work entitled *Notizie Istoriche delle Chiese Fiorentine Divise ne' suoi Quartieri* (*Historical Notes on Florentine Churches Divided into its Districts*) written by the eighteenth-century historian/antiquarian, Giuseppe Richa. Richa's *oeuvre* is basically a historical survey of Florentine churches and is contained within ten volumes. Richa appears to have been given rare access to some of the inner spaces of the Annalena convent complex and his notes concerning the early history of the convent can be found within volume ten. He provides some biographical details about Annalena and he also describes in some detail the convent that she founded. Interestingly, his account of the Annalena convent is longer and more detailed than many of the other churches in his survey including that of Le Murate which was the largest convent in Florence in the fifteenth century. Invaluable as Richa's work is, it is important to be aware that his account of the Annalena convent was written some three centuries after Annalena had actually founded her convent. By the time Richa visited in the eighteenth century it had been greatly modified. Additionally, he was able to use sources from the Annalena convent that no longer survive today, for example an account written by one of the sisters in the convent called Suor Laudomina di Ludovico Antinori written in the sixteenth century. Naturally, such information about the convent that was made available to Richa is vital for any study of the Annalena convent but sadly, since this information no longer survives, it means that it cannot be interpreted further today. In sum this serves as a vital reminder to us that the use of any source whether it be primary or secondary must be exercised wisely and with caution. To my knowledge, Richa's *oeuvre* is only available in the Italian language and of course it goes without saying that the translation of this work requires extensive labour on behalf of the researcher (unless he/she is fluent in Italian). I had to work laboriously to translate the relevant sections for my research. The translation of this vital historical resource into the English language would prove to be a more than useful project for any scholar of Italian Renaissance history, Italian language or Italian studies. At this point it is worth dwelling a little upon the translation of sources, since this would make up a significant part of my research. Many of the sources that I would have to deal with, whether they were in the form of marriage contracts, letters, *catasto* (Florentine tax records), convent documents etc., would be written in the Italian language and fifteenth-century vernacular Italian at that! Others, particularly those documents that had been recorded by notaries, would often be written in a fusion of fifteenth-century Italian and medieval Latin.

All of the research and translation of documents and manuscripts has been undertaken by myself. Unfortunately, since I am an independent art historian I do not have the luxury of having a research assistant to help with such work. I have spent many hours within some of the great bastions of knowledge both in Italy and in England and some of my favourite haunts were the *Archivio di Stato Florence* (ASF), *Biblioteca Nazionale Centrale di Firenze* (BNCF), British Library London, Courtauld De Witt Library London, Sackler (Bodleian library), Oxford and the Victoria and Albert Museum London (V&A). It would be in the ASF that I would examine a plethora of sources including fifteenth-century *catasto* records, convent records written in virtually indecipherable script and bound together in ancient ledgers, and ancient maps. At times the translation and interpretation of some of these sources would prove difficult and so occasionally I would have to seek the advice of eminent scholars in the field. For the reasons described above, the writing of this book has perhaps taken somewhat longer than I'd have hoped for. However, I rest satisfied in the knowledge that the research that I have completed has been undertaken with due care and attention.

As I probed deeper into finding out more about Annalena it became evident that she was a young woman who was quite remarkable in her own right. The convent that she founded actually became one of the most beautiful and important convents in Renaissance Florence and it has even been written by the academic Stefanie Solum that Annalena Malatesta was Florence's most important living female spiritual role model. With this information in mind I began to re-evaluate my own initial thoughts about this young Renaissance noblewoman. Yes her life had indeed been a tragic one, but from the depths of sadness something glorious had been born. Her story was not only one of tears of sadness but also one of tears of joy.

It was important that the positive elements of Annalena's life and her achievements should be recognised and celebrated. I now knew more than ever that it was my duty to tell a more complete story of her life and not only the tragic tale that had been popularised over the centuries. It was essential that everyone, including Florentines, should be aware of the important role that Annalena Malatesta had played in the history of the city. It is quite opportunistic then that the year 2020 also marked the 600th anniversary of Annalena Malatesta's birth.

The resulting book is one that is based upon a combination of academic research interlaced with a fictive voice to express the thoughts and feelings of Annalena herself. Although we will never know exactly what she may have said or thought, this 'voice from the past' as it were (which I have added in italics at the start of selected chapters) is entirely based upon my own speculations, which are rooted in my historical knowledge of the period and available surviving evidence. I have also endeavoured to provide a plausible insight into her life through those who were perhaps closest to her. Furthermore, this book is the story of my own personal journey in search of Annalena, and it has indeed been a challenging and fascinating one. A journey that has taken me down many routes and brought me into contact with many interesting people and places along the way.

Above all I have tried to live and breathe the air that Annalena herself might have done, visiting and exploring many of the places she may have known. One of the most interesting is the Castle of Sorci in the province of Arezzo, which was once the home of Annalena's murdered husband Baldaccio d'Anghiari, who is believed to haunt the place. My husband and I bravely spent the night there and quite literally 'lived to tell the tale', all in the name of research of course and I shall recount this experience in a later chapter.

CHAPTER 2:

The search for Annalena begins

I discovered that the Pensione Annalena brochure contained a few biographical details of Annalena Malatesta that would appear not to be from the hand of Machiavelli; I was puzzled, where had this information come from? I was aware that there may indeed have been some embellishment of the truth, after all it made for a fine story for the pensione, but there had to be some underlying basis for their claims. I endeavoured to find out more.

According to the brochure Annalena was of aristocratic birth, since her father was *Conte* (Count) Galeotto III Malatesta Lord of Rimini and her mother was *Contessa* (Countess) Maria degli Orsini. I had been able to confirm these details from a variety of other sources. The name Malatesta may be familiar to some and indeed, most scholars of Renaissance Italy will have heard of one of the main members of the Malatesta family, the infamous tyrant Sigismondo Pandolfo Malatesta (1417–1468) who was Lord of Rimini in the fifteenth century. The name *Malatesta* means 'evil-head' or 'wrong-head' and certainly there were many 'evildoers' in the Malatesta family. Many of the family were notorious for their crimes and cruelty. However, Annalena appears not to have inherited such malevolent traits. Like many of the celebrated Italian families, the Malatesta were divided into many branches and Annalena's family belonged to a secondary branch, namely the Ghiaggiolo, Cusercoli/e and Valdoppio branch. All these names are districts of Civitella di Romagna in the Romagna region of Italy.

Annalena's father Conte Galeotto III was born in 1375 and he was the son of Conte Niccolo (Nicolai) di Ghiaggiolo who in turn was the son of Ramberto, all of whom were *condottieri* or mercenary captains. Indeed, many of the male members of the Malatesta family were great mercenary soldiers. Annalena's father and his brother Malatesta had been orphaned at an early age and their guardian had been Galeotto I Malatesta Lord of Rimini who was the son of Pandolfo I Malatesta. It appears that following the death of his guardian in 1385, Annalena's father was later cared for by Carlo Malatesta in Cesena. Annalena's father is recorded as being in the service of the Florentines and in a document dated April 21st 1402 it is written that he had been placed in command of ten Florentine lancers in the war against Gian Galeazzo Visconti.

According to what was written in the pensione brochure, Annalena also had been orphaned at an early age since her mother had died in childbirth and her father died soon afterwards after being seriously injured in battle. I found this not to be entirely correct since Annalena's father appears to have died after 1441 at an advanced age, since the last known reference to him appears in a letter that he addressed to the *Podesta* (Mayor) of Galeata dated September 4th 1441. It may indeed have been the case that Annalena's mother had died in childbirth since women dying either during or following childbirth was commonplace during the Renaissance. However, to date I have been unable to confirm whether this may have happened to Annalena's mother. It had also been noted that Annalena had been raised in Florence under the care and guardianship of members of the Medici family including Cosimo de' Medici and I will discuss this in a later chapter.

One of the most fascinating pieces of information that I discovered relating to Annalena's father, was that he was a descendant of the famous feudal Lord Paolo Malatesta, known as *Il Bello* (the handsome), whose tragic love story with Francesca da Rimini was immortalised by the great Florentine poet Dante Alighieri in his literary masterpiece the *Divine Comedy*. Some of you may be familiar with this mysterious story of love and death since it has fuelled the imagination of countless artists and poets over the centuries. It certainly has been a tale that has captivated me, however, I would never have imagined that one day there would be a link with the subject of a book that I would be writing.

The story goes that Paolo Malatesta was murdered in 1285 by his brother Giovanni who suspected him of having committed adultery with his wife Francesca. The connection with Annalena's father is through Paolo's wife Orabile Beatrice the last Contessa of Ghiaggiolo whom Paolo had married in 1269. She was the daughter and heiress of Uberto the last Count of Ghiaggiolo and as a result Paolo's heirs were the Counts of Ghiaggiolo, which included Annalena's great-grandfather Ramberto and her grandfather Count Niccolo/Nicolai di Ghiaggiolo. Thereafter, there was a division of states and a new branch of the family was started with Annalena's father who became known as the Count of Cusercoli. Dante may possibly have seen or perhaps even had met Annalena's ancestor Paolo Malatesta when the latter was Capitano del Popolo in Florence from February 1282 to February 1283. It was exciting, albeit somewhat disturbing, to think that Annalena was a descendant of *Paolo il Bello* and that his blood ran deep within her veins. Interestingly, it has to be said that if this terrible episode had not been written about and made popular by Dante, then this secondary branch of the Malatesta family (Annalena's ancestors) would surely have slipped into complete oblivion.

It is not known exactly where Annalena was born although it is believed to have been either in Rome or Rimini. There is also uncertainty regarding her exact date of birth with most authors citing either 1416 or 1426. Based on a birthdate of 1426 Annalena would have been a mere child when she was widowed following the murder of her husband in 1441, indeed she would only have been fifteen years of age. Certainly, it was the case that females did marry young in the Renaissance and many women were widowed at a young age, however this later birthdate of 1426 would seem highly improbable. I hadn't been the only one to have questioned this later birthdate since one scholar had speculated that it must have been an error and that it was more probable that Annalena's birthdate should be the earlier one of 1416. Therefore, it is most likely that Annalena was older than fifteen when she was widowed but I will return to this matter in more detail in a later chapter.

Annalena's parents also had a son named Uberto who is sometimes known as Roberto and even Ramberto (I shall refer to him as Uberto from now on). Annalena's father also appears to have been the father of a further five children who were called Pandolfo, Antonio, Giacoma, Giovanni and Guido. Once more uncertainty surrounds who the mother or mothers of those children were. One thing that is known for certain is that Annalena was related to the Medici family, both on her maternal and paternal sides. Annalena's grandfather Niccolo/Nicolai was married to a Medici (the daughter of Vieri de' Medici) and Annalena's mother Contessa Maria degli Orsini is said to have been linked to the Medici through her maternal line. Additionally, Cosimo de' Medici was Annalena's godfather.

My research into the genealogy of Annalena Malatesta has led me to discover one of the most important sources for anyone wishing to know more about the ancestry of the major Italian families of the Renaissance period, namely Litta's *Celebre Famiglie Italiano*. This work, which consists of several volumes, was collated in the nineteenth century by Count Pompeo Litta who was himself derived from the noble house of Visconti of Milan. It basically is like a Debrett's and it has been described as 'Italian peerage on a gigantic scale'. I was delighted to discover that a set of the Litta folios was available in a library that was virtually on my doorstep namely, the Sackler library, which is part of the Bodleian library in Oxford. I had arranged in advance to consult the folios relating to several of the Italian families that I knew to have familial associations with Annalena Malatesta: Orsini, Medici, Guidi and of course Malatesta. I had used the Bodleian library previously but I had never been to the Sackler building before. On the day of my visit the library was a hive of activity and the librarians appeared to be run off their feet. As soon as I was able to I asked one of the librarians if the Litta folios were ready for me to collect. The librarian told me that indeed they were ready and I waited patiently as she dutifully disappeared into a back room to retrieve them. After what seemed to be an eternity but in reality was probably no longer than ten minutes, she reappeared from the back. I noticed that she was empty-handed; I looked visibly concerned, where were my books? My heart sank when she told me that she had been unable to access them. It transpired that a meeting was in progress in the room in which the folios were stored. Could I possibly return later? I had no choice, so I left the library feeling rather annoyed and whiled away the time by doing some unnecessary shopping. Seriously, did I really need to buy that new top?

I returned to the library after a couple of hours and as soon as I approached the reception desk the librarian with whom I had spoken earlier swiftly got up from her seat and with a broad smile on her face told me that the books were ready for me. In a blink of an eye, she slipped off into the back room once more. Second time lucky, within seconds she had returned carrying the most enormous tomes, indeed they must have measured over two feet tall. They were by far the largest volumes that I had ever encountered, with the exception of some ancient choir book manuscripts that I had seen in Italy. I watched as she gently eased the heavy volumes on to a nearby trolley and then wheeled them over to a desk for me to look at. Boy, was I relieved that I didn't need to carry them!

I followed her over to the desk and sat down. I thought it strange that the area allocated for the reading of rare books should be located in the busiest part of the library, right next to the information and reception desk in the foyer. I guess the reason for this was so that the librarians could keep their beady eyes on what was going on. I rummaged through my bag for my dictionary, magnifying glass, pencil and paper in readiness for the task in hand. It was going to be a long afternoon! I carefully lifted the folio, which was dedicated to the Malatesta family, from the trolley and slid it carefully, ever so carefully, on to the desk. It weighed a ton! With trepidation, I opened its enormous cover to reveal page after page of genealogical tables all painstakingly written in the Italian language and in miniscule print. The tables invariably spanned two pages at a time and charted the various members of the different branches of the Malatesta family, their dates of birth, death and when the family became extinct. There were also more detailed biographical pieces of information next to some of the names of the individual Malatesta family members and, just to break the monotony, as interesting as all this may be, there were a few pages devoted to the illustration of tombs, monuments and portrait medals, all beautifully executed.

With my magnifying glass in hand I scoured each genealogical table in turn in the hope of finding the name Galeotto III Malatesta, Annalena's father. Eventually, I did manage to find his name, which I am pleased to say was accompanied by a few additional snippets of information, which I diligently noted. Although, I didn't make any major discoveries I was at least able to confirm much of what I already knew. In particular, Litta had also noted that Conte Galeotto III had died after 1441 at an advanced age. Litta had also recorded that Conte Galeotto III had married Maria degli Orsini but he did not give a date of their marriage, nor did he give any further details about Annalena's mother. I observed that Litta had been one of those who had given the earlier date of 1416 as Annalena's birthdate.

There was also confirmation that Annalena's father did indeed have other children besides Annalena and her brother Uberto and each of their names were listed with a brief biographical entry. I was interested to read that Annalena's brother or half-brother, Antonio, had six children including three daughters: Bartolommea, Barbara and Iacopa, who went to Annalena's convent. I scribbled this information down knowing that it would prove useful at a later date when I would be writing about her convent.

Next I turned to the folio dedicated to the Orsini family who were an important and wealthy family from Rome, in the hope that I might find Annalena's mother's name listed. Once more I had to plough through endless pages devoted to the different branches of the family but sadly, I was unable to find any record of Annalena's mother's name. I then had to check out a couple of family names that had connections with Annalena and so I turned to the folios dedicated to both the Medici family and Guidi families, which proved to be more fruitful and I will explain my findings in the following chapters. After more than an hour of painstakingly searching through the folios, fatigue set in. My brain was awash with names and dates, and I was fast becoming cross-eyed from scanning page after page of miniscule print. It was no use, I just couldn't absorb any more. I had had enough and I was in need of some fresh air.

I leaned back in my chair, closed the volume in front of me and breathed a sigh of relief. As I did so, I observed that as the weight of the book's cover fell upon the pages inside, it released a puff of air and it was as though it too felt relieved that my task had finally come to an end. I remained seated for a few minutes and gently cupped the palms of my hands over my eyes; boy did it feel good. I then gently levered each of the folios back on to the trolley, and told the librarian that I had finished with them. In all honesty I felt glad to see the back of them!

In reality, this would not be the one and only time that I would have to consult these volumes since I would return to them often during the course of my research. It would, however, be the only time that I would see them on home ground, as it were, since thereafter I would use those in the BNCF (see **Figure 5**). I packed up all of my belongings and promptly left the building. It was a true delight to step out into the late afternoon sunshine. My eyes welcomed the break after the intense workout I had just subjected them to.

CHAPTER 3:

Annalena's birthdate revealed

In the hope of perhaps discovering more about the life of Annalena we headed for Florence. We had rented an apartment for a month in the lovely medieval street called the Via delle Terme, located just off the elegant Via Tornabuoni with its fashionable designer shops. On this occasion we had chosen to rent somewhere instead of staying at the Hotel Annalena, only because our stay would be of a longer duration than usual. The Via delle Terme is a charming, quiet street very close to the historic centre of the city and is named after the ancient Roman baths that were once located there.

I simply couldn't believe that we would be staying in Florence for a whole month and I often had to pinch myself just to make sure that it was really true. Our apartment was small, bright, modern and conveniently placed for all of the museums and galleries as well as the state archives and libraries that I would have to visit during our stay. From our kitchen/sitting room window, we could clearly see the crenellated top of the Palazzo Vecchio with its clock set within its slender tower that was built by Arnolfo di Cambio. I looked out over the sea of red terracotta roof tiles and across at what I knew to be the back of the loggia of the Palazzo Davanzati. This palazzo is one of my favourite places in Florence and I always recommend it to people when asked where they should visit. 'It's the best two euros that you will ever spend in Florence!' I would tell them. In more recent times this entrance price has been increased to the princely sum of six euros but it still remains excellent value for money! The palazzo was built for the Davizzi family in the fourteenth century and was later purchased in the sixteenth century by the Davanzati family. It is an example of the transition between a medieval tower house and a Renaissance palazzo. In 1956 the Florentine State opened it to the public as a most excellent museum. It is full of marvellous frescoes and furnishings and offers a glimpse into the domestic aspects of the Renaissance and really serves to bring this period to life. Although perhaps earlier in date, I imagine this to be the type of palazzo in which Annalena might have resided before she dedicated her life to God and built her convent.

Annalena was constantly on my mind and both our days and nights were consumed with my quest to find out more about her. Even my husband Richard had fallen under her spell. It is almost worrying when an interest develops into an obsession but that is what Annalena had become for me. I laughed nervously when my husband jokingly borrowed the infamous line used by the late Princess Diana saying that 'there were three of us in this marriage'!

One evening as we just happened to be trawling through the internet we discovered a reference to a very interesting paper written by the scholar and author Arnold Victor Coonin, Professor of Art and Art History. Its subject concerned some new discoveries linked with an important artistic commission that Annalena Malatesta had been involved with. Naturally, without hesitation I contacted him and he very kindly emailed me a copy of his paper together with some additional information that he thought might be of interest to me. I was particularly intrigued by a footnote that he had included in his paper which gave a reference to an entry for Annalena Malatesta in the Florentine *catasto* dated 1442. The *catasto* was a Florentine tax census which required all Florentines to provide information regarding their wealth. The fact that there was a *catasto* entry for Annalena obviously was of prime importance to me and the entry was one which I would of course have to draw upon. The detail held within this document could for example provide me with some more certainty regarding Annalena's actual birthdate. The Florentine *catasto* records are stored in the ASF and I had already decided that we should visit there the following day.

The very next morning I rose early and looked out of the window and with no exaggeration I was greeted by the most breathtaking sight. The sky was of a glorious, vibrant magenta hue. Dawn had certainly worked her magic chasing away the night sky! I gasped at the sight of the tower of the Palazzo Vecchio which stood silhouetted against the magnificent backdrop. It really was such a poetic experience and one which I would always remember. Indeed, it was one of those moments when it felt good to be alive. Feeling buoyant following such an inspirational start to the day it was business as usual as we set off for the ASF. It was a delightful September morning and because it was so lovely, we chose to take a slightly longer route than was necessary in order to savour the peacefulness of the city at this early hour and to explore a little. We strolled along Via Ghibellina in the area of the great Franciscan church of Santa Croce (Holy Cross), passing by the huge complex known as Le Murate which deserves a special mention here. The Benedictine convent known as Le Murate was the largest and the most important convent in fifteenth-century Florence and it has been of great interest to scholars in recent years. Le Murate means 'walled-up' and was so called because of the nuns who once lived there. The convent had been established by a small group of hermit nuns who had previously lived in small cells along the old Rubaconte bridge (replaced by the present-day Ponte alle Grazie). This bridge was often subject to flooding and the nuns were relocated to the new convent building on the other side of the river in 1424.

Le Murate is an excellent example of one of the convents which had changed both its purpose and aspect over the centuries following its suppression by the French in 1808. In keeping with the 'walled-up' heritage of this building this former convent even served as Florence's prison up until 1985 when it was relocated outside the city. In more recent years the complex changed its aspect once again when it became the subject of a creative and very successful architectural programme. As a result the former convent/prison is now home to shops, cafes, restaurants, open spaces and public housing. Indeed, this former convent site has become somewhere cool to hang out and enjoy a drink and a pizza! We had been on a guided tour of Le Murate the previous summer and had enjoyed learning about the history of the complex. I was disappointed, however, to discover that today nothing really remains to be seen of the fifteenth-century convent. Nevertheless, it was fascinating to see how much of the former prison including the actual prison cells had been incorporated into the residential accommodation.

Wandering around Florence I have become quite expert at spotting these former convents and it never fails to amaze me how much land these establishments actually occupied in the city. I can understand fully why modern architects have used and remodelled these establishments to suit modern-day requirements. Most tourists, and indeed even some Florentines, remain totally unaware that the building that they walk past, study in, dine in or even shop at, may once have formed part of an old convent complex.

Leaving Le Murate we continued on our way and within a few minutes we caught sight of the ASF building. This large, modern, light brown cement and glass building sits on an island in the centre of a very busy *Viale* (periphery road) near the Piazza Beccaria, just beyond the San Ambrogio area of the city. Originally, the vast archival collection, which dates from the eighth century to the present day, was stored in the Uffizi but following the disastrous floods in Florence in 1966 it was transferred to this new purpose-built building. It was a shame to leave the warm early morning sunshine behind us as we climbed the steps to enter the building, however, at the same time we welcomed the opportunity to leave the hustle and bustle of the traffic outside. Since this was my first visit (but certainly not my last) to the ASF we were required to show our passports to the staff at reception. We then took the lift up to the third floor of the building where the consultation, distribution and reading rooms are located. After signing in we were directed to some lockers where we could leave our belongings. Easier said than done, since it was almost impossible to find a locker that wasn't broken. After trying out each in turn we eventually found one which seemed to be satisfactory and we stuffed our belongings into it only to discover that it too was broken. We then found one that worked but it took all of our intelligence and more just to work out how to operate the combination mechanism. Just when we thought we had 'cracked' it, we carelessly forgot to note down the combination number making it totally impossible for us to reopen the locker. Out of sheer desperation we had to call on a member of staff to try to open it with a master key. Phew, after all this I actually felt quite worn out and I hadn't even begun any work yet! (I am relieved to add that on a recent visit to the ASF in January 2019, they were in the process of changing over to a simple, more normal… wait for it…'key in lock' mechanism. Clearly, we hadn't been the only ones to have struggled with the complexity of the former system.)

As if we hadn't suffered enough, I then had to learn how to circumnavigate the archive's mind-boggling classification system. We passed through the consultation room and we made our way up to a bright, raised area. A few scholars had congregated around a small number of desks with computers;

this appeared to be the nerve centre of the room. An officious-looking staff member, who was clearly the research officer on duty, was seated at a separate desk nearby. She was engaged in a lengthy discussion with a fellow researcher. We patiently waited in turn to speak to her, totally unaware that our wait would be a long one. We looked on frustrated as the woman suddenly got up from her desk and accompanied the researcher through to the back of the room. She rudely brushed past us without even acknowledging our presence. We were at a loss as to what to do next. Clearly, we must have looked troubled since a couple of assistants dressed in white lab coats appeared from out of nowhere and quickly took us under their wing. In my best Italian (and it needed to be, in such a scholarly place, otherwise one appears like a fraud), I explained that I had never used the archives before and that I was doing some research on Annalena Malatesta who had lived in Florence in the fifteenth century. The two assistants quickly led us over to one of the computers and they very kindly talked us through the process of obtaining a reader's card. Before long I was in possession of one and as soon as I had chosen a password it allowed me to access the online archive system. I was then shown how to use the classification system on the computer so that I could order any archival sources from distribution. Clutching both my passport and my newly acquired pass we then wandered over to the back of the room, which was lined with shelves containing an array of ledgers and files full of inventories and other archival listings. At a quick glance there didn't appear to be anything obvious that could help with my research on Annalena Malatesta. Once more I was at a loss as to what I should do next and again I sought the help of a member of staff. A certain Dottore Martelli came to my assistance. I had already been in contact with him via email with regards to visiting the ASF and arranging to view a document. Almost immediately he fished out a ledger from one of the shelves. It contained the inventory regarding the Napoleonic suppression of Florentine convents. A quick look through this revealed that, indeed, there was a section that contained records from the Annalena convent, but they were dated from the sixteenth century and later.

I looked down upon the reading room below and envied the rows of illustrious scholars poring through ancient manuscripts and documents. I had rather hoped that I would soon find myself amongst them, but this clearly was not going to happen instantly. Fortunately, I had arranged in advance to consult the main source that I had come to see, which was the *catasto* for 1442. Dottore Martelli had very kindly emailed me the relevant details for this including the microfilm number on which the *catasto* was stored. From my correspondence with him I was rather amused to be reminded that the word for reel in Italian is '*bobina*'; which is rather like our word bobbin. '*Bobina*' is such a lovely word!

The Florentine fifteenth-century *catasto* records are organised according to the various districts of the city. From 1343 Florence was divided into four *quartieri* (quarters or districts) and these were named after the main church of the district thus there were the quarters of San Giovanni with the cathedral and the Piazza della Signoria to the north, Santa Maria Novella to the east, Santa Croce to the west, and to the south of the river Arno, Santo Spirito. These quarters in turn were subdivided into four *gonfaloni*, literally banners, which were effectively neighbourhoods or districts. In 1442 Annalena was living in the Santo Spirito quarter of the city in the *gonfalon* known as 'Ferza', which included the areas of San Felice in Piazza and San Pier Gattolino. I typed in my request for the *bobina* which contained the *catasto* details for Annalena. Fortunately I could collect the microfilm immediately since it was stored in a nearby filing cabinet. At least something had worked in my favour! Within minutes I had collected the microfilm and an assistant led us over to one of the glass-fronted cubicles flanking the reading room so that we could view it. The reel contained the *catasto* records for both the 'Ferza' *gonfalon* of Santo Spirito and another called 'Nicchio'.

I have to confess that I am absolutely hopeless when it comes to the use of technology, even old technology as clearly this was! Thank goodness that Richard was on hand since he knew exactly what to do. He secured the reel into place, then fast-forwarded the tape, rewound it, fast-forwarded it once more then stopped it… and so on. The contents of the *catasto* were displayed on a screen beneath the projector and we excitedly searched through each and every name. It was no use; try as we might we just couldn't find the name Annalena Malatesta listed anywhere. In desperation, we scoured through the reel once more. Then much to our surprise and jubilation there it was in front of us: '*Chontessa Annalena*' (Countess Annalena) with a listing of her assets at the time the *catasto* had been conducted. Just the mere sight of her name brought me to tears. The *catasto* record of 1442 is one of the very few existing primary sources related to the life of Annalena. I had so longed to see evidence of her name and here it was.

It was almost impossible to read the miniscule, spidery handwritten entries in black ink and so we increased the magnification in the hope that this would help. Unfortunately, it still proved to be extremely difficult and even with the aid of a magnifying glass it remained so. With great effort I managed to decipher the contents before me. However, just to make sure that I hadn't missed some vital detail and to support my translation of the script, I sought the assistance of a member of the archival staff. Within the claustrophobic confines of the tiny booth the three of us, heads bowed, searched through the text before us. In unison we chanted out the words that we were able to make out. Then if ever there was a 'eureka' moment, it was this: before us were the words: '... *Annalena d'eta danni ventidue*' (Annalena aged twenty-two years); see **Figure 6**. At last here was the evidence which would clarify the confusion surrounding the exact birthdate of Annalena. We now know that Annalena was born in 1420 and that she was twenty-one years of age when she became a widow in 1441.

CHAPTER 4:

Who was Annalena's guardian?

'I do not remember a great deal from those very early years save for a memory of my father sweeping me up into his arms and hugging me tightly. I felt safe and secure within his strong embrace and I didn't want him to release me ever. I asked when Mother would return; at first he did not respond but he only pulled me closer. It was at this point that I would hear those ill-fated words for the first time: "Poverina Annalena" ("Poor little Annalena"). These words would remain in my mind forever. The journey to Florence was long and tedious but father tried his hardest to make it seem like an adventure for me. As we rode together on horseback he would recount stories of brigands and valiant soldiers. I cherished those moments of laughter and happiness. All at once, however, familiar landscapes soon changed into ones that appeared strange to me. Mostly I can remember feeling the warmth of my father's cloak as he wrapped it around me to ward off the night chills. It felt good to nestle close to him.

'As night became day we arrived at the threshold of a solid grey-stoned palazzo, which would soon become my new home. As my father gave me one final hug, I swear he had a tear in his eye but I cannot be certain. I recall asking him why he was so sad but he said nothing. He handed me something; it was a tiny book of hours and he told me that it had belonged to my mother and that

I should treasure it always. It was then that he told me that sadly my mother had departed from this earth and that she was now in the company of angels in celestial paradise. He assured me that one day I would indeed see her again. I have kept that book of hours and I have often found solace within its covers. Many a time I have gazed upon the image of the sweet Virgin found therein and substituted her face for that of my own mother or at least from what I think I can remember of her. In reality I have no memory of her except that she must have be kind and tender just like Our Lady.

  '*Every day I prayed to the Madonna that my father might return soon to take me home with him. Every night I would cry into my pillow only to be comforted by a countenance so gentle that soon found me drifting peacefully off to sleep. Months, indeed years passed, but my father never came back and I remember thinking that perhaps he never wished to see me again. To placate me, once more those who had been charged with my care and well-being furnished me with soothing thoughts. They told me that both my father and mother loved me dearly and that they thought of me constantly. They assured me also that one day my father would most certainly come to see me. Needless to say time passed, and that day would sadly never come. It soon came to be that with every hour the memories of that ever so brief episode in my young life would fade more deeply into the mists of time and it was as though I had stepped into another life, another world.*'

Annalena's early life is plagued with uncertainties and the matter of who really had been responsible for her care whilst she was in Florence is just one example. It is believed that following the death of his wife, Annalena's father, who is said to have been greatly engaged in war and politics and frequently absent due to his military commitments, must have felt that he was unable to look after his young daughter alone. He seemed to have thought it best that she should be cared for by his kin in Florence. It is not known whether Annalena's brother and the siblings (or half-siblings) also transferred to Florence at this time.

  Annalena arrived in Florence as a child and this would become her adopted city. This was where she grew up and lived all of her life. Most sources including the Annalena convent memoirs, which were probably written in the sixteenth century, claim that she was raised initially in the household of Attilio di' Vieri de' Medici who was a member of a distant branch of the Medici family. Other sources suggest that Annalena was later cared for by Cosimo de' Medici. The pensione brochure actually claims that Annalena had been adopted by Cosimo de' Medici and his wife Contessina de' Bardi. One other individual known as *Contessa* (Countess) Elisabetta da Battifolle has also been credited with being her guardian. I shall now consider each of these three candidates who might have played a vital role in shaping Annalena's life.

Attilio indeed had strong familial connections with Annalena. Firstly, his grandfather was Vieri de' Medici who was a distant relative of Cosimo de' Medici. It had been Vieri who had been responsible for the founding of the great Medici bank and indeed modern banking as we know it today. Vieri was one of the richest and principal citizens in Florence. Vieri's wife (Attilio's grandmother) was Bice de' Medici (1359–1433) who interestingly was of the Malatesta family. Attilio's mother, like Annalena's, was an Orsini. Additionally, Annalena's grandmother on her father's side was the daughter of Vieri de' Medici and therefore Attilio's aunt. Attilio's father Niccolo, sometimes known as Nicola, (1384–1454) together with his brother Cambio had inherited his father's banking business. Regrettably they didn't inherit their father's business acumen since their careers in banking ended up a complete failure and they lost any fortune they had inherited from him. It transpires that Attilio's father was an extremely learned man and was more interested in culture than in business. He was a friend of humanists including Leonardo Bruni, Leon Battista Alberti, Poggio Bracciolini and possibly Carlo Marsuppini. By 1427 Attilio's father was selling off his assets to pay off debts and in the ensuing years he and his descendants fell into poverty. Of course it is all relative and how poor they ended up is unclear. They may just have fallen from the upper echelons of financial wealth in the city. As well as his business and cultural ventures Attilio's father was also involved in the political life of the city and held offices in government. His roles in government, however, became more limited after the return of Cosimo de' Medici from exile in 1434 and as a result of the failure of his company. From my studies of the *catasto* records I had already discovered that Attilio's father was recorded as being age forty-three in 1427 and living in the quarter of San Giovanni in the ward of the Leon d'Oro. At that time he was widowed and there were thirteen people in total in his household.

Attilio followed in his father Niccolo's footsteps by pursuing a career in government and he held important political offices both in Florence and elsewhere in Tuscany. His political career climaxed with him attaining the role of *Gonfaloniere di Giustizia* (the highest office in Florence) in 1481. He married twice, firstly to Benedetta di Daniela Canigiani with whom he had three children and then to Agnoletta di Bernardo Soldani. Unfortunately, we do not have the exact date of birth for Attilio. However, on learning that his father had been born in 1385 alarm bells began to ring in my head. Could Attilio have been old enough to have been Annalena's guardian? Men of Niccolo's status generally would have been aged about twenty-five to thirty years at the time of their first marriage and based on this Attilio could not have been born before 1411. I will remind the reader that Annalena was born in 1420 therefore Attilio would only have been a few years older than her making it unlikely that he could have been her guardian. There doesn't appear to be an entry in the *catasto* dated 1427 for Attilio thus it is a reasonable assumption that he wasn't of adult age and was still part of his father Niccolo's household at this time. It is not known when Attilio married but it must have been after 1427. It is my conviction that it was Attilio's father's household in which Annalena might have been raised and alongside Attilio, rather than in the household of Attilio himself. It is possible that the reference found in the aforementioned convent memoirs may have been incorrectly transcribed and the name Attilio di' Vieri should have read Niccolo/Nicola di Vieri. This apparent mistake seems to have been perpetuated by authors over the centuries without examination or question.

If Annalena did spend any time at all in Attilio's father's household then it would have been for a brief time before 1427 when Niccolo is known for certain to have been a widower. Niccolo's mother, Bice de' Medici, lived for more than thirty years after the death of her husband Vieri and she may have helped to govern Niccolo's household. She may even have assisted in the care of Annalena. Bice de' Medici was by all accounts a remarkable woman; even at her death in 1433 the great humanist Leonardo Bruni praised her accomplishments during widowhood. He described her as being wonderfully kind: '… her charity towards her own, her affection to all…' Bice de' Medici would have been a more than suitable role model for Annalena or, indeed, any of the women who became part of that Medici household.

As to whether Annalena entered her godfather Cosimo de' Medici's household at a later date following being in Attilio's father's household, this is indeed an exciting prospect, however, sadly, I have been unable to find any documentation to support this. It is interesting that in 1421, the sons of Tommaso Portinari (an agent for the Medici bank in Bruges) were placed in

Cosimo de' Medici's household following the death of their father, therefore it is possible that Annalena may also have been cared for in Cosimo's household. If she did enter Cosimo's household then I believe this must have been of short duration and had to have been between 1427 and 1429. After 1429 Cosimo de' Medici was greatly engaged in the wars of Lucca (1429–33) and Milan and he wasn't even in Florence in 1430 since he left the city to escape the plague. He was also actively engaged in business both at home and throughout Europe during this period. It is my belief that the years after 1429 would also have been too disruptive for Annalena to have resided in Cosimo de' Medici's household and furthermore Cosimo was exiled in 1433. He was ousted from Florence by his enemies the Albizzi family led by Rinaldo degli Albizzi who disliked the economic, social and political power that the Medici family were beginning to hold in the city. Cosimo de' Medici and other prominent members of the Medici family were expelled from the city and Cosimo spent this time in Padua and Venice. Cosimo's exile was short-lived since he returned and was welcomed back to the city in 1434. Even when he returned from exile it would have still been too dangerous for Annalena (who would have been fourteen years of age at this time) to have stayed in his household since he was still in the process of building up his power base in the city.

If Annalena did spend any time at all with her godfather then it would have been in the Medici ancestral palace known as the *Casa Vecchia*, which lay in the same neighbourhood as that of Niccolo di Vieri de' Medici, that is the San Giovanni ward of the Golden Lion area of Florence. The new Medici palace which Cosimo commissioned from his favourite architect Michelozzo had not yet been built. Cosimo was passionate about culture and learning and was a friend of humanists and a great patron of the arts and benefactor of public works. Cosimo's household would have been an extended one which included not only Cosimo de' Medici and his wife and children but also his brother Lorenzo and his family, other relatives, tutors, doctors and secretaries. The *Casa Vecchia* was not just a home but it was also where the Medici had their central office and there would have been a constant stream of visitors to the palazzo. If Annalena did reside here at any time she would have been exposed to a great many influential and important people. Although we have no concrete evidence to support that she was cared for by Cosimo, as her godfather he would have played some part in her overall welfare. We know that he and indeed the Medici family would have a continued interest in her life.

The other individual who has been linked with the care of Annalena and, indeed, may have been her main guardian is the previously mentioned Contessa Elisabetta da Battifolle. Litta cites her as being the sole guardian of Annalena whilst she was growing up in Florence and gives no mention of Attilio or anyone else. Additionally, the author Carlo Brizio who wrote a historical novel about Annalena's husband Baldaccio d'Anghiari mentions that Elisabetta was the closest person to Annalena in her life. Contessa Elisabetta da Battifolle (sometimes written as Lisabetta) was the Contessa of Borgo alla Collina, a hillside village near Poppi in the Casentino, a fertile valley about twenty-five miles north-east of Florence. She was descended from the ancient noble lords of Guidi who were holders of territory in the Casentino. The Guidi family, like many aristocratic Italian families, had eventually split into different branches, which included the Counts of Poppi, Romena and Battifolle. Contessa Elisabetta's grandfather was Conte Simone II da Battifolle and her father was Conte Roberto di Battifolle. Contessa Elisabetta's father was known for his military prowess and his passion for culture and learning. Indeed, he had been a contemporary and friend of the great poet Petrarch. Contessa Elisabetta is also known to have been an intelligent woman and she had inherited her father's interest in antiquity.

After careful examination of Contessa Elisabetta's ancestry it would appear that she too was related to Annalena since one of her uncles, Carlo, was married to Margherita di Giovanni Orsini, a member of the Bracciano branch of the Orsini family. This association with a member of the Bracciano branch is important since it may suggest that Annalena's mother also belonged to this branch of the Orsini family. Contessa Elisabetta married twice, firstly to Ranuccio di Dolce da Montemarte and then to Giovanni di Messer Conte Gabrielli, a member of an ancient family of Gubbio; both had been great mercenary soldiers. She also appears to have been related to Annalena's father through the Dovadola branch of the Guidi family via her second husband's family the Gabrielli, who had married into both the Guidi and Malatesta families. Contessa Elisabetta was widowed firstly in 1392 and since it is known that her second husband was often involved in warfare, she appears to have lived much of her time alone; it is believed that she remained childless.

Contessa Elisabetta's family branch of the Battifolle (Guidi) had very interesting relations with Florence. In 1357 her father had signed a pact of 'accomandigia', which was a political and military contract meaning that in exchange for their loyalty and servitude the Battifolle would enjoy the perpetual protection and defence of Florence. Contessa Elisabetta would continue this tradition of servitude to the Florentines since she too would sign a similar contract in 1392. Although she was subservient to Florence, the Florentines appear to have held her in high esteem. She was considered to be a lady of great standing and of considerable strategic importance to the Florentine government and her name appears in many important leagues drawn up with other powerful Italians.

Contessa Elisabetta seems to have led a very colourful, albeit dangerous life, one which was embroiled in family feuds over the inheritance of goods and territory following the death of her father in 1375. The poor woman was terrorised by her evil cousin Roberto Novello who was the son of the Contessa's aforementioned uncle Carlo and his wife Margherita. Roberto Novello was Lord of nearby Poppi and in 1395 he besieged Contessa Elisabetta's castle at Borgo alla Collina and imprisoned her in his castle at Poppi. It was only thanks to the protection that she enjoyed from the Florentines that she was released. However, even after her release she continued to be tormented by her kinsman and one day whilst out on a hunting expedition she was attacked by her cousin. Litta provides us with more details about this terrible episode and adds that the poor woman was shot at by a shower of arrows which actually pierced her clothes. Fortunately, the Contessa managed to narrowly escape thanks to the speed of her horse and she would eventually take refuge in the city of Florence. Such in-fighting amongst the Guidi family branches would eventually bring about their downfall and ultimately open up their territories in the Casentino to Florentine domination in 1440.

My research has shown that Contessa Elisabetta was certainly residing in Florence in 1424 as she is recorded as living (in secular clothes) among the nuns of the Santa Felicita monastery (now lost) in Florence. She lived as a boarder at the monastery. As we shall later discover it was quite common for noblewomen to seek refuge in monasteries for a period of time. Based on this piece of information, Annalena therefore couldn't have been staying with her at this date.

A fascinating and curious anecdote related to Contessa Elisabetta's life at this time exists in the archives of the Santa Felicita Monastery, which tells of her helping a young noblewoman called Contessa Cecilia who together with her three children had taken refuge in and near the Santa Felicita monastery. Contessa Elisabetta appears to have assisted this woman and her children in 1423 by appealing to noble Florentine families for their support and Contessa Cecilia and her children were given a small house near the monastery. This information is useful since it serves to demonstrate the charitable side of Contessa Elisabetta and that she had connections with the noble families of Florence. An interesting artistic commission exists which I believe may relate to this episode in Contessa Elisabetta's life. It is an altarpiece known as *The Mystic Marriage of St Catherine*, which is traditionally believed to have been painted by an artist called the Maestro da Borgo alla Collina and is dated 1423. The altarpiece was given by Contessa Elisabetta as a gift to the chapel of her castle in Borgo alla Collina as a demonstration of her continued allegiance to her native land and it is also believed to have been a votive offering on her behalf. It has been said that a detail in the predella (the small narrative panel below the altarpiece), which includes the archangel Raphael leading a cloaked figure from a gateway, may possibly represent the Contessa Caterina da Romena, the cousin of Contessa Elisabetta. Legend has it that Caterina da Romena, who was the widow of one of the later Counts of Romena, together with her children had been cruelly treated by the Conti Guidi of Bagno. Like Contessa Elisabetta, her fellow kinswoman, she too had been imprisoned by her kinsmen. The Contessa is said to have been freed thanks to the intervention of the archangel Raphael. In reality it is believed that the Florentine Republic had apparently intervened and come to her aid. According to the legend both Contessa Elisabetta and Contessa Caterina lived together whilst in Florence.

Could it be the case that the name Contessa Cecilia that is mentioned in the Santa Felicita monastery documents was in fact Contessa Elisabetta's cousin Caterina da Romena? This would serve to support the detail depicted in the predella of the altarpiece. Of course it is possible that Contessa Cecilia did exist and that Contessa Elisabetta did assist her and her children but the fact that these two individuals were helped in the same way seems too much of a coincidence. The date 1423 which is inscribed on the altarpiece must commemorate the year Contessa Elisabetta assisted her and not the date that the altarpiece was painted. It is known that Contessa Cecilia (possibly Caterina) had requested help from Contessa Elisabetta's relative Beato Carlo da Montegranelli and he greatly promoted the cult of the archangel Raphael, which may explain the inclusion of this saint within the altarpiece. The archangel Raphael was also the patron saint of the Santa

Felicita monastery. The inscription on the altarpiece informs us that indeed Contessa Elisabetta had commissioned the work and reads: *Hoc opus istius capele fecit fieri egregia dna cometissa helisabeth de batte MCCCCXXIII die pma augusti.* It has been thought in the past that the altarpiece is likely to have been an offering of thanks from Contessa Elisabetta for the safety of her friend and kinswoman Contessa Caterina whom I believe to have been the aforementioned Contessa Cecilia.

In her role as protectrice for Contessa Cecilia (possibly Caterina), Contessa Elisabetta had shown great piety and kindness. Contessa Elisabetta seems to have inherited her religiosity and piety from several of her aunts who were nuns in the old convent at the monastery of Monticelli, which was located just outside the present-day Porta Romana in Florence. Her sister actually was elected abbess of that convent at the end of the fourteenth century. It is also known that Contessa Elisabetta raised her great-niece Gherardesca, the daughter of her nephew Conte Ruberto da Raginopoli who was a member of one of the major branches of the Guidi family. Contessa Gherardesca lost her mother in 1426 and had a father who went mad. Contessa Elisabetta had been entrusted with her care. When Contessa Gherardesca reached marital age it was also Contessa Elisabetta who gave her in marriage to a Florentine called Gualterotto dei Bardi. Contessa Elisabetta probably had done so in fulfilment of servitude to the Florentines in exchange for their perpetual protection. As we shall see, Contessa Elisabetta would also play a significant role in the eventual marriage of Annalena. From all that I've read about Contessa Elisabetta, she had a strong desire to help others and in particular young orphaned female family members.

From the *catasto* of 1442 we know that Contessa Elisabetta was residing in the Popolo of Santo Spirito in the *gonfalon* of Scala. Her entry includes a listing of her possessions, which included some estates in and around Florence near Impruneta. She is recorded as being seventy-five years of age when the *catasto* was carried out. The 1442 entry for Contessa Gherardesca is equally fascinating, since there is a connection with her entry and the monastery of Santa Felicita. I have also discovered that even in later years Contessa Elisabetta continued to have links with Contessa Gherardesca and, more significantly, Annalena. It is highly probable that both Contessa Annalena and Contessa Gherardesca would have known each other and perhaps had even grown up together in Contessa Elisabetta's household.

Annalena is said to have received a good education and was taught to read and write and was also probably taught Latin and the humanities. The Annalena convent memoirs mention that 'Annalena was educated in letters, and every other thing…' This reference to 'every other thing' probably relates to the fact that Annalena would also have been taught morals and received instructions in sewing, dealing with household servants and preparation for when she would become a wife and mother. All three of Annalena's potential guardians were passionate about culture and learning and her background would have been shaped by those around her.

In conclusion, I think that Annalena may have stayed initially in the household of Niccolo rather than that of his son Attilio up until 1427 and she may possibly have resided for a brief time in the household of Cosimo de' Medici between 1427 and 1429. However, unless any document is found that states otherwise, it is my belief that Contessa Elisabetta was closest to and played a greater part in the care of Annalena whilst she was in Florence. I am convinced that Contessa Elisabetta was actually Annalena's main guardian. I think it likely that Annalena entered Contessa Elisabetta's household from 1429 onwards. Contessa Elisabetta didn't have any children of her own and I rather think that she was desperately seeking to satisfy her deep-seated maternal instincts and therefore may have acted as a surrogate grandmother/ parent for Annalena. Contessa Elisabetta was a wise, intelligent woman who had shown tenacity, great piety, charity, determination and fortitude in her life. As we shall see these would all be qualities which would define the character of Annalena. Contessa Elisabetta was a woman so full of love and charity and I think she would have relished the opportunity to care for the young Annalena as though she were one of her own.

CHAPTER 5:

Growing closer to Contessa Elisabetta

I must confess that after everything that I had discovered about Contessa Elisabetta I found myself particularly drawn to her, much in the same way that I had to Annalena, and I felt a great desire to visit her territory in the Casentino. The connection between Annalena and a member of the ancient and important Guidi family had left me hungry to explore more. I also wanted to see for myself the altarpiece that Contessa Elisabetta had commissioned.

The Casentino valley is a part of Tuscany which is little visited by tourists today; even we had never visited the area before. Indeed, it is often referred to as *La Toscana Nascosta* (Hidden Tuscany). Amazingly, this beautiful countryside can be reached by car from Florence in about an hour. It is here in this land of the Guidi that the great fourteenth-century poet Dante Alighieri fought as a cavalryman in the Battle of Campoldino. During his travels through the Casentino valley Dante had even been a guest of Contessa Elisabetta's ancestors, the great Guidi feudal barons. Such was Dante's attraction to the Casentino valley that he describes the Casentino territory graphically in his greatest work the *Divine Comedy*, where he traces the course of the great river Arno from its source at Mount Falterona.

We had travelled from Bagni di Lucca in north-west Tuscany, and had planned to spend a couple of days travelling through the Casentino territory. As we drove, I mentally recorded the passing landscape which truly was quite lovely. A green, fertile valley unfolded before us with gentle slopes studded with forests, hidden monasteries and punctuated with ancient castles. We headed straight for Contessa Elisabetta's home town of Borgo alla Collina, which appeared more like a hamlet. I had imagined that it would be small but it was even smaller than I had expected. As we drove into Borgo alla Collina I noticed a church with its doors flung wide open. I felt the excitement grow within me; I knew that there could only be one church in such a small place and I hoped that this would be where I would find the altarpiece. It was almost 11.00am and I urged my husband to quickly find a parking place so that I could visit the church before it closed. Most churches in Italy usually close at noon (if indeed, they are open at all in the first place); there was no time to lose! I swiftly ran to the church, which was the parish church of San Donato, and as I entered, I was disappointed to discover how bare the interior was. Having said that, it made it easier to spot the altarpiece I had so longed to see. I quickly found it on the left-hand side of the nave above an extremely plain altar. I reverentially walked over towards the altarpiece (see **Figure** 7) and crept between the pews so that I could stand before it. Tears filled my eyes, I was so overcome with emotion. I gazed up at the central panel with the Madonna and child and noticed that the Madonna's robe was devoid of colour since it had obviously lost any pigment it ever had over the centuries. There remained only a hard, dark outline which was incomplete in parts. A nearby information panel reminded me that the Christ child was of the type described as '*Bambino Vispo*' or 'Wriggling Baby' and yes, here indeed was a real live baby in as much as it was represented as straining away from the Virgin to place a ring on the finger of the kneeling Saint Catherine who was dressed in a brilliant red mantle. It was, however, on seeing the inscription written in Gothic characters and scrolled across its surface just above the predella (see **Figure 8**) that I became overwhelmed with emotion. I couldn't believe that I was reading Contessa Elisabetta's name. I fixed my eyes upon each and every letter and numeral that lay before me which read: '*Hoc opus istius capele fecit fieri egregia dna cometissa helisabeth de batte MCCCCXXIII die pma augusti*'. This, indeed, made the whole thing real for me. I had of course previously seen a photograph of the altarpiece in a book but nothing could ever come close to seeing the actual work 'in the flesh' as it were. Standing before the altarpiece itself, I felt that I had been allowed access into Contessa Elisabetta's world and through her, Annalena. The fact that Contessa Elisabetta had commissioned this work and probably would have prayed before it made her presence tangible. In a similar way that the Madonna or the saints had served as intercessors to God for people during the Renaissance, the presence of Contessa Elisabetta through her altarpiece brought me closer to Annalena. She was my intercessor to Annalena.

I stood before the altarpiece for some time since I found it really difficult to part from it. I knew that I would probably never see it again since, undoubtedly, there would be no reason for us to return to Borgo alla Collina. This made me feel sad and I had to muster up the strength to walk away from it. Before leaving the church itself, I stopped to pay homage to one of the great celebrities from the Renaissance, the humanist Cristoforo Landino whose tomb can be found on the left-hand side of the inner facade of the church. His tomb is the main reason why visitors come to the church of San Donato. Landino had been the teacher of Lorenzo the Magnificent and afterwards he became the chancellor of the Republic of Florence. There just happens to be a connection between Contessa Elisabetta and the great Renaissance humanist since Cristoforo Landino spent the last years of his life in Borgo alla Collina. In the fifteenth century he had been awarded Contessa Elisabetta's castle by the Florentines for his services.

Stepping out into the hot midday sunshine we set off to explore Borgo alla Collina itself and in particular what would have been Contessa Elisabetta's castle (and later Landino's home). It was crazy to think that this pleasant little place once witnessed terror and cruelty. It didn't take long for us to locate where her castle had once stood, even although its appearance had changed significantly since she lived there. The castle was restored during the 1950s and now assumes a well-preserved aspect and is today the seat of the *Accademia Casentinese di Lettere-Arti-Scienze ed Economia*. Most certainly the castle would originally have been of a larger size than we see today and was probably surrounded by a moat. Before Contessa Elisabetta became the owner of the castle, which is sometimes referred to as *Il Palagio* (The Palace), it was used as a pleasure house or hunting lodge by the Guidi Counts.

Despite the restoration that has been carried out it is still possible to obtain some idea of what it may have looked like since a few ancient architectural features remain, including a rather lovely entrance doorway with a carved *stemma* or coat of arms above. We wanted to see what the back of the castle looked like and so we walked just outside the confines of the castle but still within range of it, then climbed down below a road and through a narrow tunnel. We emerged into some open fields with vines. In actual fact the aspect at the back of the castle is much more interesting from an architectural point of view since more of the original features can be seen including some ancient windows and lintels. I looked up at one of the windows and I imagined Contessa Elisabetta in happier times looking out over the countryside that would have belonged to her. However, such thoughts were very quickly replaced with the sense of danger that she must also have felt in this place, fearful that her evil cousin might attack her at any time.

I gazed over at the vineyards and plots of land given over to the growing of vegetables. In my mind's eye I replaced the vines with a thick forest and thought of Contessa Elisabetta out hunting on that terrible day when she narrowly escaped death. Almost immediately though, I erased such terrible images from my mind. It must have been a huge relief for her to have been liberated from the continual terrorising she had endured from her cruel kinsman. At the same time it must have been quite an ordeal to have been forced to leave her homeland and retire to the city of Florence; it must have seemed like a whole new world to her.

We returned to the front of the castle and I was in the process of busily scribbling down some notes when we noticed an elderly gentlemen and a lady (most certainly his wife) carrying some plants. They were making their way up to their house, which stood adjacent to the castle. I watched as the woman slipped into the doorway of the house and the gentleman made his way down towards a nearby workshop where he began chatting to another slightly younger man. I plucked up the courage to ask them if they could tell me anything about the history of the castle. I must pause here to add that I do have this terrible tendency to assume that everyone I meet in Italy has an in-depth interest and knowledge of Renaissance history! Unfortunately, they didn't really know anything at all about it except that there had certainly been connections with the Florentines. I had already espied a piazza close to the castle called the 'Medici Piazza'.

I asked them about some lovely carved *stemme* and some stone statues of lions that I'd noticed dotted around the entrance way leading up to the castle. At this point the slightly younger gentleman proudly patted his old friend on the back and told me that it had in fact been his friend who had made these. His friend then explained that only one ancient coat of arms remained and this was above the entrance door to the castle. As much as I had admired the elderly gentleman's work, I would have of course much preferred to have heard that it was from the time of Contessa Elisabetta. I very quickly remarked that he was a very talented man indeed to be able to carve with such skill. He was evidently touched by my appreciation of his work and he invited us to look around his workshop. Within a short space of time we found ourselves chatting in Italian about the art of stone carving. We learned that the area around Borgo alla Collina had a long tradition of this skill but sadly nowadays it was quite literally a dying art. The elderly gentleman, who was eighty-seven years old, was the only remaining stone carver in the area. He appeared to delight in this opportunity to reminisce with us about the 'old days' and proudly told us that in his heyday he had been headhunted to undertake important work in Florence. He then added: 'Today, I only demonstrate my skills at *festas*,' and he shook his head in dismay.

I glanced around at his workshop, which was full of skilfully carved statues, bas reliefs and fountains. They had all been carved using the beautiful, elegant bluish-grey type of sandstone known as *pietra serena* (literally 'serene stone') probably alluding to its serene blue-grey colour. This stone was made fashionable in Annalena's day by the great architect and engineer Filippo Brunelleschi. It was used mostly for internal and external architectural details. We chatted about the stone quarries that used to be worked at Fiesole, Settignano and Maiano in the hills immediately above Florence. In the Renaissance, *pietra serena* was quarried to the north of the Arno. We also spoke about *pietra forte* (literally 'strong stone'), that other great stone of Florence. This warm honey-brown type of sandstone was used to build many of the medieval palaces in the city giving them an appearance of fortitude and strength. This stone came from south of the Arno. The old gentleman then led us over to a small sculptural piece he had recently carved and proudly pointed out that it had been made from *pietra forte*.

On seeing the piece I was puzzled since it didn't look like *pietra forte*, it looked more like *pietra serena*. I watched as he wiped at a small area of its surface with his own spittle so that I could see the stone better. He explained that the colour change was due to a coat of silicon he had applied to the piece. He was clearly enjoying our interest in his craft and while I examined the object in more detail he suddenly produced an old black and white photograph from out of nowhere for us to look at. I instantly recognised the image; it was Michelangelo's famous statue of a 'Head of a Faun' dating from approximately 1489 and now lost. Michelangelo had carved it when he was very young and it had won him the patronage of the great Lorenzo de Medici. I noticed that the photograph was creased and crumpled; it had obviously been the object of discussion on many an occasion. 'I know where this is,' the elderly gentleman gleefully told us whilst pointing to the photograph of the statue. At this point I was convinced that he was going to astound us by announcing that he had the sculpture hidden away somewhere in his workshop. 'The Germans took it to Berlin and it is now in Russia,' he continued. I quickly breathed a sigh of relief that he hadn't been the one who had stolen the sculpture but at the same time I was a little disappointed that my name wouldn't go down in history as the person who had found Michelangelo's lost masterpiece! On this note we said our goodbyes and parted, then Richard and I headed for Poppi, the land of Contessa Elisabetta's ancestors, the Counts of Guidi.

The castle of Poppi sits proudly atop the town and its lofty bulk dominates the landscape enabling it to be seen from miles around. We had booked to stay in a hotel just outside the town for that evening. It was early afternoon when we arrived in Poppi and the place was deserted. We strolled beneath the shade of some enchanting ancient porticoes, which incidentally are a rare architectural feature in Tuscany, before making our way up to the castle itself. Poppi castle is one of the highlights in the Casentino valley and is certainly worth visiting since it is steeped in history. It is one of Tuscany's most important examples of medieval architecture. The castle was designed by the celebrated Di Cambio family of architects and served as the prototype of the Palazzo Vecchio in Florence, which was designed by Arnolfo di Cambio. Today the castle is in an excellent state of preservation since it has been greatly restored over the years. An enormous bronze bust of the poet Dante Alighieri greets the visitor on the approach to the castle. I shall remind the reader that Dante had been a guest of the Guidi Counts here. Sadly, Contessa Elisabetta didn't receive the same hospitality from her kinsfolk. I felt like a defector as we entered into what was once the stronghold of her evil cousin Roberto Novello since, as mentioned previously, it was within the walls of Poppi castle that he had imprisoned her. The Guidi family is omnipresent within its walls, and of particular note is the beautiful bas-relief sculpture in stone of Conte Guidi Simone da Battifolle (Contessa Elisabetta's ancestor) at the top of the stairs. He is shown with a shield and a sword at his side. It was Count Simone da Battifolle who transformed the castle at Poppi into one of the most beautiful in Tuscany.

Naturally being an art historian my favourite place within the castle was the Guidi chapel with its wonderful fourteenth-century frescoes depicting scenes from the Gospels. These have been attributed to Taddeo Gaddi, the leading pupil of Giotto di Bondone. One of the scenes from the fresco cycle, in particular, had caught my attention; this was the scene depicting the *Feast of Herod* with a figure of Salome dancing. Just as Salome must have captivated her audience with her dancing I too was captivated by the attention the artist had given to the details surrounding her dance; he had even depicted her clicking her fingers as she moved. Several years ago I had taught a course on dance in Italian Renaissance art and this particular detail would have been of considerable interest had I known about it. I made a point of photographing the image for future reference. Of far more significant value for my present purposes, however, was a detail within the fresco cycle which showed members of Contessa Elisabetta's family. Within the scene depicting *The Prophecy of the Baptist* in the *Annunciation of the Coming of Christ* it has been observed that there is a portrait of her father, Conte Roberto da Battifolle.

As much as the castle appears magnificent today and visitors like myself can admire its treasures through modern eyes, it must be remembered that Contessa Elisabetta would have regarded it very differently. Oh how she must have hated those cold, dense, solid walls that were once her prison. How she must have despaired never knowing if she would ever see the light of day again. I shall remind the reader that in 1440 the Republic of Florence took control of the Casentino including gaining possession of Poppi castle, along with other Guidi territories, when the whole area came under Florentine domination.

During our stay in the Casentino we visited several other strongholds that had once belonged to the Guidi Counts including the castle at Romena, which is where Contessa Elisabetta's cousin Caterina once resided, and the town of Battifolle and its castle: the namesake of Contessa Elisabetta's branch of the Guidi family. I say town, however, in reality there are only a small cluster of homes nestled high in the hills surrounding Borgo alla Collina. Some rubble and an old cistern are all that remain of the old Battifolle castle.

Some local inhabitants informed us that many of the old stones and other building materials that had been used in the construction of the ancient castle of Battifolle had actually wound up in their gardens.

I was pleased that I had taken this pilgrimage to the land of the Guidi Counts since I believed that I had inched closer to Annalena through Contessa Elisabetta. It had been important for me to gain an understanding of the person whom I am convinced played a significant role in the life of Annalena. In keeping with the analogy of 'foundations' I am certain that Contessa Elisabetta, who was much older than her ward, was her 'rock' and remained so until her death in 1448.

CHAPTER 6:

Growing up and living in Florence

'At times the household was full of people, many of whom would remain complete strangers to me, but there were also others whose faces I came to know well since they would visit often. I welcomed their presence since they would greet me warmly. Of course it is no lie to say that I hoped that one day my father would be amongst those who graced our threshold. I understood nothing of the conversations that filled the air and thus I would oft slip off into another "camera" within the palazzo. It was here amongst the rich furnishings that I would find my playthings including a small altar, which would become my pulpit. As I knelt before it I became the great preacher whom everyone came to listen to in the huge piazza, holding up my mother's beautiful book of hours for the crowds to see. But it was the forzieri that I loved most of all with their colourful painted figures and animals and these became my storybooks. In this make-believe world I could be anyone I wished to be and I could populate the scenes before me with all of those I loved most of all. A beautiful lady wearing a red and gold gown and a headdress of peacock feathers and pearls became my mother and a gentleman wearing shiny silver armour my father. They spoke sweet, kind words to me and I to them.

'As I approached my early teenage years I became aware that I possessed a beauty that others felt a need to comment on. Instead of hearing those words that

I had come to dread: "Poverina Annalena", I was now "Bellisima Annalena". I will not deny that I secretly took pleasure in hearing such words. Of course like other fair maidens of my social standing I also became the object of scrutiny for the matrons of our great city who had taken it upon themselves to seek out potential brides for their beloved sons. At Mass within those hallowed walls of our fair Santa Reparata I would be the recipient of their attentions. I could feel their eyes survey my whole being. It was as though I were a bolt of the most precious crimson velvet or silk that must clear inspection before receiving its seal of approval. I was a flower in bud about to blossom forth and had to be plucked whilst at my best. However, my future had already been decided upon and my husband was already chosen.'

The city of Florence and the circumstances that Annalena as a child would have found herself in must surely have appeared foreign to her. Although she was cared for by her own kin, they too must have seemed like strangers to her initially. Growing up in a fine palace whether belonging to Attilio's father Niccolo, Cosimo or Contessa Elisabetta, her life would have been shaped by her surroundings and those around her. It is worthwhile considering the city during her lifetime.

In Annalena's day Florence with its population of between 40,000 and 50,000 was one of the largest and wealthiest cities in Europe. The city had grown prosperous due to textiles, trade and banking and it was full of merchants, bankers, humanists and artists. The Florentines were fortunate since the river Arno, which crosses the city and neatly divides it into two, was the city's principal resource. The Arno provided power and water for the textile industry and it also gave access to the sea for imports and exports. During the fifteenth century a great many Florentines were involved with the silk industry. All sectors of Florentine society whether they be rich or poor were tuned into the preciousness of cloth since the textile industry involved workers who made the cloth as well as rich citizens who wore luxurious clothes. The status and wealth of people was expressed by means of their clothing. Even today we can get a sense of how important the textile industry was from the street names of the city which include Via dei Velluti (Street of Velvets), Via dei Tintori (Street of Dyers) and Via de' Vagellai (Street of the Dyers' Vats).

The time and circumstances during the years when Annalena was growing up were just ripe for a flourishing of the arts and Florence became the 'cradle of the Renaissance'. Already by the time Annalena was a child, the first Renaissance masters had established themselves and some of the most important early Renaissance masterpieces had been created. Later, great names such as Lorenzo de Medici, Botticelli, Michelangelo, and Leonardo da Vinci would emerge from this great city that had become her home. Although not a Florentine by birth, Annalena along with her Florentine contemporaries would witness great changes as new Renaissance monuments rose up against the medieval backdrop of that city. There must have been something completely new to marvel at virtually every day and at times the city must have seemed like one vast building site. Undoubtedly, one of the greatest artistic and architectural achievements that Annalena would have witnessed during her lifetime was the completion of the cathedral of Santa Maria del Fiore (see **Figure 9**) with its magnificent new dome constructed by Filippo Brunelleschi, the star of the new era. The Florentines were immensely proud of their cathedral and rightly so; Filippo Brunelleschi's cupola or dome was a great feat of architectural engineering and remains so to this day. He had achieved what others had failed to do since he built his dome without the use of wooden centring to support the masonry. At the time of its construction it was the largest dome in the world. The great architect and humanist Leon Battista Alberti wrote that it 'rideth high in the heavens and can shelter all the people of Tuscany'. It must have been truly incredible to behold when people saw it for the first time. Who knows, the young Annalena may have been amongst the crowds that came to rejoice and celebrate the consecration of the reconstructed cathedral, the old Santa Reparata under its new name of Santa Maria del Fiore, topped with its newly completed cupola on March 25th 1436, the start of the Florentine new year. More than 200,000 people apparently flocked to the city from the countryside and nearby towns to witness the celebrations.

From the mid-fifteenth century, building was commenced on many of the great Renaissance palazzi including those of the Medici, Strozzi and Pitti since this was the great age of private building (it was Cosimo de' Medici's new palace that had first ignited the interest in palace building and would serve as a model for others). Of course not everyone was wealthy enough to live in a fine palace and certainly not of the size and prestige of that belonging to Cosimo de' Medici. The visitor to Florence in the *quattrocento* would also have met with a cityscape made up of more modest dwellings, tower-houses, and tenements. Until the mid-sixteenth century there was no exclusively wealthy area in the city, with the exception perhaps of the area of Via Maggio in the Oltrarno, since the rich and cultured built their homes amongst the more modest buildings.

During the fifteenth century the city of Florence was divided into quarters and the cathedral of Santa Maria del Fiore, together with the baptistery of San Giovanni and Giotto's *campanile* (bell tower), made up the religious centre. This site was rich with artistic treasures and during her lifetime Annalena must have seen and admired many of these including the magnificent bronze doors known as the *Porta di Paradiso* created for the baptistery by Lorenzo Ghiberti and completed in 1452.

Although this was an age of grandeur and magnificence this was also a period which was punctuated with political tension, territorial expansion, warfare, plague and famine. In the late 1420s and 1430s during the time when Annalena was growing up wars were commonplace and there was the constant threat of plague. Indeed, there were at least eight plague epidemics during the fifteenth century. Of course none were as bad as the 'Black Death' of 1348 but they were still terrible enough to claim many lives. As we will see in a later chapter, even Annalena's life would not escape the consequences of this horrible disease. Death was omnipresent and Renaissance culture was inextricably linked with religion, and people at this time believed that the Virgin and saints could act as intercessors to God in times of danger or disease. This was a time when medical knowledge was not as advanced as it is today and people felt vulnerable, so they harnessed the power of both God and saints as well as what was known medically. I like to think of Florence during this period as being rather like a richly woven tapestry with threads of black to denote the fatality of plague, red to symbolise the blood shed in warfare, a combination of black and white entwined threads to conjure up the intricacy of political tension, and glistening gold and shiny metallic threads to reflect the artistic splendour of the age.

Annalena, like all Florentines of her day, would have grown up in a city where time was regulated by the sound of church bells. Bells both sacred and secular marked the rhythms of urban daily life. They called citizens to prayer, marked the beginning and end of the working day, summoned men to war and called the members of the city's council to their meetings. Everyone at the time would have understood this 'language of bells' and it is worth reflecting on such for a moment. Whereas in modern times we may be accustomed to using GPS (Global Positioning System) on our mobile phones or in our car to locate where we are, during the Renaissance, people relied upon the sound of the different bells to know which part of the city they where in. Bells still ring out in the city of Florence today, however, they no longer have the significance that they once did. Additionally, in our own modern times we are so used to social media and twenty-four-hour news bulletins, which alert us of any danger to our lives. In the Renaissance once again bells would have come into their own. Annalena and her fellow citizens would have known immediately that if they heard the deafening boom of the great bell known as *La Vacca* (the cow) ring out from the tower of the Palagio della Signoria (the present-day Palazzo Vecchio), then danger or community discord was afoot. Indeed this was a sound of grave importance to the Florentines. It must have been like during the war years in our own modern era when air-raid sirens resonated through the skies and danger filled the air.

The tolling of bells could also mark more joyous occasions for Florentines, for example the principal bell known as *La Campana del Leone* was rung unceasingly on the announcement of a victory or on the celebration of marriages. Interestingly, although Florentines relied heavily on the bells of the city, there was also a mechanical clock in the tower of the Palazzo Vecchio. In the same way that we use clocks alongside the newer technology of mobile phones today, people in the Renaissance continued to use bells and sundials as backup to their newer technology. Indeed, there is a lovely example of a medieval sundial which can still be seen on the Ponte Vecchio. Continuing with the theme of time, the Florentine calendar would have centred around saints days and church festivals. One very important date for the Florentines was the feast of St. John the Baptist (the city's patron saint), which took place on June 24th. This date is still celebrated in Florence today.

So let us stop a while to think about a world without television, mobile phones, newspapers or radios. In Annalena's world, city heralds and preachers would have been the conduit through which people would have heard of any news. Storytellers in the piazzas and street corners would have captivated listeners with their tales, and musicians would have entertained crowds with their melodic tunes. Business discussions, politics, everyday gossip and other matters would have taken place in the taverns, piazzas, street corners and the marketplaces. During the daylight hours the streets of Florence would have been full of people and bustling with activity. People would arrive from the neighbouring countryside to sell their wares at the bustling *Mercato Vecchio* (Old Market), the commercial centre of the city. In the fifteenth century this was located in the present-day Piazza della Repubblica. A monumental arch known today as the *Arcone* dominates the piazza nowadays. This was erected in 1895 following major renovations which swept away much of the medieval parts of the city including the *Mercato Vecchio*. Today the piazza is lined with restaurants and cafes including the famous Gilli Caffe and Hard Rock Cafe. Tour guides frequently stop at the only remaining trace of the old medieval market: a stone column called the *Colonna dell'Abbondanza*. In Annalena's day this column was topped with a figure of *Dovizia* (Abundance) by Donatello which has been replaced with a copy today. In the centre of the present-day piazza a colourful, old-fashioned carousel spins around. Watching this, it is easy to allow one's imagination to be transported back through the centuries, back to the fifteenth century when we can substitute all of the aforementioned features of modernity with the sounds, smells and sights of what was once the *Mercato Vecchio*. Images from that most distant past flash before me: fruit and vegetable vendors jostle alongside second-hand clothes dealers, a pickpocket disappears into the crowd and in the shadows a couple of prostitutes ply their wares beneath the lecherous gaze of a nobleman dressed in fine clothing. In the surrounding narrow *vicoli* (alleyways) gamblers play dice. Of course Annalena would definitely not have frequented such a place and I will discuss the restrictions placed upon Renaissance women later.

If we allow our mind to wander further, we can also imagine what was going on in the other piazzas of the city. In the vast open spaces attached to the great churches huge crowds would gather to hear the mendicant preachers deliver their sermons. Preachers were the 'movers and shakers' of fifteenth-century Florentine society and in their great booming voices they would speak about all manner of things not only religious matters. These spaces were also the sites of horse races, tournaments and other festivities. On such occasions as these, the city would unfurl itself in full technicolour with a splendid display of gaily coloured costumes and joyous fanfare. Trumpeters, drummers and flag throwers would parade through the streets and excitement would fill the air.

Modern designer shops such as MaxMara are quickly substituted with those of silk merchants shops and storerooms crammed full of richly coloured bolts of cloth. Those wealthy enough may choose from collections of velvets, patterned brocades, crimson silks and more. If less flush with money, then you won't miss out, since the *riggatiere* or second-hand clothes dealers do a roaring trade in the city. Indeed, there is something to fit everyone's budget! Talking about money, for those wishing to change money or engage in some other financial activity then bankers are 'two a penny'! You can find the money men dressed in their long red gowns with their money purses by their sides and their ledgers atop tables in and around the *Mercato Nuovo* and the *Mercato Vecchio*. Or is it the case that you have some other business matter to attend to? Then a suitable meeting place might be Santa Maria del Fiore (the cathedral), if it isn't already too full of people and dogs that is?

The visitor to modern-day Florence will have noticed, I am sure, the horses and carriages which await tourists in the Piazza del Duomo and in other parts of the city. Those who are prepared to pay the rather extravagant prices will enjoy a leisurely meander through the streets. If the visitor should take the time to block out the sound of the modern-day traffic and listen instead to the clip-clopping sound of the horse's hooves upon the paving slabs, then this would have been the sound of traffic in Annalena's day. Horses and carts laden with fruit and vegetables, with perhaps a dog barking at its heels, would have been a common sight in the city.

Today, we are fortunate enough to enjoy the luxury of modern sanitation both in our homes and in our towns and cities. In terms of urban sanitation modern-day Florence owns a fleet of curious, small vehicles which are equipped with radial brushes and water sprays. What these vehicles lack in size they make up for in the thunderous noise they emit, a warning to any pedestrian who might fall in their path. These tiny vehicles patrol the streets both day and night as though performing some ritual of purification, cleansing the city of its daily grime. In the fifteenth century, Florence was by European standards a remarkably clean city and already had some paved streets. However, the filth and stench of horse manure, rotting fruit, vegetables and other waste materials still pervaded the air. Some measures were actually put in place to partially address the problem, for example in 1442 the Florentine authorities ordered the butchers to move their shops to the Ponte Vecchio. This isolated them from the centre's palaces and houses, and their new location on the bridge meant they could dump their waste directly into the river Arno. Previously, the foul-smelling scraps from the butchers' carts would have fallen straight on to the streets. Ultimately in

1593 (well after Annalena's time), the butchers were evicted from the bridge and replaced with the much more respectable goldsmiths shops that can still be seen today.

As the spinning of the carousel draws slowly to a halt so too does this little vignette of the city which Annalena came to call her own. In my mind's eye the day draws to a close and it is curfew at sunset. The great wooden and iron gates of the city are tightly bolted and soon day slips into night. Only an occasional lamp burning before a sacred image on the corner of a roadside or torches adorning the exterior of some of the larger palaces illuminate the darkness. People are asleep in their beds until the next morning when at dawn the day begins all over again, heralded in with a peal of church bells and the reopening of the city gates.

CHAPTER 7:

The marriage of Annalena and Baldaccio

'It is truly as though everyone in our fair city has come out to behold us; never before have I seen so many people. High above the streets well-wishers greet us from their handsomely decorated windows whilst in the streets below crowds gather as far as the eye can see. The air pulsates with excitement and the bell of the Leone rings out incessantly for all to hear. Everyone's gaze falls upon my new husband and me. Oh how strange it is to utter that word "husband"!

'My body trembles with both apprehension and joy and my heart spilleth over with sadness. Sadness since my mind is consumed with thoughts of my parents and in particular my dear mother. How it would please me dearly to have her close on such a joyous occasion. I imagine her warm kiss upon my face and the gentleness of her fair hands as she helps to arrange the magnificent gem-studded and feather ghirlanda upon my head. May God protect her. I look over at dear Contessa Elisabetta who is always here for me. God protect her since she is but frail in these, her twilight years. Oh how I welcome her reassuringly warm and gentle smile. How many more years will she live to see, I wonder, but this is not the time to dwell upon such matters...

'Music fills the air and the words "Bellisima Annalena!" reverberate amongst the crowds. I rejoice on hearing the gasps of admiration from the *mouths of women as they behold my gown of the most precious crimson. I feel my cheeks warm slightly and I fear that they too will take on the colour of my gown.*

A slight chill interrupts the air since it is true that the early spring sunshine has not yet awakened from its slumber. I feel grateful that my gown is of the best heavyweight cloth; Baldaccio has indeed chosen well.

The route before us appears distant and our pace is somewhat slow but the atmosphere is vibrant. God alone knows what the future may hold; may he guide me and protect me always.'

Florence in the fifteenth century was one of the most patriarchal societies in Europe and as a young noblewoman Annalena would have had limited freedom in contrast to men, older women and her poorer female counterparts. Compared with women of a lower status, Annalena would not have been able to work. Additionally, women in general were also unable to participate in the political affairs of the city. There were only two real options available to women of Annalena's noble rank and this was either to become a wife, or to enter a convent.

Noblewomen such as Annalena were also unable to move about freely in the city and were generally restricted to their homes. The only places considered acceptable to frequent were churches and piazzas to attend sermons and even then she probably would have been chaperoned. Recent research into the gendered spaces of women have revealed, however, that in actual fact women of higher status may have had more freedom than previously believed. Upper-class women did venture out and about on occasions, for example they would have travelled to their villas in the countryside. As I have already mentioned, Annalena would never have experienced the hustle and bustle of shopping at the *Mercato Vecchio*, the city's old market, nor would she have been exposed to the idle gossip of the people who worked there (perhaps not a bad thing!). Only women from the lower classes would have frequented such a place with some of them working as either street vendors or prostitutes. This was hardly the place for a young aristocratic woman! At this point, it is worth considering for a moment how fortunate most women are in our own modern age to enjoy the freedom of movement denied to our Renaissance sisters.

During the Renaissance period marriage was considered a key event in the lives of Florentine citizens, especially women. Indeed, marriage was the bedrock of Italian Renaissance society. Recurring episodes of the plague had greatly affected the population and so procreation was the main purpose of marriage. When speaking about the upper classes during this period it is vital for us to understand that marriage was both a social and economic contract between families. In contrast to today, marriage wasn't simply about the union of two individuals who had fallen in love, it was considered far more important than this since it also involved the building of family alliances. Thus a husband would have been chosen for Annalena. Of course although marriages were arranged it was naturally hoped that the couple would eventually grow to love each other. Usually the two families would be of similar social, economic and political standing. In Renaissance Florence matchmaking was considered a serious activity and it was a constant preoccupation of Florentine mothers who saw it as their civic duty. In the case of Annalena such duty would probably have fallen to Contessa Elisabetta, her main guardian.

In the surviving letters written by the fifteenth-century widow Alessandra Macinghi Strozzi, we can gain a clear insight into how much trouble she went to in order to seek out a suitable bride for one of her sons. She attended Mass every morning in Santa Maria del Fiore to sit behind the girls whom she would like her son to marry and scrutinised each one of them. The health and good looks of the bride were uppermost in her mind since according to Alessandra such qualities made for a beautiful and safe delivery of a child.

It is also important to point out that marriage during the Renaissance was very much a secular affair and it was conducted as though it were a business transaction. Before the Council of Trent in 1563, marriage didn't even require the intervention of the clergy nor did it need to take place in a church, although sometimes the ceremony was conducted on the church steps. For this reason no extant marriage registers exist in Italy until the Council of Trent. However, from the thirteenth century, communal law in Florence required the civil notarisation of all marriages and some of these records survive scattered within the *Notarile Antecosimiano* (notarile archives), which are held in the ASF. Notaries played an important role in Italian Renaissance society and were called upon to draft and record all kinds of legal documents including those related to marriage and dowries. Additionally, it is often the case that marriages are recorded in private books of *ricordanze* (remembrances).

Marriage during this period involved several stages through betrothal to consummation. As is the case today marriage was an occasion for great celebration and it involved huge expenditure particularly so amongst the wealthy classes and the aristocracy. Large sums of money would be spent on a dowry, clothing, jewellery, banquets and other festivities. According to some later accounts, which most likely were based on sources no longer surviving today, Annalena's nuptials were arranged by her godfather Cosimo de' Medici (see statue in **Figure 10**) who apparently pledged her to Baldaccio d'Anghiari, one of the most respected and best-known soldiers of the day when she was fifteen years old. Indeed, Cosimo de' Medici is recorded as having acted as a marriage broker in the city. Although it is impossible to corroborate this particular detail, we have reason enough to believe that Cosimo de' Medici did play a vital part in Annalena's marriage arrangements.

Baldaccio d'Anghiari was a *condottiere* or mercenary soldier, a valiant captain of infantry and one of the rising men in Florence. Incidentally, *condotta* in Italian means contract and hence the word *condottiere* means a contracted soldier. Niccolo Machiavelli in his *Florentine Histories* calls Baldaccio (translated) an 'excellent soldier, not to be surpassed, either for courage or conduct in all Italy at that time'. The city of Florence had no army of its own during this period and therefore was reliant upon mercenary soldiers such as Baldaccio.

Both Baldaccio and Annalena were of noble birth; she was a Contessa and he was a wealthy aristocrat. It was usual for *condottieri* such as Baldaccio to belong to old feudal, aristocratic families. He was the son of Piero da Vagnone Bruni, Lord of Ranco castle in the province of Arezzo and his wife Donna Assunta. Baldaccio like Annalena was also a non-Florentine since as his name suggests he was from the territory of Anghiari in the province of Arezzo. Annalena's guardian Contessa Elisabetta (who by this time was a mature woman) played a vital role in the marriage arrangements and her advice would have been greatly respected by Cosimo. She would have prepared her young ward well for her future role as wife and mother. It may have been the case that Contessa Elisabetta gave Annalena in marriage to Baldaccio in servitude to the Florentines as she had done so previously in the marriage of her great-niece Gherardesca. Additionally, she may have had her own vested interest for bringing the two together. As we have seen from an earlier chapter, it was during these years that Contessa Elisabetta was in a vulnerable position with regards to the status of her territory in the Casentino, the same land to which Baldaccio belonged. She probably would have known Baldaccio and admired his military prowess. Perhaps she hoped that if Annalena married him he might help her win back her castle and her territory. We may never know the full details of Baldaccio and Annalena's marriage arrangements but it goes without saying that a great deal of thought and planning would have been behind the choice of both bride and groom. Equally, we will never know Annalena's own feelings for her husband-to-be when their marriage was arranged or indeed at the time when she married him. It is possible that she may have met him before their marriage; if not then she must certainly have heard about him from Contessa Elisabetta.

In 1437 Cosimo de' Medici and the citizens of Florence had recognised Baldaccio's worth and he had been made a Florentine citizen. Cosimo de' Medici had given him a house behind the church of San Firenze in the heart of the city and upon his own request Baldaccio had been exempted from taxes. This house was the Palazzo Anguillara, which is located close to the present-day Bargello Museum and can still be seen today (there are conflicting sources as to whether or not Baldaccio held the title of Count of Anguillara and had a castle in Anguillara near Rome). Baldaccio had also been given a life pension of 900 *fiorini* above payment for his services. Such rewards were typically given to *condottieri* at this time. Furthermore, a decree dated June 19th in this year records that Baldaccio was exempt from the usual requirement for non-Florentines to have a house built of a minimum value of 400 florins as stipulated by the Statutes. On December 16th 1438 Baldaccio bought a house for 700 *Scudi d'Oro* from the Monte Comune di Firenze. This palazzo with *orto* (garden) was in the Popolo S. Felice in the Oltrarno, and had previously belonged to Pietro dei Bardelli. This was the house that would form the nucleus for the convent that Annalena would later establish.

As previously mentioned the 1430s were punctuated by a series of wars and Baldaccio had often risked his life in the service of the Florentines. He had gained victories for the Florentines over the Lucchesi and in the Romagna. However, in the fashion of a true *condottiere* he had no scruples in selling his sword to whoever paid him the most money. It would have been in the Florentines' interest, and indeed in the interest of Cosimo de' Medici who was still in his ascendancy, to keep Baldaccio sweet. Cosimo would have wanted to keep Baldaccio in his services and he is known to have used his connections and network system to strengthen his power base within the city. Annalena was most probably a 'pawn' in a game of strategy by Cosimo. Since Annalena belonged to a branch of the Malatesta family, one of the most celebrated Italian families and a kinswoman of Cosimo, his giving of her in marriage to Baldaccio would have been reward indeed for him.

With her proposed marriage to Baldaccio, Annalena would be stepping into a familiar world since, as I have previously mentioned, the men in the Malatesta family were renowned for their military prowess and their roles as *condottieri*. As we have already seen Annalena's own father was a *condottiere* and both of Contessa Elisabetta's husbands had also been mercenary soldiers. Undoubtedly, Contessa Elisabetta would have helped prepare her young ward as best she could for living her life as the wife of a 'soldier of fortune'. However, we will never know if Annalena would have felt comfortable with such a prospect or whether she would have preferred to have been betrothed to a banker or merchant instead. Annalena was nineteen years of age when she married Baldaccio on February 7th 1439 and her groom was in his late thirties or forty (he was born either in 1400 or more probably in the 1390s). This age gap was typical for the period, since brides in Florence were mere girls when they married and their husbands were generally about twice their age. The average age of a Florentine bride in the Renaissance was about eighteen years of age; Annalena would have been considered to be of the ideal age to maximise her childbearing potential, which as I have already mentioned was the primary purpose of marriage at that time. Men on the other hand, who were much older at the time of their first marriage, were expected to attain a level of status and show that they were able to provide for a family before they married.

It was important that Annalena should have been a virgin at the time of her marriage to Baldaccio. Virginity before marriage and fidelity to her husband afterwards was considered vital to ensure the purity of a husband's lineage and the legitimacy of any heirs, not to mention the reputation of his family. Baldaccio, her husband-to-be, on the other hand, being so much older than his young bride, would undoubtedly have been more sexually experienced than she. Double standards were at play during the Renaissance since it was acceptable for men like Baldaccio to take mistresses, concubines or even prostitutes prior to marriage. Concubinage was fairly widespread during this period and was tolerated even by the clergy. Interestingly, during the course of my research I discovered that Baldaccio probably did have a *concubina* (concubine). I found this revelatory detail recorded by a notary called Ser Giusti who was also from Baldaccio's territory of Anghiari. It appears in an entry written in his diaries known as: '*I Giornali di Ser Giusto Giusti d'Anghiari*' and is dated September 1442: '*Monna Giovanna, figliuola che fu di Vannuccio da Notra di Pisa e femmina che fu di Baldaccio d'Anghiari e moglie al presente d'Iacomo da Cento*', which translates as '*Monna Giovanna, daughter of Vannuccio da Notra of Pisa and who was the femmina and present wife of Iacomo da Cento*'. The term '*femmina*' in this context means mistress or concubine. Confirmation of this detail appears in a later source of the seventeenth century which was written by the chronicler Lorenzo Taglieschi. However, it is wise to note that Taglieschi is known to have used Ser Giusti's Giornali as a basis for his own work.

There is one further, highly interesting detail recorded by Ser Giusti and this is that on Sunday February 15th in the year 1439 '*detto di Baldaccio d'Anghiari meno moglie in Fiorenza con dispensazione del papa perche erano serrate le linee*' ('Baldaccio d'Anghiari took a wife in Florence with dispensation from the Pope... '). As well as the more general meaning of 'to take a wife' the use of the word '*meno*' may in fact specifically relate to the term '*menare a casa*', which was the more public part of the marriage celebrations which involved Baldaccio taking his new wife to his home. Initially, I struggled to comprehend exactly the meaning of '*erano serrate le linee*' and I had to seek the assistance of an eminent scholar in the field so that I could understand it more fully. I am grateful to Nerida Newbigin, translator of Ser Giusti's diaries, for providing some clarity for me in this matter. She proposed that within the context of the source, the meaning of these words probably meant that Baldaccio and Annalena were 'closely related'. It was undoubtedly for this reason that Baldaccio had required special dispensation from the Pope to allow him to marry her. My excitement reached fever pitch on hearing this since I had long had my suspicions that there might have been some familial link between Annalena and Baldaccio. I had thought that this link may have been through the House of Anguillara, a branch of the Orsini family and the one which Annalena's mother possibly belonged to (Bracciano/Anguillara).

Indeed, a papal dispensation would be required if spouses were related to one another by blood within 'four degrees', or connected to one another through godparentage, marriage or sexual relations. I had read about one other example of a marriage of the fifteenth century requiring papal dispensation because the bride and groom were related. This is recorded in the *libro di ricordi* of Cino di Filippo Rinuccini (a member of one of Florence's prominent families) and is dated 1461. I checked to see if the aforementioned seventeenth-century chronicler Lorenzo Taglieschi had also recorded that Baldaccio had received a papal dispensation to marry Annalena and indeed he had done so. Taglieschi wrote that Baldaccio had received the papal dispensation because of '*Alleluja*'. This must have been an error on behalf of either Taglieschi who probably misread Ser Giusti or someone who had mistranslated Taglieschi, and this translation had been discounted by Nerida Newbigin.

I was delighted to have discovered this new piece of information regarding the fact that Baldaccio and Annalena were related in some way, and this would be of prime importance not only for my own purposes but indeed to scholars interested in the life of Baldaccio d'Anghiari. I thought it might be useful to pursue this further and so I arranged to visit the Dominican library in Florence. This library is located next to the Tourist Information Office and Visitors' Centre, opposite the station of Santa Maria Novella. I had contacted the library there by email in advance of my visit to explain what my research purposes were. On my arrival, a very helpful librarian pointed me in the direction of some documents that might prove useful for me. She also handed me a huge tome which she told me contained a list of papal dispensations. She also gave me a paperknife so that I could separate the pages of the book. I felt terribly nervous at undertaking such a task for fear of destroying the document. I was more accustomed to handling books and manuscripts with great care. Surely I couldn't have been the first person who ever wanted to take a look at this book? Unfortunately, I was unable to read every page in the book since this would have required me to prise open too many of its pages. In those that I was able to check there didn't appear to be any entry for a papal dispensation granted to Baldaccio. I surmise that Cosimo, who had close links with Pope Eugenius IV (the Pope in office at the time and who also was in Florence at this date), may have helped Baldaccio to obtain his dispensation or indeed, it may have been Baldaccio himself.

It is prudent to point out that 1439 was a very important year since the ecumenical council (union with the eastern and western churches) took place in Florence. Ser Giusti had also noted that on Thursday February 12th the Pope entered into Florence with great pomp and on Sunday 15th (during Baldaccio and Annalena's wedding festivities) the Emperor of Constantinople and about 400 Greeks were in Florence. The city was jubilant and decked out for the occasion and must have been quite splendid.

Amazingly, despite the paucity of sources relating to the life of Annalena, we are fortunate to have an extremely important contemporary document which relates to her marriage. This is the *Carta degli Sponsali* or marriage contracts for Annalena and Baldaccio dated February 7th 1439. In this precious document Annalena's noble status is recorded since she is addressed as: '*Magnifica domina domina comitissa Annalena...*' The title '*Magnifica*' was used to signify her wealth and status. Additionally, we have further confirmation that she was the daughter of Count Galeotto the Count of Cusercole: '*... filia magnifiei comitis Galeotti de comitibus de Glusercule...*' The *Carta degli Sponsali* is revealing on many levels since it records that both Annalena and Baldaccio were present in the company of witnesses for the giving and receiving of the rings and to make the marriage legal. It records the names of the witnesses, agreement on dowry issues such as who paid the dowry and the amount paid, as well as details concerning inheritance listing the houses and property of the young couple, which were to be settled upon their heirs. This latter detail appears to have been agreed upon two days before on February 5th 1439 in the house of Baldaccio located in the parish of San Felice in Piazza. This part of the contract was conducted in the presence of representatives from Borgo alla Collina most likely on behalf of Contessa Elisabetta and a representative from Borgo Sansepolcro for Baldaccio and his family. Baldaccio also appears to have exchanged a castle in Gubbio, which was given to him by Contessa Elisabetta as part of Annalena's dowry, for a castle in Ranco.

The *Carta degli Sponsali* informs us that the giving of the ring part of the marriage ceremony (*anellamento*) and the exchange of vows took place in Contessa Elisabetta's house in the Parish of Santa Felicita. Usually this took place in the bride's father's home. This detail confirms that Contessa Elisabetta was involved with the marriage arrangements. Additionally, it supports the fact that Annalena must have been staying with Contessa Elisabetta certainly at the time of her marriage and probably before. Furthermore, it most definitely serves to support my belief that Contessa Elisabetta was Annalena's main guardian. At this time Contessa Elisabetta was probably living in a house that had belonged to her father Conte Roberto da Battifolle (other sources cite that it was her husband's house or a house given to her by the Florentine government). Undoubtedly, her residence was a fine one since she was a person of great standing and she knew some of the most influential and elite families of Florence; she certainly mixed with the 'crème de la crème' of Florentine society.

The Parish of Santa Felicita encompassed a large area which included houses along the river Arno and behind the present-day church of Santa Felicita, which is on the site of the former Santa Felicita monastery. It extends up to and beyond the present-day Via San Giorgio and San Niccolo. Although the exact location of Contessa Elisabetta's house is not known, it may possibly have been located on Via dei Bardi leading up to the area of San Niccolo since many of the palazzi belonging to some of the ancient families of Florence could be found there. Equally, it could have been situated near the present-day church of Santa Felicita with which, as I have already mentioned, Contessa Elisabetta had associations.

In Renaissance Italy a girl needed a dowry to marry; no dowry, no marriage! Generally it would have been the bride's family, more usually her father, who would have provided the dowry, which was a reflection of the wealth of the family. The purpose of the dowry was to provide for the bride's upkeep during marriage and to give support for the widow after her husband's death or to facilitate her remarriage. Dowry prices had spiralled upwards throughout the fifteenth century and were a constant source of worry for fathers providing for their daughters. To help alleviate the burden the Florentines set up a state dowry fund in 1425 known as the '*Monte Delle Doti*' (literally the 'Dowry Mountain'). Fathers or sometimes other family members, relatives or godparents could pay a deposit into this communal fund when the girl was very young (usually before she was ten years of age) and this together with interest would be paid out at the time of her marriage. Even wealthy families including the Medici and the Strozzi paid into this fund.

Annalena's dowry was a substantial one and reflected her status as a Contessa. Interestingly, we learn from the marriage contracts that it was Contessa Elisabetta who gave Annalena's dowry, which was comprised of 'movables' and money to a value of 2,000 gold florins. The value of the florin during the 1430s would be the equivalent of about £20 today so Annalena's dowry was about £40,000! Curiously, Annalena's father played no part in the proceedings even though it is known that he was still alive at this time. It remains a mystery why he appears to have been absent on the most important day of his daughter's life. Perhaps he was simply too old or even too ill to attend. Or it may even have been the case that since he had entrusted the care of his daughter to Contessa Elisabetta many years before, he no longer had any contact with her. In giving and paying the dowry Contessa Elisabetta appears to have taken on the role of surrogate, albeit elderly, parent. It would have been Contessa Elisabetta, too, who would have provided Annalena with the wise guidance on how she should love her husband to be and how she should behave in his presence. At this time there existed a set of rules, almost 'commandments', for the bride-to-be regarding her duties as a wife. The words of the aforementioned Alessandra Macinghi Strozzi come to mind, since in a letter to her daughter she had written 'Do as I say and you shall be as a crown of gold to your husband'.

The notary would have recorded the union of both Baldaccio and Annalena. He would have asked the ritual questions and both Baldaccio and Annalena would have answered '*Volo*' ('I wish to') followed by an exchange of rings (wedding rings were given to both husband and wife at this time). An insight into this part of the ceremony can be gained from the many paintings and frescoes from the period which represent the marriage of the Virgin. I tried to imagine the beautiful young bride Annalena offering up her delicate, ivory-smooth right hand so that the wedding ring could be placed upon her finger. Did she tremble with fear or would she have felt some curiosity of what it might feel like to be enveloped within Baldaccio's strong embrace?

The couple may have attended Mass after their marriage. The marriage of Annalena and Baldaccio would clearly have been a very important and grand occasion and if magazines and newspapers had been around in those days then their union would have been greatly reported upon, since they would have been regarded as a 'celebrity couple'. Amongst the witnesses present were some of the most eminent citizens of Florence including Niccolo di Bartolomeo Valori, Neri di Gino Capponi, Luca di Maso degli Albizzi, Piero di Luigi Guicciardini and Francesco di Cionaccio Baroncelli. With the exception of the latter all were members of leading Florentine Oltrarno families (the area in which Contessa Elisabetta resided). It may well have been the case that some of the aforementioned witnesses had also been involved with the marriage arrangements of the bride and groom.

A further observation is that many of them had been involved with the Florentine expansion into the Casentino (Contessa Elisabetta's territory). This suggests that there must indeed have been a strategic reason for the union of Annalena and Baldaccio. The witnesses were of course friends of the couple to be married but most importantly, they were all strong supporters of Cosimo de' Medici. Talk about 'all the President's men', this was no ordinary marriage ceremony. It is worth taking a closer look at the witnesses since they were some of the major players in Florence during this period.

Niccolo di Bartolomeo Valori belonged to the ancient Valori family, which had originated from Fiesole. Although the Valori family were relatively small in size they had made a huge impact on the city of Florence both culturally and politically. Niccolo Valori's father Bartolomeo had close ties with Cosimo de' Medici and had in fact actively assisted with Cosimo's return from exile in 1434. Indeed, members of the Valori family had been rewarded with political offices as Medici allies, and with the ascendancy of the Medici family to power during the fifteenth century their status and their authority had also risen. Niccolo himself was a top player in Florence's political and cultural life and held important positions in government. It appears that Niccolo served as Baldaccio's 'best man' since he seems to have been in charge of the ring.

Neri di Gino Capponi (1388–1457) was a close friend of Baldaccio's and a frequent visitor at the home of Contessa Elisabetta. Capponi, like Baldaccio, was a war captain; he was also a patrician, politician and merchant. He was the third son of the merchant and banker Gino di Neri Capponi and he was one of the city's wealthiest citizens. After the return of the Medici in 1434, Capponi became one of the most important figures in the Medici regime, second only to Cosimo. A measure of how important a person he was is the inclusion of his portrait within the fresco by Benozzo Gozzoli in the Medici–Riccardi palace in Florence. Capponi also features in Domenico Ghirlandaio's fresco of the *Resurrection of the Notary's Son* in the Sassetti chapel in the church of Santa Trinita in Florence (he is the man standing with his back to the viewer dressed in the purple robe; Neri Capponi's grandson married one of Francesco Sassetti's daughters).

Luca di Maso degli Albizzi (1382–1458) was also a close friend of Baldaccio and like Capponi he was a frequent visitor to the home of Contessa Elisabetta. Luca belonged to one of the oldest, most influential and powerful families in Florence. It had been his brother Rinaldo who was responsible for the exile of Cosimo in 1433, only to be sentenced himself to exile the following year. In contrast to his brother, Luca was a strong supporter and friend of Cosimo. He shared Cosimo's passion for classical learning (humanist studies) and good conversation. As a reward for his friendship Luca had been given a Medici bride. Aurelia di Niccola de' Medici was Luca's second wife and she was Cosimo's cousin and the sister of Attilio di Vieri de' Medici (whom Annalena may have grown up with) thus Luca's second wife was a distant relative of Annalena. Luca held important political positions and he also enjoyed an extensive diplomatic career and was even a diplomat to the Pope in Bologna.

Piero di Luigi Guicciardini (1378–1441) was one of Florence's most distinguished diplomats. He was often away from the city and indeed died whilst on a diplomatic mission in Lombardy in 1441. He married three times and his first wife was called Laodomia di Donato Acciauoli, whom he married in 1395. Sadly, she died in 1398 eight days after giving birth. Piero's second wife was Giovanna di Bartolomeo Valori, who was a relative of Niccolo Valori, but this marriage was also short-lived since Giovanna died of the plague in 1400; she was six months pregnant. Piero's third wife was Angela di Andrea Buondelmonti. Piero's daughter Costanza married into the Medici family. Although, Piero was a great politician he was an unsuccessful businessman and appears to have run into financial difficulties and ultimately died poor.

Francesco di Cionaccio Baroncelli belonged to an ancient Florentine family and he appears to have held government positions. He was resident in the quarter of San Giovanni. His name appears in a Venetian register dated 1428 which was linked to the wars of Lombardy alongside others including Contessa Elisabetta. He had investments in the textile industry and owned a silk company.

Following the union of Annalena and Baldaccio there would have been a feast probably provided by Contessa Elisabetta and thereafter a great deal of pomp and further festivities, which may have continued for several days. The celebrations concluded with a very public display of the new bride leaving her home to go the home of her new husband ('*menare a casa*'). This term could also refer to when the marriage was consummated. Annalena would have left Contessa Elisabetta's palazzo in the parish of Santa Felicita for the home of her new husband Baldaccio. It is thought by some that the couple lived initially in the previously mentioned Palazzo Anguillara whilst their new home in San Felice in Piazza was being enlarged and renovated. However, my interpretation from the marriage contracts is that since Baldaccio had agreed the conditions of the dowry etc. in his palazzo in San Felice in Piazza only a couple of days before the actual giving and receiving of the ring, it must be deduced that the palazzo in San Felice in Piazza must have been ready for moving into. Whether the couple stayed at the Palazzo Anguillara or at the palazzo in San Felice in Piazza, Annalena would probably have ridden upon a white horse and paraded through the streets of the city to her new home for all to see. Porters would have carried colourful painted '*forzieri da sposa*' (marriage chests) glistening with gold leaf and packed with riches. A crowd of family, friends and well-wishers would have accompanied her along the route. This was the most public part of the whole marriage ceremony and served to announce the new alliance between the two families.

The Palazzo Anguillara has of course undergone many alterations and changes of ownership over the centuries. This is a building we have come to know well since it just happens to be located very close to one of our favourite *gelaterie* (ice cream shops) in Florence. I've lost count of the number of ice creams that we must have consumed whilst musing over this palazzo! At the time of writing, the palazzo was undergoing yet further refurbishment. We peered inside the entrance door, which had been left slightly ajar, in the hope of glimpsing the interior of the building. I then glanced up at one of the windows and wondered if, indeed, Annalena had ever spent time within its walls. As I did so I was reminded of a very lovely dual portrait entitled *Portrait of a Man and a Woman at a Casement* attributed to Filippo Lippi and now in the Metropolitan Museum in New York. This is believed to be a betrothal or marriage portrait dated to about 1440, roughly the same date of Annalena's marriage. Since no known betrothal or marriage portraits exist of Annalena (portraits to commemorate an engagement or a wedding were relatively unusual in Florence during the fifteenth century), I paint a portrait of her in my mind based upon contemporary details of Florentine Renaissance wedding attire. Undoubtedly, Annalena would have possessed many of the feminine ideals of the day: blonde hair, high forehead, plucked hairline, thin eyebrows, pale, flawless skin and a good figure. Even if she had been a brunette Annalena probably would have dyed her hair blonde since even in the Renaissance gentlemen preferred blondes! Baldaccio would have paid for Annalena's wedding clothes and jewels. As befitting of her high-ranking status and that of her new husband, Annalena would have been dressed in a richly coloured embroidered silk and velvet gown adorned with jewels and perhaps with her new husband's insignia embroidered on a sleeve. Her jewels would have included pearls, which were considered to be a symbol of purity and a typical wedding gift during this period. To complete her bridal attire Annalena would also have worn a magnificent headdress possibly of feathers and pearls. Her whole outfit would have been many months in the making and would have involved tailors, embroiderers, metalworkers and makers of headdresses. Baldaccio would have paid for all of this to show that she was now part of his family since when a woman was married, she, like her clothes, was considered the property of her husband. Interestingly, Baldaccio had received a vast consignment of cloth a few years before the wedding perhaps in readiness for his marriage. He may also have had some involvement in the textile industry as many Florentines did and thus we can imagine that he was particularly knowledgeable about textiles. Annalena and Baldaccio like other wealthy nobles placed great emphasis on clothes and appearance. On average, wealthy families invested 40% of their income on clothing with men spending as much as women.

Annalena, perhaps with the help of Contessa Elisabetta, would have brought her wedding *donara* (trousseau) of personal items, which she would have prepared some months before. This trousseau would have included more fine gowns and other items of clothing, jewellery, linen and some personal objects including combs, a mirror, devotional books and sewing implements.

Regarding Baldaccio's house in San Felice in Piazza, this would become the couple's home and later would form the nucleus of Annalena's convent (see **Figure 11**). We can gain some idea of what it looked like from the contract of February 5th 1439. From my translation it is described as being a great house, with a wooden decorated ceiling, service rooms, principal rooms, cistern, vaults above and below ground, courtyard, other buildings and a garden. As was customary for the times, lavish sums of money would have been spent on decorating the '*camera*' or nuptial chamber and this would have been paid for by Baldaccio. The painted '*forzieri da sposa*' would have stood pride of place in the '*camera*' alongside other pieces of furniture including the marriage bed and other rich furnishings especially purchased for their marriage.

Baldaccio pledged to give Annalena a '*Morgincap*', a counter gift in accordance with the Statutes of the Republic of Florence, in return for the dowry Annalena gave to him. He would have given his gift to his bride on the first morning after the wedding to mark the consummation of their marriage. Further festivities including an elaborate banquet held at the home of Baldaccio would have followed. This may have taken place out of doors, perhaps under a loggia in the piazza. Florentine husbands and their families spent on average about one-third to two-thirds of the promised dowry on nuptial gifts and wedding festivities.

So what kind of a man did Annalena marry? By the time of his marriage to her Baldaccio's military career was impressive and in the *Carta degli Sponsali* he is recorded as holding the high rank of '*equitum peditumqice conductor*' translated as 'conductor of horsemen and infantry'. It is known that Baldaccio was in fact general commander over the entire infantry of the Republic of Florence. Baldaccio's father was a '*sindaco procuratore*' (government official) for the Florentine Republic in the land of Sorci in Anghiari territory, and he had hoped that his son, who had been baptised 'Baldo', would follow in his footsteps or reach even greater heights in government. Alas, Baldaccio preferred to be a soldier and even in his younger years he already had a thirst for blood and warfare. In his early years he would amuse himself by robbing people and sacking their homes and castles in and around his home territory of Anghiari. By 1430, only nine years before his marriage to Annalena, he had become ruthless in his exploits and narrowly escaped decapitation for the death of a certain Tardiolo Marescotti. But like a cat with nine lives, Baldaccio seems to have always managed to escape any consequences of his wrongdoings. Before long such mere 'dabbling' was not enough for Baldaccio. The 'aristocratic bandit' wanted to fight on a much grander scale and on a more serious level. He therefore increased his little group of brigands who had gathered around him into a fine infantry and seriously pursued his career as a *condottiere*. Baldaccio often risked his life in the service of the Florentines, beginning with the war against Lucca in 1433. He travelled around and fought far and wide and during the course of his military career he had also been in the service of Carlo Malatesta and even the Pope. In his professional capacity Baldaccio was obviously a valiant captain but clearly he was also ruthless, cruel, and a cunning risk taker. We do not know with any certainty what he was like as a husband but it is true to say that some *condottieri*, although ruthless on the battlefield, did make good husbands.

Intriguingly, I have read that the marriage contract included the clause that Baldaccio was bound 'never to make cause of quarrel against his wife'. Could this have been inserted because Baldaccio, on or off the battlefield, may not have been able to control his aggression? Significantly, Litta states that Annalena had an unhappy marriage and this is supported by a few other sources too. Almost immediately after their marriage Baldaccio was away far from home and he was greatly engaged in the war of Romagna in the two years leading up to his murder. We can only hope that if their marriage had been an unhappy one then it was due to his long absences from home rather than any acts of aggression towards Annalena. In modern times we have the expression 'golf widow' and thought of in this light Annalena was certainly a '*condottiere* widow'. I am of course not suggesting in the least that if she had been lonely and unhappy due to her husband's frequent absences then this would have been easy for her.

CHAPTER 8:

Annalena and Baldaccio: the honeymoon years

With Florence many miles behind us we entered into the province of Arezzo in the heart of Tuscany. It was a beautiful July morning and there was already the promise of yet another hot day. The Aretine countryside was delightful with its gentle forested slopes dotted with the occasional patch of yellow *ginestra* (broom) amongst tall pine trees. The landscape would probably have appeared more rugged and desolate in the days of Annalena and Baldaccio. As we drew closer to the town of Anghiari in Baldaccio's territory, the terrain seemed different with fields appearing against the backdrop of the verdant green trees. Just outside the town of Anghiari itself, I was excited to see those iconic symbols of Tuscany, rows and rows of sunny yellow *girasoli* (sunflowers) and tall *cipressi* (cypress trees). The sunflower is one of my favourite flowers; they radiate positivity and their smiling yellow heads make me feel happy. The Italian word *girasole* means 'turn to the sun' as indeed these tall flowers do, in the height of summer.

The town of Anghiari itself is famous for being the site of a very important battle between the Florentines and the Milanese, the so-called 'Battle of Anghiari' (sometimes called the Battle for the Standard), which took place on June 29th 1440. The Florentines led by Neri Capponi and his Papal troops had fought victoriously against the Milanese troops who were led by Niccolo

Piccinino. Yes, this was the same Capponi who was Baldaccio's closest friend and who had been present at Annalena and Baldaccio's marriage. Following the battle of Anghiari, Capponi became even more exalted for his military prowess. This victory by the Florentines meant that central Italy would remain in the hands of the Florentines rather than under the control of Milan. The battle was a major triumph for Cosimo de' Medici, Annalena's godfather. The art historian Dale Kent describes the celebrations that took place in Florence following this major victory, which included the illumination of various public buildings as well as Filippo Brunelleschi's newly completed cupola. Even at the beginning of the sixteenth century the victory was still remembered and celebrated, since the Florentine leaders commissioned the great Renaissance artist Leonardo da Vinci (who was then at the height of his career) to paint scenes depicting the battle on the walls of the great Council Hall of the Palazzo Vecchio in Florence. Leonardo's fresco of the *Battle of Anghiari* was to have been his largest painting, however the artist abandoned the project a year after he started it, probably due to the failure of a new experimental technique he used for fresco painting. Leonardo's lost fresco is still believed to exist under a later fresco painting by Giorgio Vasari, who was involved in renovations of the building and who some believe was reluctant to destroy Leonardo's work. Even today the battle is still remembered in the town of Anghiari itself, with a re-enactment on June 29th every year. Amazingly, Baldaccio did not seem to have taken part in what was probably the greatest battle of the age. Contrary to what some have written, he appears to have been tied up with other matters and was actually making his way to Suvereto in Piombino at the time.

Today the town of Anghiari is a delight to visit with its picturesque houses and quaint narrow streets. We decided to visit the small museum, which is dedicated to the battle. In all honesty, as a museum dedicated to such an important historic event, it is rather low-key and insignificant. Its main display is focused around a tabletop reconstruction of the battle formation as had been adopted on the actual day. Those interested in military history will enjoy such details; I, however, have neither expertise nor strong interest in such things. I did, nonetheless, note down some details about the various different items of armour and weaponry that would have been used by the soldiers involved in the battle. Even if Baldaccio hadn't fought at that famous event, this information would at least give me some idea of what he must have worn and used during his military campaigns. In all truth it didn't take us too long to look round the tiny museum, so we then decided to see seek out where the battle itself took place. A museum assistant kindly pointed us in the direction of the city walls where we could look down on what would have been the site of the battle. Sure enough from that vantage point we could clearly see the plain surrounding the long straight road leading to San Sepolcro, against its backdrop of hills. Fortunately, there was an information board with a key to the site, so we were able to work out exactly where the battle took place. We looked long and hard at the view before us and marvelled at the thought of that very important victory for the Florentines all those centuries ago. It was crazy to think that if the outcome hadn't been favourable for the Florentines then the whole course of Renaissance history would have been very different. This was the battle that saved the Renaissance.

With this thought still uppermost in our minds we left the view of the battle scene far behind us and wandered through the narrow streets of Anghiari, admiring terracotta roofs and beautiful blazing-red geraniums cascading from terracotta pots along the way. We also popped into the cool, dark shadows of a church or two to escape the midday heat. With it fast approaching noon it seemed a good point to seek out somewhere to eat. We made our way back down into the main piazza of the lower town, which is aptly named Piazza Baldaccio after the town's famous son. Just as Annalena would leave her name indelibly on the map of Florence, Baldaccio had done so here in Anghiari. Everywhere we went we were constantly reminded of Annalena's husband and even the place where we chose to have lunch was called Bar Pizzeria Baldaccio. I guess it was its colourful sign of a *condottiere* on horseback that lured us in! I was greatly amused to learn afterwards that even the town's football team is called Baldaccio Bruni. This was also annoying since just when I thought that I had been able to find out even more information about Baldaccio, invariably it would merely be a reference to the town's football matches!

After lunch we headed for the Castello di Sorci, once the property of Baldaccio and our accommodation for the evening. It didn't take us long at all to reach there since it isn't very far from Anghiari. As we approached the road leading to the castle, we were greeted with a sign with a cartoon-like image of a phantom on it. I must confess at this point I really wasn't too sure what to expect. I had read online that the castle was believed to be haunted by their most famous owner, Baldaccio d'Anghiari, as well as being the site of other paranormal activities. The thought of spending the night amongst such unwanted guests was not something I was really looking forward to, but my search for Annalena had brought me here and I just had to deal with it. When we arrived at the actual castle there was a strange, quiet stillness so typical of siesta time in Italy, when everybody seems to disappear behind closed doors. You could have heard a pin drop, the place was deserted. We felt unsure as to what we should do and so we sat in the warm sunshine for a while and waited to see if anyone might notice us. Before long a gentleman with a dog appeared from a nearby building. After I briefly explained to him that we had booked to stay at the castle that evening he pointed us in the direction of the nearby *locanda* (restaurant or inn) where someone would help us.

We made the short walk over to the *locanda*, which appeared to be just in the process of closing up after lunch. A couple of waitresses were busy tidying things away, and didn't even notice our presence. However, a young woman appeared from the back of the restaurant and she introduced herself and welcomed us. She had obviously been expecting us since she was holding a bundle of freshly laundered towels and a bunch of keys. She accompanied us back over to the castle and we chatted as we walked. Unsurprisingly, we had booked to stay in the '*Stanza di Annalena*' (Annalena's room). The young woman led us to our room and handed us the key, which was attached to a chunky key ring. It is believed that Baldaccio brought Annalena to the castle of Sorci for safekeeping when he went off to fight her relatives, although there is no evidence to confirm this. In 1439 Baldaccio had been engaged by Guid'Antonio di Montefeltro to fight with the Visconti against Annalena's distant relatives the Malatesta of Rimini who were at that time allied with Florence. The room was simple but lovely and the window, which had been prised open, looked out over the countryside beyond the castle. Our host placed the bundle of crisp, clean towels she had been carrying at the foot of the bed. She then explained to us that breakfast would be served over at the *locanda*. She wondered if we would like her to show us around the castle. In unison we very quickly replied with an excitable '*Si grazie!*' ('Yes please!'). Without any hesitation we followed her through the narrow, labyrinthine corridors of the castle. We were informed that we would be the only guests there that evening and so we could enjoy the whole place to ourselves. I didn't quite know if this would be a good thing or not and I was left musing over this thought for some time.

As we followed her, I tried to remember the way so that we might explore the castle's rooms for ourselves later on. Our host opened a multitude of heavy wooden doors and allowed us to peer inside as we went. Most of the rooms had wooden ceilings and terracotta tiled floors, one even had a chandelier hanging askew from the ceiling. We stepped inside the room which was adjacent to the *Stanza di Annalena*; this just happened to be named the '*Stanza di Baldaccio*' (Baldaccio's room). It was fairly small and filled with darkness when we entered. She purposefully threw open the shutters and all at once the afternoon sun flooded the room with light. We were now able to see that the room was furnished with a small four-poster bed and had a ceiling with wooden beams. At the foot of the bed was a Savonarola chair (a wooden collapsible chair named after the Renaissance preacher Girolamo Savonarola). The reader may be familiar with such chairs since reproductions of these are used by custodians in many Italian museums.

A bust of a woman who appeared to be dressed as a nun rested on top of a wooden writing bureau opposite the foot of the four-poster bed. Our host proudly told us that this represented Annalena. The sitter of the bust's face was strange, not ugly, but not beautiful either. Our host believed that Annalena had been a very nice lady, just like me! I'm not sure whether she meant that I resembled the bust of Annalena or her character. I rather hoped the latter since I personally thought the sitter of the bust looked very peculiar! I studied the face in detail with its clearly defined painted eyebrows, rosy cheeks and red lips. The face was asymmetrical with one side appearing thinner and having smaller features than the other. One eye appeared wider than the other and the nose seemed extremely pinched, long and narrow. We only stayed in this room for a short time since our host was keen to show us more of the castle. She quickly closed up and once more she led the way with us following on at her heels. We passed through what appeared to be a dining room with a huge stone fireplace with a carved coat of arms above, and in the centre of the room there was a large wooden table. We then looked around another couple of bedrooms before she left us to settle into our own room. On our return to our bedroom we quickly set about unpacking our things before retracing our steps and exploring the castle once more on our own. As we fumbled our way along the dark, narrow corridors, we soon found ourselves back at Baldaccio's room. I hesitantly opened the door, half expecting to see his ghost. One of the shutters that our host had opened earlier had been left open and a shaft of sunlight offered just enough light to enable us to look around. I must confess that I did feel quite uncomfortable, even scared, whilst standing within this room. I sat down on the Savonarola chair at the foot of the bed and gazed once more upon the bust. This, I have to say, was a truly incredible experience. I felt a real sense of unease whilst sitting before it and I don't know whether I was imagining it or not but I felt a cold shiver creep along my spine. Richard quickly took a photograph of me sitting before the bust and on seeing this later the image is quite extraordinary. It is as though some strange aura surrounds my upper body. Needless to say, we didn't spend too long in this room! I pulled the door to and double-checked just to make sure that I had closed it firmly behind us. I wasn't taking any chances, the last thing I wished to encourage was a restless ghost!

We returned once more into the all-encompassing darkness of the corridor and shuffled along in single file, feeling the walls as we went. I could feel my heart beating fast. We stopped at some stone steps that led downwards into the depths of the castle. Instinctively we began to descend; was I a 'glutton for punishment' or what? I was frightened but not enough to put me off. It was a strange sense of fear, one tinged with curiosity and excitement. The stone steps led down into the dungeons; there was no going back now. As we climbed forever downwards, suddenly, in the darkness we could just make out a skeleton suspended from the ceiling of a dungeon cell. This was really freaky and not the sort of thing I wanted to see. If this was not enough, we next encountered a skull which had been carefully placed upon a stone ledge together with an assortment of other creepy items. At our next turn, and on a less frightening note, we could just make out what seemed to be a well-stocked wine cellar with some old dust-laden bottles stacked on racks against damp-encrusted stone walls.

I felt quite relieved when we returned to the main part of the castle and as we passed through its rooms and corridors I wondered if indeed Annalena had ever stepped foot within its walls, as legend says she did. Could this ancient stone stronghold once have felt the merriment and happiness that is generally associated with newlyweds? Or was Annalena unhappy in her marriage as stated by Litta? The fact that Baldaccio had been fighting against her kinsfolk must surely have upset her, leaving her confused and deeply concerned about the situation. Could these castle walls have been witness to her sadness? Whatever the case, if indeed Annalena did stay at Sorci, the castle and the surrounding countryside must have seemed strange and so far removed from what she had grown accustomed to in Florence. Sorci must have seemed desolate and rugged in contrast to Florence with its fine monuments and relatively clean paved streets. I thought of her lying afraid in bed during the hours of darkness, awakened by the unfamiliar sounds of the

Aretine countryside: the grunting of wild boars, screeching of owls and the distant howl of a wolf.

When we had made our reservation to stay at Sorci castle I had explained that I was doing some research on Annalena Malatesta and I had enquired whether anyone at the castle might be able to assist me. Indeed, someone would be available to help me with my enquiries I was told and I met with that person later that afternoon. Coincidentally, it just so happened that the gentleman whom we had met on our arrival was that person. His name was Alberto and he seemed more than keen to assist. He led us over to a small building next to the castle which was crammed full of books related to Sorci and its history. He pulled a couple of them from a shelf which he thought might be of interest to me. We then slipped outside into the late afternoon sunshine, and sat under the shade of an olive tree. We discussed Baldaccio and Annalena for a great many minutes. It was wonderful to meet with someone else who was as enthusiastic about this celebrity couple from the Renaissance as I was. A curious, fleeting thought entered my head: what would Annalena and Baldaccio have made of us discussing their lives some 500 years or so after their death? As we were chatting Alberto just happened to mention that he was in the process of writing a book about Baldaccio and that perhaps one day when I had finished my book and he his, we might give a presentation together. We both agreed about certain details relating to the couple, for example that there had probably been an error surrounding Annalena's birthdate that had been perpetuated through the ages. He believed that a birthdate prior to 1426 would be more likely. I of course already knew Annalena's exact date of birth but did not disclose this at the time. He also told me that he didn't believe Baldaccio had been at the battle of Anghiari since he would have been in Suvereto at the time of the battle. I was pleased to hear this since this supported what I had also read.

Crucially, Alberto had something else up his sleeve, namely the identity of the person who he believed to have been responsible for the murder of Baldaccio. As the reader will discover, mystery surrounds this intriguing episode and I will explore this in a later chapter. Unfortunately, he was unwilling to elaborate further on this piece of the jigsaw but he assured me that it would be revealed in his forthcoming book. As much as I really would have loved to have obtained this information from him I knew I couldn't push him on it. I had gleaned as much as I possibly could so I thanked him and said goodbye. Richard and I returned to our room within the castle and it was only at this point that I truly became aware that we were indeed the only ones within its ancient walls.

That evening we enjoyed a delicious meal at the nearby *locanda*, where we feasted upon hearty Aretine cuisine. From the verandah where we were sitting, we welcomed the sight of a family who were also enjoying their meal. At least we weren't the only diners that evening. It was comforting to hear the voices of the children as they played near an ancient wine press, a relic from when the *locanda* had once been a farm. Feeling well and truly satisfied after our wonderful repast we headed back to 'our castle' and to our room. Call me crazy, but I thought that it would be a good idea if we explored the castle at midnight and I suggested this to Richard. Suffice it to say that he didn't appear to be too enamoured with that thought.

Since we had already explored the grounds of the castle and there really wasn't anything else to do, we went to bed fairly early. Of course I still had the intention of getting up at the stroke of midnight. However, as the hours slipped into the darkness of the night that idea very quickly disappeared. What had I hoped to gain from it anyway? Perhaps I thought that the ghost of Baldaccio would be friendly and provide answers to my questions about Annalena. I smiled nervously at this thought. Call me a 'scaredy cat', but I couldn't believe that I had even suggested such a stupid idea in the first place. I tried to sleep but in the deathly silence of the night I found my mind racing with thoughts about Annalena and Baldaccio. I tossed and turned and tried with all my might to calm my mind but it was no use. Suddenly, I heard the screech of an owl and I felt frightened. I sat up in bed and looked over at Richard who had already dropped off to sleep and was totally unaware of my plight. The room was unbearably hot since it didn't have any air conditioning and even although we had brought a portable fan with us it did nothing to alleviate the situation. I now know that even ancient, thick-stoned Tuscan castles which are freezing cold in the winter can be as uncomfortable to live in during the hot summer months. I lay back down, turned over and closed my eyes hoping that this time I might be able to drift off to sleep. However, once more I was prevented from doing so. I felt certain that I could hear music playing faintly in the room. It was strange music, not of a type that I was familiar with. It wasn't modern, or even from the time of Annalena and Baldaccio. The gentle melodic tune appeared to be from a flute or some other wind instrument. I pulled the bedcovers up tight around myself in an attempt to block out its strange sound. I must have eventually dozed off to sleep for a short while, however, since all I remember is being brusquely awakened by the sensation of a slight movement or shaking of the bed. I panicked and sat bolt upright, and promptly woke Richard to tell him what had happened. Annoyed that I had interrupted his slumbers, he responded with a mere utterance of, 'Oh go back to sleep, you're just imagining it!' He duly turned over and returned to the 'land of nod', whilst I, needless to say, remained awake until the first sight of sunrise, my saviour!

Our stay at Sorci castle had certainly been memorable at least for me. However, as fascinating as it was I don't think that I will be rushing back there again soon. Before heading back to Florence we of course had to visit nearby Ranco and its castle, the possible birthplace of Baldaccio. Unfortunately, we were unable to walk up to the castle (which now exists only as a ruin and is privately owned). The only view we were able to get of it was from the car window as we sped by on the road. I looked over at the desolate ruin resting atop a croppy spur. It was difficult to believe that it had actually belonged to Annalena after Baldaccio's death. In the *catasto* of 1442 it is recorded that Annalena was in possession of the castle at that time. However, she is known to have sold it in 1443 and I wondered if she had actually ever visited this place at all. As we drove past I caught sight of a sign indicating the direction for Monterchi which I knew to be the location of one of Piero della Francesca's greatest masterpieces, his fresco known as the *Madonna del Parto* or Pregnant Madonna, which I had wanted to see for as long as I can remember. Since we were so close it would have been a crime not to make a detour. Today a tiny museum serves as a shrine for this hugely important work by one of the leading artists of the Renaissance. We were amply rewarded since we were the only visitors in the museum and able to enjoy Piero's beautiful figure of the pregnant Madonna, all to ourselves. As I gazed upon the fresco I have to confess that tears trickled down my cheeks, so enraptured was I by its beauty.

This chance detour along the Piero della Francesca route may seem like a mere digression and an act of self-indulgence on my part and indeed it was, but permit me to say that there may in fact also be some connection between this great artist and the story of Baldaccio and Annalena and this will become apparent in due course.

CHAPTER 9:

Celebrations on the birth of a son

'Long before I had even felt any movement in my womb I heeded the wise counsel of those who knew about such things and I thank God that their recommendations of herbal remedies have indeed served me well.

'On hearing that I was with child, my heart became so full of joy that only such good news could bring. But it is also true to say that this same joy had fear as its companion, since I knew not the path ahead. I know that I should not complain about such insignificant matters but if truth be known I am growing quite tired of consuming so many chickens and capons. Even the fragrant Trebbiano wine doesn't make such blandness any more palatable. However, it is more than enough reward that God has safely delivered of us our dear little Guidantonio and for that I am truly grateful.

'As I gaze upon his sweet, dear little face I am afraid that he should cry or show signs of distress or even pain since I know not what to do. I watch him intently from my bed, frightened lest he should breathe his last breath. God only knows the relief that I feel when I see our dear little son safe and secure, wrapped ever so tightly in swaddling bands and held in the arms of his nurse. May God grant that he be healthy. I ask God and his mother Madonna Saint Mary and all the other Saints in Paradise to make him a good boy in the grace of God'.

From the moment Annalena married Baldaccio there would have been immense pressure upon her to fulfil her duty to become a mother. Alongside marriage, the birth of a child, and particularly the birth of a son, was a moment to be celebrated during the Renaissance. The birth of a son ensured the continuation of the family name. Baldaccio had not needed to wait long for his heir and therefore one can imagine the great joy that must have filled the couple's household when their son Guidantonio was born. Richa informs us that the name for their child was authenticated in the convent archives and the *catasto* record for Annalena dated 1442 had also revealed to me that Guidantonio was fifteen months old when the *catasto* was written.

Annalena herself must have felt both happy and relieved to have given birth safely at a time when mortality during childbirth was commonplace. Possibly even Annalena's own mother had died in childbirth. Giving birth to a healthy child was a 'badge of honour' for a woman in the Renaissance. Death in childbirth affected women from all classes and wealth did not act as a deterrent. Medical care was obviously not as advanced or as sophisticated as it is today and women actually feared that they may not survive the birth of a child. Indeed, many women even took insurance out against the eventuality of their own death during childbirth and possibly Annalena had done the same. From a study of Florentine death registers scholars have found that nearly one-fifth of the recorded deaths of young married women in early fifteenth-century Florence were linked in some way to childbearing. There was also a high mortality rate among newborns and young children during this period.

The elderly Contessa Elisabetta must have shared in the happiness of Annalena and Baldaccio when she heard about the new addition to the family. Although she had been childless herself, she most certainly would have offered words of reassurance during this very important and difficult episode of Annalena's life. Even before the birth of her child, Annalena would have prayed before an image of the Virgin and child in the comfort of her own bedchamber, in the hope that she like the Virgin would give birth to a healthy baby. Sacred scenes showing the birth of the Virgin or St. John the Baptist abound in the Renaissance and such scenes of a safe birth, set in familiar contemporary surroundings, offered comfort to young women like Annalena. However, such images also offered an idealistic and sanitised representation of childbirth since they do not actually show the birth itself and as such, technically, they depict confinement scenes.

An insight into the actual reality of the dangerous nature of childbirth during this period can, however, be seen in what is probably one of the most poignant and harrowing works of Italian Renaissance art. It is the marble relief known as the *Tornabuoni Relief* or *The Death of Francesca Tornabuoni*, c.1478–79, by the workshop of Andrea del Verrocchio now in the Bargello National Museum, Florence. Within this relief we witness the sorrow and despair experienced by Giovanni Tornabuoni (who was the papal treasurer and manager of the Medici bank in Rome at the time of his wife's death) on learning that he had lost both his wife and child in childbirth. The relief depicts two separate scenes: on the right-hand side we see the slumped, dishevelled, dying figure of his wife Francesca surrounded by grieving female attendants and in the left scene we see the presentation of the dead baby by the midwife to the father and group of onlookers.

Annalena was indeed one of the fortunate young women to have given birth safely. Baldaccio must have felt thrilled that he had an heir and that his wife had survived the ordeal. On hearing the announcement of the birth of a son to Annalena and Baldaccio friends and relatives would have arrived at the couple's home in their splendid palazzo in the parish of San Felice in Piazza to present gifts to the new mother and of course to welcome the new child. This was a social event and was rather like a post-natal 'baby shower'. Visitors would have brought gifts of sugar-coated sweetmeats in beautifully decorated boxes specially purchased from the apothecary shop and probably also gifts of silver spoons. Most of the women that came to visit (since birth and confinement was essentially female-centred) would have been from influential and elite families; perhaps Annalena had even sought advice from some of them during her pregnancy. Annalena would have received her visitors and guests in the '*camera*' or nuptial bedroom, which was the heart of the household. In a wealthy Florentine household such as that belonging to Annalena and Baldaccio this space would have served as both a private space for sleeping and as a more public one for receiving visitors. In the same way that marriage was an opportunity to show off the wealth of the family, so too was the birth of a child. The '*camera*' would have been richly furnished and decorated for the occasion. Rich tapestries would have hung from the walls and a sumptuous red and gold bedcover with intricate designs and specially embroidered birth sheets and birth pillows would have dressed the bed. Annalena would have worn a special veil head covering and a *mantello da parto* (birth cloak) specially purchased for the event and she would have greeted her guests from her bed during this 'lying-in' period, as it was known. Once more those sacred Renaissance images come to mind and one in particular, the *Birth of St. John the Baptist* (1486–1490) painted by Domenico Ghirlandaio for the Tornabuoni Chapel in the church of Santa Maria Novella. In this image we can easily substitute the figure of St. Elizabeth with that of Annalena or indeed any other affluent mother from the fifteenth century.

At last Annalena could make good use of the *desco da parto* (wooden birth tray), just one of the many gifts she may have received on the occasion of her wedding or at the birth of her baby son. These birth trays were almost trophy-like in their significance since they were markers of this very important episode in a woman's life. They were generally painted on both sides with images which could depict birth scenes, games and naked babies. Such images held symbolic meaning related to the safe delivery of a child. Not only were these trays decorative but they were also functional since they were used to bring treats to the new mother following the delivery of her child. In the aforementioned fresco by Domenico Ghirlandaio we can see such birth trays in use; one is shown with a cloth on it to protect it whilst another laden with fruit is being carried on the head of a woman. Once they had served their original function these trays could be hung on the wall since they were often treasured and handed down in families. Several of these birth trays exist today and can be seen in museums and galleries. At this point it seems pertinent to remind the reader that these trays and many other objects that were made during the Renaissance period are sometimes still displayed as though they are works of art with the purpose of being viewed in a modern gallery. Although aesthetically beautiful in their own right, it is important to consider their original function and purpose in order to appreciate them fully.

As Annalena was a noblewoman she most probably would have had a live-in nurse to help care for little Guidantonio since only the very wealthy would be able to afford this. More usually, babies were sent out for up to two years to a wet nurse in the countryside. As was customary for the times, little Guidantonio was baptised within a few days of his birth and this took place on June 1st 1441. Guidantonio was therefore born at the end of May 1441. It is recorded that Astorre II Manfredi Lord of Faenza (whose mother Gentile incidentally belonged to the Malatesta family) was named as the child's godfather. Although he was incarcerated in the *stinche*

(Florentine prison), it appears that Baldaccio enabled him to be released and Manfredi also nominated two notaries to be present at the baptism to record the event. All infants who were born in Florence would have been baptised in the baptistery of San Giovanni. However, it is not known for certain if Guidantonio would also have been baptised here or, as has been suggested by some, in Baldaccio's homeland. In Baldaccio's day the people of Anghiari didn't have a baptismal font and the community usually baptised their children at the parish church of Micciano or Santa Maria alla Sovara, which were located outside the town. It has been noted that Guidantonio may have been baptised in Micciano.

Annalena and Baldaccio would have paid careful attention to their choice of *compare* (godparents) for their young son. Since the couple belonged to the upper echelons of society their choice of godparents would have been based upon their usefulness and importance to the family. Choosing godparents was considered a form of networking in the Renaissance. Annalena would not have been present for the actual baptism itself since she would have been still recovering after the birth. Baptism was largely a public and masculine affair in contrast to birth and confinement, which were private and female-centred. Most likely a godmother would have stood in for Annalena at the baptismal ceremony. The infant Guidantonio would have had special baptism clothes: fine linen swaddling bands specially ornamented for the ceremony and the finest baptismal mantle perhaps of rich gold velvet with trimmings on top. The baptism of a child was yet another occasion for gift-giving. Undoubtedly, the godparents of little Guidantonio would have given gifts including boxes of sweetmeats, forks and candles. Following the baptism of Guidantonio his godparents would have visited Annalena at home.

Perhaps in the hope of the safe delivery of a son as his heir, Baldaccio is known to have contributed financially to the building of a baptistery in his homeland of Anghiari. It is recorded that in April 1439 Baldaccio gave '400 *grossoni* masses of silver' for the construction of the old baptistery of San Giovanni, which is located in the former Via del Borghetto, today the Via Taglieschi in Anghiari. The church and baptistery of San Giovanni in Anghiari was actually only completed in 1442, a year after Baldaccio's murder, so unfortunately he didn't live to see the inauguration of the building; the architrave over the entrance to the building that was the former baptistery bears the date 1442. The door that can be seen today is a replica of the original, which is held in the *L'Istituto Statale d'Arte* in Anghiari and has been restored in recent times. I couldn't believe that Baldaccio could possibly be capable of such a charitable act; perhaps beneath his cold, war-like exterior there was a element of kindness after all! The discovery of this kind gesture to the people of Anghiari on behalf of Baldaccio led me along a completely new and unexpected but exciting path. I actually found myself following along the trail of the great Renaissance painter Piero della Francesca once more. According to one school of thought, there would appear to be a possible connection with the commission of Piero's masterpiece the *Baptism of Christ* now in the National Gallery in London and the Baptistery of Anghiari funded by Baldaccio. The painting can be dated to after 1437 and it may be one of Piero's earliest extant works. In fairly recent times a fascinating hypothesis connected with this altarpiece has been postulated by Roberto Manescalchi, an art historian and a leading scholar of Piero della Francesca, who wrote that this work may have been commissioned by Annalena's husband Baldaccio and might have been intended for the high altar of the baptistery in Anghiari. The author provides plausible evidence for his hypothesis, including the fact that Piero della Francesca was in Florence in 1439 when Baldaccio was also there. It would have seemed quite reasonable for Baldaccio to have commissioned a work from an artist who was a contemporary and from his native land. Interestingly, some new documentation has emerged which suggests that the Pichi family who were known to Baldaccio may have acted as a middleman for Baldaccio and the artist. Manescalchi offers a reason why the altarpiece was never delivered to the baptistery in Anghiari: Baldaccio had been murdered in 1441 before the baptistery was actually built. There is even the suggestion that the altarpiece may have once been in the home of Annalena in Florence.

Today the now deconsecrated old baptistery in Anghiari is a private home and at the time of writing it could be rented out as a holiday apartment. I was interested to read about the property online, which included some significant historical information peppered amongst the more practical conditions of renting the property. Of particular note was that Piero della Francesca's altarpiece of the *Baptism of Christ* is believed to have once adorned one of its walls. I think that it was this information that had helped to provide a basis for the hypothesis above. I was amused to read that a forty-two-inch television screen now occupied the wall on which the Piero painting was hung (if it was ever there). If the hypothesis by Manescalchi should be verified one day, then this would be groundbreaking material for the art world and it would be an unexpected finding of immense significance for me. The possibility that the subject of this book, Annalena Malatesta, may have been linked to one of the greatest masterpieces in Western art is something that I could never have imagined.

Sadly, not a lot more is known about these very brief years that Annalena and Baldaccio shared together as husband and wife. As we will discover in the next chapter, tragically Baldaccio's life was cut short due to his assassination in 1441.

CHAPTER 10:

Intrigue, conspiracy and murder

'Dear God abandon me not in this my hour of need. Grant me strength to choose the right path ahead since I know not the way to turn. I beseech thee to grant forgiveness to those who are in need of it. May they find refuge in your love. I am comforted in your guidance and seek thy protection always. You are my beacon of hope, my anchor at sea and my only salvation. I am forever your humble servant. Find it in your heart to give unto me and all others who live on this earth the unconditional love that is eternally yours.'

As pointed out in the first chapter of this book, the life of Annalena and the foundation of her convent has only really been told as a mere footnote to the more sensational story surrounding the murder of her husband, Baldaccio d'Anghiari. Hopefully, I am progressing well in my quest to readdress the situation and I am rather pleased to say that here, possibly for the very first time, his story will be told as a mere chapter or so in the story that is hers.

The assassination of Baldaccio in 1441 was one of the top crimes of the fifteenth century and it caused a great sensation both in the city of Florence and throughout Italy. It was a crime like no other and many important personages from the Renaissance including Cosimo de' Medici and even Pope Eugenius IV have been associated with it. The crime was considered significant enough to have been recorded by several contemporary chroniclers and historians including Giovanni Cavalcanti in the fifteenth century and Niccolo Machiavelli in the sixteenth century. Incidentally, it is worth pointing out that Machiavelli in his *Florentine Histories* based much of his account of the murder of Baldaccio on what Cavalcanti had said before him. If newspapers had existed in those days then this crime would have provided fodder for many of the tabloids, and tales of conspiracy, bloodshed and blame would have been splattered across their pages.

For our purposes it would be impossible to discuss the life of Annalena without giving any mention to this terrible event since it did indeed have a direct impact on her life. This was Annalena's husband after all and the father of her child. Baldaccio d'Anghiari was assassinated on September 6th 1441, a date that would not only go down in history but would change Annalena's life forever. His assassination took place not in some back street in the city but right in the very political heart of Florence: within the monumental Palazzo Vecchio (see **Figure 12**), which was called the Palagio de' Signoria in Annalena's day. This palazzo has enjoyed an interesting past and over the centuries it has been known by many other names each reflecting the political characteristics of the city at the time. The building that we see today has been greatly altered since it was first built in 1290 after designs by the architect Arnolfo di Cambio, when it was originally built as the residence of the priors (the city's highest governing body) and then called the Palazzo dei Priori. The massive crenellated fortress-like appearance is a reminder of the instability of the government during these early times. In the fifteenth century the palazzo housed the government of the Florentine Republic or *Signoria* hence the change of name to the Palazzo (Palagio) della Signoria. The palazzo stands in the Piazza della Signoria which again reflects the name of this palazzo in the fifteenth century. In the sixteenth century the palazzo became the residence of Duke Cosimo I, who commissioned his court artist Giorgio Vasari to double the building in size. The Grand Duke and his family then moved to the new Pitti Palace in 1540 and the Palazzo della Signoria became known as the Palazzo Vecchio (the Old Palace). Even today the Palazzo Vecchio still serves to seat the Florentine city government. All visitors and tourists to Florence will be familiar with the Piazza della Signoria with its aforementioned monumental palace and outdoor museum of sculptures. In centuries past this was the hub of the city and it remains so today. Everyone from all over the world, it seems, flocks here: a seething mass of tourists, tourist guides, souvenir vendors and police officers patrolling from the comfort of their vehicles. On a daily basis tourists descend on this Florentine 'Mecca', and armed with selfie sticks, cameras and mobile phones they jostle with each other to photograph the replica of Michelangelo's giant statue of David, which stands proudly outside the Palazzo Vecchio itself. Sadly, many of those who excitedly snap photos of the statue will remain totally unaware of the history behind it, and may even believe that they are seeing the original statue of David itself rather than a copy. Michelangelo's statue of the young shepherd boy who fought against the giant Goliath was originally intended to be placed high up on the cathedral facade but was considered to be too perfect for such a position and so it was placed before the Palazzo Vecchio where it was unveiled in 1504. The statue was later removed from this site to preserve it from the elements and taken into the Galleria dell'Accademia in Florence where it can be seen today.

During the years Annalena was living in Florence, the Florentine government or *Signoria* (sometimes written as Signory) was made up of eight elected government officials known as *priori* or priors plus an individual who was elected to the highest position of *Gonfaloniere di Giustizia* who, as the name suggests, was responsible for the maintenance of law and justice. Each of these individuals held office for two months and were then replaced with a new group. Thus the city had six changes of government in a year. The Florentine *Signoria* also enjoyed support from various other office holders which included the 'twelve good men', sixteen *gonfaloniere*, a war office which was comprised of the 'ten' and another body called the 'eight' who served as a criminal and political police.

The Piazza della Signoria would have looked quite different in Annalena's day, since obviously there wouldn't have been all the trappings of modern-day life. Outside the palazzo itself on the front and on the north there would have been an L-shaped platform called a *ringhiera* and it was from here that orators spoke, hence the name *ringhiera* meaning a haranguing place. It was here too that the Signoria would assemble for public ceremonies. The *ringhiera* was only demolished at the beginning of the nineteenth century when the present steps and platform replaced it. Additionally, the statues that we admire today, including the original David sculpted by Michelangelo, and those within the adjacent Loggia della Signoria (also known as the Loggia de' Lanzi and Loggia dell' Orcagna), were not yet in place. We can gain some idea of what the piazza with its palazzo and the adjacent Loggia della Signoria looked like in the fifteenth century before the statues were in place from a fresco depicting *The Granting of the Charter to St. Francis*. This was painted by the fifteenth-century artist Domenico Ghirlandaio and is in the Sassetti chapel in the Florentine church of Santa Trinita.

If walls could talk then the Palazzo Vecchio would have many tales to tell but none more secretive and brutal than the execution of Baldaccio in 1441. Although the palazzo had witnessed many turbulent episodes throughout its history, including the Ciompi revolt in 1378 and the imprisonment of Cosimo de' Medici in 1433 in the bell tower of the palazzo, nothing would compare with the murder of Baldaccio. This atrocious crime appears to have been unique and extremely dramatic for the times. For this reason the narrative of this 'murder most foul' has more or less been handed down through the centuries and has attained legendary status. People remain fascinated by the assassination of Baldaccio d'Anghiari since indeed this was a crime like no other. Just as today, many people remember where they were and what they were doing when John F. Kennedy was assassinated; this must also have been the case for the Florentines and other Italians when Baldaccio was murdered. Everyone would have been familiar with the name of this famous *condottiere*.

How could it all have gone so horribly wrong? How could it have been that Baldaccio d'Anghiari, valiant captain of infantry and one-time hero of the Florentines, came to meet such a terrible end? His assassination has all the makings of a gripping Hollywood blockbuster movie but this was no movie, this atrocious act did indeed happen. This episode has been told many times before but since this crime was so sensational and did have a major impact on Annalena it is worth recounting in detail. On September 6th 1441, Baldaccio was summoned by the *Gonfaloniere di Giustizia*, Bartolomeo Orlandini, to the Palazzo Signoria. Some say that Baldaccio went to the palazzo without suspicion of anything untoward, since this was a place that he was familiar with. He would often have gone there to attend to matters relating to conditions of his contracts, for example the pay of his soldiers.

According to legend Baldaccio was with his wife Annalena at home when the summons from Orlandini came and some accounts state that he had been warned by his wife of the dangers threatening him in the city, because of his recent misconducts, and that he should prepare himself for the worst. It is impossible for us to know if this was the case but Richa noted that in the

Annalena convent memoirs it was written that Baldaccio had been at home with his wife and that he had turned to a crucifix of Christ which was in the room and he begged pardon for his sin on the eve before his death. When Richa actually visited the convent of Annalena in the eighteenth century, he specifically noted that a crucifix that had once belonged to Baldaccio was kept in the rooms of the infirmary of the Annalena convent along with other precious things including further crucifixes. So perhaps there is some truth to this part of the story.

However, if Baldaccio had been given a 'heads up' as it were by Annalena, it is tempting to question why he did respond to the summons. In response to this, it may have been the case that he thought that he probably would escape the consequences of his misconducts as he had always had a habit of doing. Perhaps he anticipated receiving a hefty fine and/or some other equivalent punishment, which would have been more usual when *condottieri* had committed any misdeeds. There must however have been some concern on Baldaccio's part since he is believed to have sought advice from Cosimo de' Medici before heading for the Palazzo della Signoria. Cosimo allegedly cunningly told him that 'obedience' was praiseworthy and was considered the greatest virtue of citizens. If this was a movie then the next scene would be the one that everyone would be waiting for. Tension would be mounting, background music would be reaching a crescendo and the audience would be drawn to the edge of their seats with excitement and fear.

Baldaccio arrived at the Palazzo della Signoria where he was met by Orlandini who escorted the valiant captain up the broad flight of stairs leading to the private chambers of the magistrates on the upper floor of the palazzo. It is said that they stopped in a corridor outside the chamber of the ruling *Signoria* and when the time was right Orlandini signalled to some armed men who had been hiding in one of the adjoining rooms who then rushed out and assaulted Baldaccio. The armed men killed Annalena's husband and then threw his body out of a window on the north side of the palace facing the courtyard called the *Cortile della Dogana* (sometimes known as *Cortile del Capitano*), which was in those days open. The executioner was sent out to strip Baldaccio's body of its clothing leaving it completely naked before finally cutting off Baldaccio's head and dragging his corpse round to the centre of the piazza in front of the main facade of the palace, for all to see. The corpse is said to have remained in the piazza for nearly a day so that the public could see it. The valiant captain who had in the not-so-distant past been made a Florentine citizen and awarded many privileges by the Florentines, was declared a rebel and a traitor to the Republic.

Amazingly, a very interesting first-hand account of the episode written by one of the priors at the time survives. Francesco di Tommaso Giovanni recorded that the Florentine government wasn't happy with how Baldaccio had been conducting himself. Baldaccio had basically taken it upon himself to override the Florentine government in his actions and thus the priors together with Orlandini, the *Gonfaloniere di Giustizia*, had decided to punish him. Giovanni recounts that many of the priors had met on the evening of September 5th to discuss the situation. The priors plotted against Baldaccio in an indirect conversation whose intent appears to have been understood by everyone. Only one of the prior's colleagues seems to have kept out of it and that was Cante Compagni, and he appears to have kept silent about the whole affair. On the day of the assassination, September 6th, the diarist recorded that he had hidden nine palace guards in his own room, and after Baldaccio arrived at the palazzo, he moved the guards into the *Saletta*. Giovanni then apparently stood at the head of a passageway pretending to read letters, while awaiting a prearranged signal from Orlandini. Once the signal was received the guards set upon Baldaccio and stabbed him. Baldaccio's body was then thrown from a window into the *Cortile del Capitano* and he was finally decapitated and his head exhibited. Giovanni claimed that the priors had simply planned to arrest Baldaccio.

The fine arts Professor Marvin Trachtenberg gives a fascinating analysis of the architectural spaces of the Palazzo della Signoria and uses information such as that provided by Giovanni and the assassination of Baldaccio to determine the actual physical layout of the Palazzo Vecchio building. He believes that Giovanni and the others must have known that their intentions wouldn't go to plan and that they would lead to something far worse. Baldaccio was a proud, valiant captain and he would obviously have sought to defend himself. Trachtenberg also points out that the very fact that there were nine guards required to carry out the deed reflects this. Supposedly, according to Giovanni, the intention was only to capture Baldaccio but he drew a knife to defend himself, which led to the guards stabbing him. Everything appeared to have been planned secretly even including the part of the palazzo where the murder should take place, i.e. within a secret passageway. The Palazzo della Signoria in Annalena's day was the very symbol of civic life and Florence's power. Giovanni and the priors served as

Florence's highest officers. They would have known that the treachery they were about to commit was immoral and illegal. The Florentine Government was divided in their allegiance to Cosimo and upholding law and justice. They obviously regarded Baldaccio as a potential threat to Cosimo and they would have been torn as to what they should do. The assassination shocked the Florentine people because it had been carried out by the Florentine Signoria, the upholders of law and justice in the city. The crime made a whole mockery of the institution of the priors and undermined the palazzo as a symbol of power and order. Despite the turbulent history of the Palazzo Vecchio the assassination of Baldaccio was extremely unusual and perhaps this was why Baldaccio had gone there in the first place without suspicion.

Why wasn't it enough just to kill Baldaccio and why was he beheaded? The beheading had been done to try to give some semblance of legality to the atrocious act, to make it seem as though the execution had taken place under normal judicial circumstances. The Florentine government had to demonstrate to the Florentine citizens the severity of Baldaccio's treason and to serve as a reminder not to challenge the authority of the government. News of the mercenary captain's murder must have raged through the city and people must have flocked to the Piazza della Signoria to see for themselves if it were true. As for 'povera Annalena' (poor Annalena), the shock of hearing about her husband's terrible fate is quite unimaginable. I thought of her together with her young son in their home on Via Romana in the Oltrarno. Her status had changed in an instant: she was no longer the wife of the most respected captain of infantry whom everyone had admired. She was now, at the tender young age of twenty-one, the disgraced widow of a traitor to the Florentine government. Did she now fear for her own life and that of her child? Would the Florentine government and the Florentine citizens now wish to have her expelled from the city too? She must have felt distraught and confused. Of course, as the wife of a soldier of fortune, Annalena would have learned to live with the fear that one day she might be the recipient of tragic news. However, it must have been devastating for her to learn that her valiant husband had not died as a great hero on some far-flung battlefield, but as an unsuspecting victim in their home city. She must have needed to draw upon all of her strength in the ensuing days, weeks and months. Her world had been turned completely upside down overnight. Undoubtedly, she must have prayed to God to help her and it would be to God that she would eventually turn in the days and years ahead. Following the assassination, the Florentine government confiscated all of Baldaccio's goods and possessions with the exception of those that had been taken by force. Strangely, it was one week after Baldaccio's death on September 13th 1441 that the *Signoria* issued a *provvisione* (provision) that listed Baldaccio's trumped-up crimes. The reason stated by the Florentine Signory was Baldaccio's disobedience to their commands while in their service.

It is not known whether or not Annalena would have sought the advice and comfort from the aged Contessa Elisabetta whom she still had strong links with or indeed from her godfather Cosimo if she did not suspect his involvement. Undoubtedly, she would have been consoled by Florence's Archbishop Antonino (Pierozzi) who, as part of his role in the spiritual welfare of citizens, gave support to widows in the city. Archbishop Antonino probably would have reminded Annalena that she would now need to be both mother and father to her child. I will discuss the important role that he played in Annalena's life in due course. On the other hand, since Annalena was of Malatesta blood she may well have been able to deal with the situation in a much more stoic way than might be expected from someone of such a young age hurled into such tragic circumstances.

The murder of Baldaccio has fascinated many throughout the centuries and continues to do so today. Set against a backdrop of conspiracy and intrigue, we know how, where and who committed the crime but it may never be known for certain who actually instigated it and the exact motive for it. The situation was a complex one with so many twists and turns. Like many other scholars before me, I have pondered long and hard over this largely unexplained episode in Italian Renaissance history. This was a period when mercenary soldiers and leaders including even the Pope would stop at nothing to cultivate their own interests. It is thus worthwhile considering some of those who might have had a vested interest in desiring that Baldaccio should be killed.

It would appear that Annalena's husband had become too dangerous to the Florentines and in particular to Annalena's godfather Cosimo de' Medici. Cosimo had returned to Florence from his exile only seven years before the assassination and he was still in the process of building up his power base in the city having not yet attained the level of power he would later achieve. He effectively surrounded himself with his supporters but these remained dangerous and tumultuous times and he still had to be on guard against anyone who may have wished to challenge his position in the city. One person in particular is believed to have posed a serious threat to Cosimo and his name was Neri Capponi. This was the same Neri Capponi who had been a witness at Baldaccio and Annalena's wedding. Capponi was considered a great soldier and his reputation had been significantly enhanced following the victory of the Florentines at the Battle of Anghiari under his leadership. It was believed by many that Cosimo had feared his growing friendship with Baldaccio and thought that if Capponi wished to oppose him he could do so with the help of Baldaccio. Both chroniclers Cavalcanti and Machiavelli wrote that Cosimo considered Capponi's friendship with Baldaccio as a threat. Baldaccio would continue to trouble the Florentine Signory headed by Cosimo and his allies since in August 1441 (only a few weeks before his assassination) Baldaccio had entered into the Florentine territory of Piombino without the permission of the Florentine government. Baldaccio had actually blamed the Florentine government for his plundering of Suvreto, which belonged to Piombino.

However, Machiavelli in his *Florentine Histories* clearly considered Bartolomeo Orlandini to be the sole author of the crime since it was Orlandini who had given the signal. Machiavelli adds that the other citizens had easily persuaded Orlandini to put Baldaccio to death… 'to avenge himself and deliver his country from a man whom they must either retain at great peril or discharge to their greater confusion…' From Machiavelli's account of the incident, the implication is blatantly that the Florentines needed to do something about Baldaccio; whether they kept him in their service or not he was clearly considered to be a threat. Interestingly, it is recorded that in April 1440 during the war with Milan, Cosimo de' Medici had sent Orlandini to guard an extremely important mountain pass called the Marradi Pass in the Apennines, in the hope of preventing the Duke of Milan's *condottiere* Niccolo Piccinino from entering into Florence. According to Machiavelli it appears to have been an emergency situation and since the Florentines didn't have troops and officers to guard all of the passes, many citizens including Orlandini were sent out to prevent Piccinino's descent into Tuscany. The Marradi was a castle situated at the foot of the mountains which separated Tuscany and Romagna and should have been easy to guard as it was in rugged terrain. For some reason or other Orlandini abandoned this pass and allowed Piccinino to enter into Tuscany, reaching as far as Fiesole, very close to Florence. This desertion by Orlandini was probably due to the fact that he was not a fighter and had been transferred from court duties to war.

When Baldaccio heard that Orlandini had shamefully abandoned the pass he became enraged and publicly branded him a coward. This caused great shame to Orlandini and it would seem he never forgave Baldaccio.

It is possible that Cosimo acted upon the strained relations between Baldaccio and Orlandini since in the months prior to the assassination Orlandini had just been elected for a second time as the city's most powerful officer (*Gonfaloniere di Giustizia*) when the crime occurred. It is worth mentioning that it has been said that Orlandini had been installed in this position for a second time in 1441 by 'jugglery' of the ballot. If this were the case it offered a favourable opportunity for getting rid of Baldaccio. The argument grows more in favour of Cosimo being complicit in the crime when we consider the already mentioned detail that Baldaccio had allegedly sought advice from him prior to going to the Palazzo della Signoria on the day of his murder. It is important to point out, however, that this part of the story, which appears to involve Cosimo in the plot and which seems to be the only known account that does, was reported by the fifteenth-century chronicler Giovanni Cavalcanti who is known to have had a hatred of Cosimo. Intriguingly, in the early part of his account of the murder of Baldaccio, Cavalcanti appears to speak highly of Cosimo; it is only in the latter part of his narrative that he seems to be more embittered towards him and indeed everyone.

What would Cosimo have gained from the crime? If indeed he saw Capponi together with Baldaccio as a possible threat to his position then the removal of Baldaccio would have weakened this eventuality. What were relations like between Cosimo and Capponi after the crime? According to Machiavelli the incident of Baldaccio's murder served to weaken Capponi's power and lost him many friends and much influence. Strangely, Capponi himself does not mention the murder even although Baldaccio was his good friend. The correspondence between Capponi and Cosimo after Baldaccio's death doesn't reveal the tension suggested by Machiavelli and Cavalcanti. Additionally, Cosimo advised his son Piero to honour Capponi after his death in 1457 and had the artist Benozzo Gozzoli paint a portrait of him among his most important clients in the *Adoration of the Magi*, in the family chapel within the Medici palace.

Annalena must have felt enraged with the Florentine government and perhaps also even with her godfather Cosimo. How could he have allowed such a thing to happen to her husband? Could Cosimo, indeed would Cosimo, go to such lengths and have his own kinswoman suffer the resulting pain and anguish? Our modern sensibilities flag this up as being unlikely, however, someone living in the Renaissance would have banished such a thought from their mind and it would have been 'business as usual'. If Cosimo did indeed feel that his power was threatened then he would have stopped at nothing to prevent this. Such things were indeed possible during these perilous times. Interestingly, Cosimo would support Annalena in later years and she would continue to enjoy the support of the Medici family long after she had founded her convent. If Cosimo did play a part in the assassination of Baldaccio why did Annalena continue to have a relationship with him? In response to this, I have read that it could have been the case that Cosimo sought to 'wash away any crimes' that he may have instigated or been involved with.

If Cosimo hadn't actually been complicit in the murder then he surely must have had an awareness of the plot to kill Baldaccio. Baldaccio after all was so famous at this time and had been held in such high esteem it just simply wouldn't have been possible to have him quietly 'done away with'. As for Orlandini's involvement, certainly all existing evidence suggests that while he gave the signal to carry out the crime it is uncertain as to whether he actually instigated it. It was possibly the case that he did hatch the plot with his fellow priors, and I have even read that whilst he was in office as *Gonfaloniere di Giustizia* he had written to his brother in Pistoia asking that he send him a gang of ruffians to carry out the atrocious deed. It would also seem that he never forgave Baldaccio for publicly branding him a coward following the Marradi disaster. One further interesting thread which has been woven into the plot was that Orlandini had been in love with Baldaccio's beautiful wife Annalena. If this indeed was true he would certainly have had more than one reason to dislike him. I will discuss Orlandini's supposed love interest with Annalena in the next chapter.

In conclusion, Baldaccio had many enemies and there has even been a suggestion that someone outside the usual circle of suspects that I have mentioned above may have been responsible for instigating the terrible crime. During the course of my research surrounding this atrocious episode in Italian Renaissance history I myself had discovered several other individuals who had shown a hatred of Baldaccio and who would have had reason enough to wish for his removal. One name in particular that springs to mind is the *condottiere* Francesco Sforza (1401–1466) who is known to have had a hatred of Baldaccio and both had experienced antagonism towards each other.

I could write at length about all the various individuals that have become embroiled within this dark episode in history but since the purpose of this book is to celebrate Annalena's life I will leave the reader to pursue this further themselves if they so wish to do so. All that remains to be said is that the assassination of Baldaccio d'Anghiari serves to remind us of how incredibly tumultuous, dangerous, complex, secretive and underhand this period was.

CHAPTER 11:

Romantic interest between Annalena and Bartolomeo Orlandini?

There remained one niggling thought that I wished to resolve before I began to address the romantic interest that supposedly existed between Bartolomeo Orlandini and Annalena. This was that if Cosimo de' Medici hadn't been complicit in the crime why didn't he punish those responsible for it?

We headed firstly to the Harold Acton Library at the British Institute in Florence. The British Institute is housed within the elegant Palazzo Lanfredini along the beautiful Lungarno Guicciardini on the south side of the river Arno. The Institute has long played a significant role in Anglo-Florentine cultural life and first opened its doors in 1917. Whenever I visit Florence for extended periods I always try to visit this little oasis of Britishness within the city. The place has a lovely 'old world', genteel feel about it that is more akin to *Downton Abbey* than downtown Florence. One feels safe here since it also has the air of an embassy and indeed, the eagle-eyed visitor who passes along its narrow corridors will not fail to spot a huge Union Jack flag adorning the back wall of one of its offices. One can easily lose oneself for many an hour within the Institute's library, which is named after Harold Acton who had long associations with the Institute and who left his portion of the Palazzo Lanfredini to house it. Shelves groan under the weight of the extensive collection of books on Italian history and Italian literature. Leaving any study aside, it is actually worth visiting the library just to admire the 'Fiamma Ferragamo' room with its beautiful eighteenth-century painted ceiling.

It has to be said that on each occasion when I have visited the Institute I have noticed that a similar crowd of people seem to congregate here. Most appear to be elderly and speak both fluent Italian and English with clipped upper-class accents. I imagine them to be ex-pats who have long resided in Florence and have never, or have very rarely, returned to their native homeland. Although the British Institute exudes nostalgia it is also forward-looking. It offers an extensive programme of cultural, language and art history programmes which attract both young and more mature students from all over the world. Indeed, many a former student (including Kate Middleton, Duchess of Cambridge) will have fond memories of having studied there. Additionally, the Institute has an attractive children's library, which serves to encourage a new generation of readers. A regular feature in the Institute's calendar, which I particularly enjoy, is the rather quaint and, yes, extremely British custom of serving afternoon tea with cake on Thursday afternoons. I always try to combine my studies with this sweet reward whenever I am able to, so it wasn't surprising that it just happened to be a Thursday afternoon on the day that we visited. We had managed to secure somewhere to sit in the small reception area of the library with its comfortable seats and coffee table laden with British and American publications, all carefully arranged as might be expected in such a place. Richard picked up a newspaper to read whilst I started to skim through a book on the history of the Medici which had been written by someone called Colonel Young and published in 1926. I had no idea who Colonel Young was, other than that he apparently had been a fan of Cosimo de' Medici and he had written a history of the family which portrayed them in a positive light. Unsurprisingly, he clearly dismissed any accusation against Cosimo's involvement in the assassination of Baldaccio. Colonel Young wrote that there was '... not a particle of evidence that Cosimo had anything to do with it'. He said that the government was guilty of the crime and that in 1441 Cosimo had not yet attained the level of power he would later reach. Cosimo was thus unable to take any action against the government. Colonel Young had provided me with a satisfactory answer to my concern as to why Cosimo had not acted to punish those who had been responsible for the crime, if it hadn't been him. He also added that since it had been the Florentine government who were responsible for the crime, any action by Cosimo against the *Signoria* would have been considered unconstitutional.

As I mused over such thoughts I suddenly became aware of a flurry of activity around me. It was 4.30pm and time for tea, and as every good Brit knows, everything stops for tea! A small group of people filtered through into the adjacent room and we in turn followed suit. A posse of ladies was poised at the ready behind a table laden with all the necessary accoutrements for serving tea. They courteously welcomed each of us as we entered the room. Instructions were given so that those unfamiliar with the Institute's weekly ritual knew exactly what to do. As we selected our tea from a coffret emblazoned with the name of that very fine British brand Fortnum and Mason, I was amused to note that there was also an almost empty box of Yorkshire Tea sitting half hidden on the table. Guests could also choose from a selection of cakes, which included Italian apple cake, chocolate torte and Italian shortbread cake. We collected our cups of tea and chose our cakes then dropped some money into a donations pot. Then, carefully balancing a cup and saucer in one hand and a side plate with a piece of cake and a paper napkin in the other, we sat down with others who were already seated in the room. Clearly, some of those present were regulars since they were chatting incessantly to each other. Others like ourselves chose simply to savour this little taste of home.

About an hour later we left the library. It was lovely to be in the fresh air and to enjoy the late afternoon sunshine. The view across the river Arno was quite magnificent since the palazzi and the other buildings across the river had become suffused with a mellow, pale golden hue. We took time to appreciate how the light had worked its magic, throwing reflections on to the river Arno itself. We stood mesmerised by this enchanting sight for many minutes since it truly was something to behold. As the late afternoon slowly drifted into the early evening hours we made our way towards the Palazzo Vecchio, the crime scene of the murder of Baldaccio. We wandered around the exterior of the massive fortress-like building and then entered into its courtyard. Just by chance there was a special late night opening of the palazzo that evening and not only that, there was free entry!

It must have been our lucky day or evening, so without any hesitation we joined the growing queue of people to collect our free entry ticket. We excitedly climbed up the great staircase leading to the upper halls, much in the same way that Annalena's husband must have done on that ill-fated day. As we wound our way around the 'innards' of the palazzo with its network of passageways, halls and rooms we paused to admire the decoration in the apartments of Duchess Eleonora. These four rooms had been given to her by her husband Duke Cosimo I, the last of which is known as the Green Room. I knew that we were fast approaching the actual scene of the crime. I grimaced as I imagined the horrific and febrile atmosphere of the moment; the scuffling of bodies and violent thuds as Orlandini's men assaulted the captain. This must have been the one and only time Baldaccio had ever experienced a sense of real fear. I felt a shudder along my spine as I visualised Baldaccio's desperate attempt to thwart off his attackers and his last gasp of breath before he expired.

In the technicolour imagery of my mind I saw Baldaccio's body being thrown from the window into the courtyard below. In the brutal final act of decapitation I saw his head sliced from his body with blood oozing from his half-open mouth and his eyes staring horrifically. As quickly as such gory images entered my mind I tried with all of my might to shut them out. It was all too horrible, it was all too real; within these very walls the person who had been closest to Annalena, her husband and the father of her child, had met his tragic end. To this day, legend has it that the ghost of Baldaccio still haunts the Palazzo Vecchio. We stepped out into the darkness of the night still thinking about the nefarious act and as we walked in the direction of our apartment I took one last glance back at the Palazzo Vecchio. There it stood innocently silhouetted against an inky dark blue sky and illuminated by a bright shiny moon. In the moonlight the palazzo appeared quite magical and it was difficult to believe that such a sinister episode should ever have occurred within its ancient walls.

Colonel Young had supplied me with a plausible reason why Cosimo had not dealt with those who were believed to be responsible for the crime and my thoughts now turned to Bartolomeo Orlandini, the *Gonfaloniere di Giustizia* at the time. The notion that he had fallen in love with Annalena was fascinating; could there be any truth at all behind this? Or could it just have been merely conjured up to add some 'spice' to the story of Annalena and Baldaccio? Many accounts of the murder of Baldaccio especially those that were written in the nineteenth century give mention of this romantic interest. Many claim that Orlandini had become greatly besotted by

Annalena and supposedly made numerous advances to her. She in turn is believed to have rejected his advances and sought the help of her godfather Cosimo de' Medici. Orlandini was left feeling embittered or in modern-day parlance 'absolutely gutted'! If indeed he had been in love with Annalena then this, together with the fact that Baldaccio had publicly branded him a coward, would have been reason enough indeed for him to hate Baldaccio. But could this have actually happened? To possibly find out more, I needed to consult a book that was in the BNCF. Early the next morning we headed straight to the consultation room in the library to collect it. The small paperback book was entitled *Annalena Malatesta, Contessa dell'Anguillara – storia ai tempi della Repubblica a Firenze* (Luigi Vivarelli-Colonna, 1877).

The book was in a precarious state of fragility and I had to exercise great care when reading it. The covers and its contents were held together merely by an elastic band and despite being mindful of its poor condition I had to rescue some of the pages as they fell away from the binding like overcooked meat from a bone. I was excited at the prospect of what I might find inside. From what I could initially make out there appeared to be ample information about Bartolomeo Orlandini and his relationship with Annalena. However, before long it became clear that all was not what it appeared to be, since before me was a work of fiction and a largely far-fetched one at that. In fairness there were some detailed and informative footnotes.

The format of the book appeared to be based upon a conversation involving Bartolomeo Orlandini and someone called Vieri. It was unclear who Vieri was but during the course of their conversation, Orlandini appears to confess to him that he had first set eyes on the very young and beautiful Annalena whilst she was in the house of Attilio di Vieri de' Medici (of course I now believe it likely that Annalena grew up alongside Attilio in his father's household). The book is crammed full of colourful details which serve to embellish the romantic attraction between Orlandini and Annalena, details which I am sure could only have been fabricated by the author to spice up the story for his readers.

After spending some time deeply engrossed in trying to translate the contents of the book I felt in need of a break. It was not yet 10.00am and I could already feel the heat from the sun as it streamed through the large windows of the consultation room. It seemed a crime (excuse the pun) to be indoors on such a hot day. I gazed up from the book I had been reading and took a tissue from my bag and wiped away some small beads of perspiration that had begun to collect on my brow. I looked around in desperation to see if there was a fan anywhere. Indeed there was one, a measly small portable standing fan, which was placed two-thirds of the way along the lengthy room. On closer inspection I was horrified to see that it wasn't actually working. I looked around at the other scholars who didn't appear to be perturbed at all by the situation. I rather think they must have all been Italians and the heat didn't bother them. I didn't want to make a fuss so I just returned to the book I had been reading. Suddenly my attention was drawn to the view from a nearby open window. It truly was quite breathtaking; there in the near distance was the beautiful romanesque church of San Miniato al Monte perched as its name suggests high on a hill above the city. It has to be said that this was again one of those moments when I just had to pinch myself to make sure it was real. For a brief period of time I felt justified in allowing my thoughts to wander awhile from the task in hand and I simply lost myself in the majesty of the sight before me. It must surely have been the case that Annalena too would have admired and surrendered herself to the beauty of this most famous landmark of Florence. Beauty: yes that reminds me, Bartolomeo Orlandini had apparently been so overawed by the beautiful Annalena… and I diligently resumed my task of reading. Interestingly, the author had also written that Orlandini had been so torn with remorse because of his participation in the murder of Baldaccio that he had confessed to the Archbishop of Florence (Archbishop Antonino) and added that he had died in the arms of his adoring daughter Ginerva soon after the death of Baldaccio. Although there are a few footnotes in the book which appear to be correct in their detail there didn't appear to be anything pertaining to this particular episode; furthermore there was no bibliography included to confirm much of what was written. I wondered if the author had been privy to any sources that are no longer available today?

Disregarding any fanciful inventions that may have been woven into the narrative it did prove, however, to be a fascinating and excellent example of the 'romanticised' take on the story of Baldaccio's murder which I had discovered to be so typical of nineteenth-century writers. Indeed, there seems to have been a real interest in the story of Annalena and Baldaccio at this time and also into the early decades of the twentieth century. I believe that it was during this period that their story reached legendary status.

Intriguingly, as I have mentioned in an earlier chapter, I had discovered a few sources which had stated that Annalena and Baldaccio's marriage had not been a happy one although no reasons had been given. Indeed, as a *condottiere* Baldaccio would have spent a great deal of his time away from his home and his wife, and we will never know if Annalena ever did attract the attentions of Orlandini, or anyone else for that matter, during her husband's absences.

One example of a Renaissance woman who attracted the attentions of another man whilst married is Lisa Gherardini, the Florentine woman who is believed to have been the model for Leonardo da Vinci's painting of the *Mona Lisa*. She supposedly had attracted the attentions of two of her husband's friends. Granted, these gentlemen had made advances towards Lisa as a joke to ridicule her husband but with such a story in mind it may have been the case that Orlandini was attracted to Annalena during the absence of her husband, if only to avenge himself.

As I continued to delve deeper into Orlandini's possible romantic attraction to Annalena over the ensuing months, I stumbled across a reference to him in a book entitled *The Story of the Palazzo Convent of Annalena*, which I hadn't come across before. As far as the title is concerned I felt sure that I had perhaps found a source which would prove to be particularly valuable for the latter part of this book, which concerns the convent Annalena would establish in Florence. The book was written by an American author called Elsa Dawson and was published in 1958. Unbelievably, there would only appear to be a few copies of this book available worldwide, and one of those just happened to be in Florence. In fact it is housed in one of the most beautiful libraries I have ever seen, the Bernard Berenson library at I Tatti in Settignano.

I Tatti was once the home of the art historian and connoisseur Bernard Berenson and his wife Mary. Today, I Tatti is renowned for being one of the elite establishments for the study of Italian Renaissance art and has the reputation of attracting only the 'crème de la crème' of art history scholars. The villa is situated in a lovely location above Florence on the borders of Florence, Fiesole and Settignano. It has one of the most beautiful Italianate gardens I have ever seen, not to mention an incredible art collection. We had visited the villa and its gardens once before purely for pleasure but little did I know that I would return there one day in my search for Annalena. I had contacted the library in advance to obtain permission to use it, and following an exchange of emails I was finally rewarded with a reader's ticket. It was like winning Willie Wonka's golden ticket, I felt so privileged. I had only ever dreamed of being able to work within this most special place.

In contrast to when we had previously visited I Tatti, which was during the hot summer months, on this occasion it was a beautiful cold but sunny morning in late January. Indeed, it was a fine day for walking and Richard and I made our way over towards the Piazza San Marco where we took the number 10 bus towards Settignano. Both Settignano and Fiesole just happen to be two of my favourite places to visit around Florence. Following a short bus ride from the centre of Florence we got off at the stop for Ponte al Mensola and we walked alongside the narrow *torrente* or stream known as the Mensola. Vegetation now fills the dried-up riverbed where the stream once flowed. We chatted as we walked, admiring the olive groves, vineyards and beautiful villas along the way. A reminder to anyone that one needn't travel far from Florence city centre to reach the Tuscan countryside.

We reminisced about our earlier visit to I Tatti and smiled as we recalled every fabulous detail of the place. I will never forget how overcome with emotion I had felt when I first set eyes upon the marvellous art collection amassed by Bernard Berenson. Everything was still so fresh in our memories; such is the beauty of the place it is impossible to forget it. Before long we approached the gate to the I Tatti premises and I pressed the button of the gate entry system to announce our arrival. The electric gates slowly opened and as they did so I revelled in the delight of being able to enter within those 'hallowed' grounds. We headed to reception and I dutifully presented our passports for identification. As soon as these were checked and I had provided some further details, we were introduced to a very pleasant young American girl who welcomed us and gave us a brief tour of the library. She even led us straight to the shelf where the Elsa Dawson book was located and she found the book and handed it to me. My jaw dropped when I saw it. I knew in advance that the book only contained a few pages but when I saw that it was in reality a small booklet I really did feel short-changed! It was tiny in every sense of the word since it measured only about five inches by four inches. Still, I had to keep an open mind, 'you can't tell a book by its cover' and all of that! That tiniest of books could be an absolute treasure trove of information for me, or so I hoped. It had to be read and read it was, very quickly indeed! In much the same vein as the novel by Luigi Vivarelli-Colonna which I had read at the BNCF, fact had been interwoven with fiction once more and since there was no bibliography it was impossible to distinguish what was real from what wasn't. Some of its contents seemed to be so unbelievable that it read like a soap opera. It is tempting to believe that Ms. Dawson, who as I later discovered from her 'booklet', had been a friend of the owners of the Pensione Annalena during the 1950s, probably wrote it as a fictional story for their benefit. I was interested to read that the author, like her literary ancestors of the nineteenth century, had also chosen to include Orlandini's obsession with Annalena, and her account of this is embellished hugely to make for an enjoyable read. According to the author, Orlandini had made 'violent love' to Annalena whilst her husband was away and Cosimo, after listening to Orlandini's false accusations regarding Baldaccio, gave his assent to the slaying of Annalena's husband. I am uncertain as to what Ms. Dawson is referring to when she writes of 'false accusations regarding Baldaccio'. There is even mention that following her husband's murder Orlandini stormed the palazzo where Annalena was living. The most interesting and perhaps the most colourful detail Ms. Dawson ascribes to the life of Orlandini is that 'his companions in crime' became tired of his leadership and ended up killing him and tossing his body into the River Arno. Where had this piece of information come from? I certainly had never encountered such a claim anywhere else.

At this point I feel I must interject my narrative with a most curious anecdote related to the Elsa Dawson booklet. Within days of the completion of writing my book and therefore a great many months after my first encounter with the aforementioned booklet, my husband discovered that a copy of Ms. Dawson's work was available to purchase through a second-hand bookseller. Without hesitation he bought it for me. When I received the copy of the booklet, which had been signed by the author and dated 1962, I found the contents within to be somewhat different from those written in the earlier copy that I had read. Some additional details including a very rudimentary bibliography had been added whilst others including a sentiment which I actually include at the very end of my book had been omitted. As before, however, I found much of what the author had written to be largely fanciful and as much as I wished that it could have been true I now knew from the research that I had completed that unfortunately most of it wasn't. I asked myself why I should have encountered this strange little booklet once again so late on in the day. I wondered if it might be a sign that Annalena herself like me was reluctant to let go of our close relationship. Although divided by centuries I felt we were as one and I believe she did too.

Since it hardly took any time at all for me to read the Elsa Dawson book we decided to explore the library. I was like the proverbial child in a sweetshop, surrounded by so many wonderful books to choose from. I just didn't know where to begin. I envied those who were fortunate enough to have gained scholarships to work here for long periods of time, for months on end and even years. Indeed, it would be no hardship at all to study in this place. What a heavenly place to call your office! I just wished I could be left here forever as I found book after book that was of interest to me. No sooner had I pulled one from a shelf than another screamed, 'Choose me!' Luckily, a decision was made for me when I espied a couple of volumes relating to the Malatesta family which I had been unable to locate elsewhere so I satisfied myself by reading through these for an hour or so. I found it difficult to leave such a beautiful place but I consoled myself knowing that I would return there one day especially now that I was the proud owner of one of their coveted 'golden tickets'! We walked back down to Ponte a Mensola embracing the warm winter's sunshine as we went. In actual fact I felt as though I was floating on a fluffy white cloud since I was still reeling in my delight at being able to fulfil my ambition of being able to study in the Berenson library.

We decided not to go back to the city centre immediately but to enjoy lunch at a nearby trattoria called *Osvaldo*. I tucked into *ravioli con crema di carciofi* (ravioli with artichoke cream sauce) and Richard enjoyed *cinghiale al ragu* (wild boar ragu). Naturally, our topic of conversation as always was Annalena and in particular the contents of Elsa Dawson's book. Our sentences were prefaced with: 'Could she…?' 'But if he…' or 'That's impossible…' Fortunately, we were the only diners in the restaurant at the time otherwise anyone who might have been eavesdropping would have wondered what on earth we were talking about. True or not, the contents of Ms. Dawson's book certainly fed our imaginations that day. Feeling well and truly 'stuffed' after our delicious lunch and as punishment for our sins we decided to walk up to the small town of Settignano instead of taking the bus back down to Florence. We took the old road which follows the ancient walls up to the town. Along the way I stopped to examine some crumbling stones that had fallen onto the path from the ancient walls. I picked up one and held it in my hands. As I did so I thought of the great sculptor Michelangelo Buonarotti who had spent his childhood amongst the stonecutters and quarries in Settignano.

Returning to my initial discussion regarding the supposed romantic interest between Orlandini and Annalena, on balance, based on the sources that I have read, there was most certainly a great interest in the story of Baldaccio and Annalena in the nineteenth century and early twentieth century and 'artistic licence' definitely appears to have been at play at this time. In summary, Bartolomeo Orlandini's romantic interest in Annalena appears to be a construct of the nineteenth century since I have not encountered any mention of it before this date. Books such as those written by Elsa Dawson and Luigi Vivarelli-Colonna belong to a body of fictional and semi-fictional literature that had been inspired by the assassination of Baldaccio. They are invaluable even if they do contain elements that may seem exaggerated and far-fetched since they are testament to how this episode in history may have become sensationalised and romanticised over the centuries.

When we returned to our apartment in the city centre I thought it would be a useful exercise to actually consolidate what facts are known for certain about Bartolomeo Orlandini. He was born in 1390 and he belonged to an ancient family that came to Florence from Marcialla. It is also known from the Florentine *catasto* record of 1427 that he was a notary since he held the title of *Ser*, which denotes a notary at this time. From the same *catasto* he is recorded as being married and having children. It is noted that there were thirteen in his household including the head of household. A *ricordanza* (private diary) belonging to the Martelli family of Florence gives the name of Bartolomeo Orlandini's wife as being Madonna Lena since she is recorded as being present at a baptism in 1440. The Orlandinis were neighbours of Cosimo de' Medici since both lived in the *gonfalone* del Drago in the Parish of San Lorenzo (quarter of San Giovanni). Bartolomeo did indeed hold important political offices within the Florentine government including the highest office of *Gonfaloniere di Giustizia* three times in his career, once in 1438 and twice in 1441. It did seem to be the case that he had been posted by Cosimo de' Medici to guard the Marradi pass and he did abandon it allowing Niccolo Piccinino to enter into Tuscany. I have been unable to discover what happened to Orlandini following his alleged role in the murder of Baldaccio since all remains quiet in the history books immediately following the crime. However, I have been able to determine some evidence that clearly indicates that he had not been killed by his 'companions in crime' and tossed into the river Arno as Elsa Dawson might have us believe. He was very much 'alive and kicking' and still in Florence following the execution of Baldaccio. He is documented as being one of the officials of the Florentine *Studio*, the city's university, and is mentioned as being one of the university officials who helped to organise an important civic poetry competition called the *Certame Coronario*. This event took place on October 22nd 1441 only a few weeks after the assassination of Baldaccio. The theme of this Roman-inspired contest of vernacular poetry ironically was 'true friendship'. At the time the competition was held, Florence was in a state of heightened tension, still grappling with the atrocity of Baldaccio's murder. The competition took place at Santa Maria del Fiore (Florence's cathedral) and poems were judged by a panel of papal secretaries. The competition also had both diplomatic and political intentions further afield since it sought to ensure the success of the marriage between Francesco Sforza and Bianca Maria Visconti (the daughter of Sforza's long-time rival Filippo Maria Visconti of Milan) whose marriage took place on the same day as the competition, but in the north as well as the related peace negotiations to end the wars in Lombardy. It was also hoped that the event might serve to quell tensions resulting from the death of Baldaccio. The competition was unsuccessful since it didn't seem to quell any tension, rather it seemed to cause more disputes among the Florentines. There was no outright winner of the competition and the cathedral itself was crowned with a prized laurel wreath.

The evidence above is interesting since it informs us that Orlandini did not appear to have suffered any in terms of his reputation following the murder of Baldaccio, since he obviously maintained his high office within the city's university. Furthermore, in later years two members of the Orlandini family are listed as holding the position of *gonfaloniere*. These were probably Bartolomeo's descendants, testament that the family name had not suffered too greatly from the Baldaccio incident. From a list of Government office holders it appears that Bartolomeo Orlandini died in 1496 at an advanced age.

Since it is documented that following the tragic murder of her husband, Annalena retreated from the world and founded a convent, it most certainly wasn't the case that she and Orlandini 'rode off into the sunset together and lived happily ever after'. In reality I rather think that there weren't any romantic links between the two (certainly none that were tangible) and any suggestion otherwise merely contributes to elevating the story of the assassination of Baldaccio d'Anghiari to legendary status.

CHAPTER 12:

The burial of Baldaccio

The seventeenth-century chronicler Lorenzo Taglieschi records that Baldaccio was buried by his wife in the old cloister of the church of Santo Spirito in Florence, in a tomb that he had prepared for himself whilst living. The Augustinian church of Santo Spirito was the main church in the ward of the same name where Baldaccio and Annalena had lived.

Luigi Passerini, in his book entitled *Baldaccio d'Anghiari* (1866) states that Baldaccio received an honorary burial. I have also read that Annalena had beseeched Archbishop Antonino to obtain permission from the Pope to allow the body of Baldaccio to be buried in a sacred place. It is believed that the tombstone of Baldaccio was originally located on the floor of the church of Santo Spirito but was later moved into the cloister. Richa records that the inscription on the tomb read: 'SEP. BALDACCI DE ANGHIARIS, ET SVOR. DESC. MCCCCXLI.' This translates as 'Tombstone of Baldaccio d'Anghiari and his descendants, 1441'.

Armed with the above knowledge it was logical that we should visit the church of Santo Spirito in Florence to try to locate the tombstone if indeed it still existed. When I began writing this book it was actually quite a mission to gain access into the cloister of Santo Spirito since this was a monastic space that was normally closed to the public. At that time public access could only be obtained by requesting permission (in 2017 the cloister was opened up to the public by means of a small admission charge).

We stepped out of the sun and into the shadows of the church of Santo Spirito. A custodian was seated at a desk just near the entrance doors. In my best Italian I asked him if it would be possible for us to visit the cloister. He responded with a combination of hand gestures and words which amusingly resembled a game of charades and which clearly indicated to us that it wouldn't be that straightforward. He then picked up his mobile phone and told us that he would try to arrange for someone to open the cloister up for us. We waited patiently by the desk and I endeavoured to eavesdrop on his equally animated phone conversation. All at once he left us and went in search of someone who might be able to help. As we stood waiting for his return I took the opportunity to survey the beautifully harmonious interior of the church, which had been redesigned by Filippo Brunelleschi. Work on the church had commenced around 1440 and it was most likely during the years when the church was being rebuilt that Baldaccio's tomb had been moved to the cloister. After what must have been a good ten minutes, the custodian returned and he urged us to follow him, making it blatantly obvious that we had already taken up too much of his time. He led us through some doors which led to the chapter house and to a door which opened out into the cloister. As he walked he rudely brushed aside some passing tourists. With a further display of his authority he brusquely lifted a red rope which was slung in front of the doors leading to the cloister and begrudgingly allowed us to enter. I must confess that we felt like VIPs, as tourists and other visitors to the church looked on at us enviously. As quickly as the custodian had removed the cord to allow us to enter he promptly put it back in place, barring further entry to anyone.

The cloister of Santo Spirito holds rather bad memories for me since many years ago I happened to get locked inside! I remember the incident clearly as though it were yesterday. As was the case on this occasion I had needed to obtain permission to enter the cloister. At that time I was led there by a rather grumpy old priest who left me to enjoy it all to myself. Little did I know at the time, however, that he had actually locked the door firmly behind him. It was only about half an hour later before I would become aware of what had happened and that was only because it was fast approaching 3.00pm in the afternoon when the church was closing. I tried to open the door from inside the cloister so that I too could leave the church, but to my horror I found it well and truly locked. I knocked on the glass pane but no one seemed to hear me. As I peered through the glass I could see some shadowy figures pass by but alas they did not see me. I started to panic and knocked at the glass even harder. Eventually, some tourists caught sight of me and I managed to draw attention to my plight by using hand gestures to replicate turning an imaginary key in a lock. After a while the grumpy-faced priest came to my rescue. To this day I am thankful to those tourists who raised the alarm. I quickly put that memory to the back of my mind as we began our task of scouring the walls of the cloister for Baldaccio's memorial stone. There didn't appear to be any tombstones within the cloister however the walls were lined with a multitude of memorial stones. After many minutes of actively searching, sadly, we had been unable to locate it amongst the many others. Indeed, most of the memorial stones appeared to date from more recent centuries and there were actually very few that looked ancient enough even to have been from the time of Baldaccio. We wandered around the cloister once again to double-check just in case we had missed it and as we were doing so an elderly man approached us and asked us in Italian what we were searching for. I briefly told him about my interest in the life of Annalena Malatesta and my search for her husband's memorial stone. On hearing the name Baldaccio suddenly the gentleman, whose name was Piero, grew quite excited. It just so happened that he knew all about the story of Baldaccio and coincidentally, his friend was in the process of writing a book about him. I struggled to understand everything that Piero told me since he spoke so fast, hardly stopping even to breathe. From what I could make out, though, he didn't think that Baldaccio's tombstone was still in place in the cloister and thought that it had probably been destroyed. As he was telling us this, he led us over towards one of the walls and pointed to a rather weather-worn fragment of a *stemma* (coat of arms) which, according to him, belonged to one of Baldaccio's contemporaries. It did indeed look quite ancient and it could easily have been from the fifteenth century. Piero was clearly fascinated with Baldaccio and indeed, we could have been talking about him for hours. Before long the conversation centred upon the castle of Sorci, which had once belonged to Annalena's husband. At this point, Piero's eyes lit up since this was a place he evidently knew well. I wondered how long I could speak to an Italian before the subject of food would arise and sure enough this was the moment. He told us that there was a marvellous restaurant at Sorci and he was almost salivating as he continued to describe the hearty Aretine cuisine that he had enjoyed there. We told him that we had in fact already savoured the food at the *locanda* at Sorci and we agreed with him that it was indeed excellent. He suggested that perhaps one day we could join him and his friend there for dinner. I nodded and agreed that certainly that would be a good idea. Our conversation came to a natural conclusion and on parting we exchanged email addresses and he promised to contact his friend and tell him about my interest.

Although our morning had been rather unproductive in the sense that I had been unable to find any trace of Baldaccio's memorial stone, we had at least met a very interesting character. When we returned to our apartment I very promptly sent Piero an email to thank him for his help and to say that I would indeed welcome any further information that his friend could send. By strange coincidence, we learned from Piero's reply that his friend just happened to be Alberto the gentleman whom I had already spoken to at Sorci castle. It must have been fate that had brought about my meeting with Piero that day in the cloister of Santo Spirito.

I later discovered a very interesting piece of information recorded by the aforementioned chronicler Lorenzo Taglieschi which is worth considering at this point since it notes that the tomb of Baldaccio had been restored in 1626 by someone from Fucecchio who was a descendant and representative of the 'inheritors of Baldaccio'. Since it is known that Annalena and Baldaccio's only son Guidantonio died in childhood, the implication is that Baldaccio did have a child or children outside his marriage to Annalena. I had already gleaned one further very important piece of information from the 1442 *catasto* record for Annalena and this was that she had also been caring for Baldaccio's daughter who is believed to have been illegitimate. The daughter's name was Catarina and she was aged six years old at the time when the *catasto* was conducted (she was born in 1436 before Baldaccio and Annalena were married). It is likely that Catarina's mother was Monna Giovanna who, as I have explained in an earlier chapter, is believed to have been Baldaccio's mistress or concubine. It is not known whether Catarina would have been in Baldaccio and Annalena's household at the time of their marriage. I rather think that Catarina entered their household after the death of her father Baldaccio in 1441. This is based on an entry made by Ser Giusti in his diaries dated 1442, where Monna Giovanna is recorded as being the wife of Iacomo da Cento. It is possible that Catarina was taken in by Annalena at the time of her mother Monna Giovanna's marriage. It may appear strange to our modern way of thinking that Annalena was looking after Baldaccio's illegitimate child, but during the Renaissance illegitimacy was commonplace. Often elite fathers would have children born to lower status women. I am certain that Baldaccio in his early years would have had ample opportunity to father a child. In Florence an illegitimate child was the responsibility of the father and the child was more than often raised in his home alongside his wife and legitimate children. Many high profile Florentine women had raised illegitimate children alongside their own including Contessina de' Bardi the wife of Annalena's godfather Cosimo de' Medici who had raised his illegitimate son, born to a slave girl, as though he were one of her own. Lucrezia Tornabuoni de' Medici had also raised her husband's illegitimate daughter and Alessandra Macinghi Strozzi had raised an illegitimate daughter of one of her son's relatives. It is also true to say, however, that many illegitimate children were abandoned, especially girls. Annalena may of course have taken in Catarina after her husband's murder in an act of charity.

Intriguingly, the aforementioned 'inheritors' must have been the descendants of Catarina or any other children that Baldaccio had possibly fathered with Monna Giovanna or indeed anyone else. Taglieschi adds that in 1626 the remaining heir, Vittorio di Sigismondo Baldacci, sought to claim a part of Baldaccio's goods and possessions in Sovrana in the province of Arezzo. The descendants of Baldaccio had added their coat of arms, a tower with stars above, where Baldaccio's coat of arms was, together with a new inscription that (in translation) says 'Vittorio di Sigismondo Baldaccio da Fucecchio restored in the year 1626'. I had discovered that there is a record of an individual called Vittorio di Sigismondo Baldacci who was made a Florentine citizen at this time.

It was clear that I would have to return to the cloister at Santo Spirito, since the memorial stone had to exist there. By the time of our next visit, which was in fact several months later, the cloister had actually been opened up to the public. However, on the day we visited we discovered that for some reason or other the cloister had once more been closed. As before I encountered a rather grumpy-looking priest and I asked him when the cloister would reopen only to be devastated to learn that it would remain closed for a month! Since I couldn't believe what I had just been told I decided to ask someone else just to make sure that I had received the correct information. I had rather hoped that the priest might have got it all wrong. I asked a custodian who was seated at the entrance to the church the same question, explaining that I was an art historian and that I was writing a book and needed access to check out a commemorative stone in the cloister. The young woman advised us to return later that afternoon when a Padre Giuseppe might be able to help me. Her response gave me some hope and we duly returned to the church later that day. We arrived just as the huge church doors were being opened up and we were greeted by the young woman and a priest who was later introduced to us as Padre Giuseppe. He had arranged to accompany us to the cloister with one of his colleagues. Armed this time with details of the actual location of the commemorative stone we made our way to where we thought we would find it. We knew it to be located on the north wall of the cloister and so we very quickly worked out which wall faced north and set about looking for the stone. It didn't take us too long to find the ancient stone with its incised coat of arms (see **Figure 13**). How could we have missed it before? This was such an exciting moment for me. I took copious photographs of it and then thanked Padre Giuseppe and his colleague profusely. I even returned to the young woman and thanked her for her help.

Before leaving the church I had wanted to seek out the tomb of Neri Capponi, Baldaccio's friend, who was also buried in the church when he died in 1457. Neri Capponi had been one of the most powerful men in the quarter of Santo Spirito in Florence; this was his territory. Indeed, he had played a vital role in the planning of the building of the new church of Santo Spirito. I had tried on several occasions before to see the wall tomb that had been built for his burial but to no avail, since the part of the church in which it is located (in the first chapel on the northern side in the eastern arm of the church) always appeared to be cordoned off whenever we visited. This time I was lucky since I was able to see the wall tomb (which had been carved by Bernardo Rossellino and his assistants around 1460) at close quarters. I felt incredibly moved as I stood before the grille-encased tomb. I could just make out the portrait roundel of Neri Capponi himself. The plaque, which is carved in relief and in profile, was most likely to have been executed from a death mask. I savoured that moment of standing before the final resting place of someone who had known both Baldaccio and Annalena well. Neri Capponi had probably seen Annalena grow up, perhaps helped to choose Baldaccio as her future husband and had stood side by side with the couple as they were married in Contessa Elisabetta's house. This man would actually have spoken to both Annalena and Baldaccio, laughed with them… I could feel my eyes well up with tears.

As I have already said, all is quiet in the history books immediately following the death of Baldaccio with the exception of the *Certame Coronario*, which I have already discussed. However, there is a fascinating detail that is linked with Baldaccio's assassination which further highlights the impact of his murder on the psyche of the people: a *modo di dire* or a saying, '*fare il salto di Baldaccio*', meaning 'to make Baldaccio's jump', entered into the Tuscan language. It means 'to be thrown out of the window' and it was also used to curse someone to whom one wished ill. I discovered that this saying came into use from the mid-sixteenth century but undoubtedly, it would have been used most probably soon after the crime itself.

Of course the story of Baldaccio and indeed Annalena would have had a very different ending should his terrible murder not have occurred and had he not been declared a traitor to the Republic. If he had lived to see out his days, commended for his valiant military contributions and brave service to the Florentines, at his death Baldaccio would most certainly have been guaranteed a state funeral or his portrait in a public place, or even a tomb monument in Florence's cathedral. If this had happened then everyone today would know the name of this great *condottiere* and his praises would be sung; visitors to the Duomo would count his monument amongst the treasures to be seen within. On the flip side, it is interesting that had Baldaccio been a true traitor and had the Florentine government not been involved with the crime, there most probably would have been a '*pittura d'infamia*' ('defamation portrait') of him. Some famous artists of the day, for example Sandro Botticelli and Leonardo da Vinci, were involved in painting such images. These ancient versions of 'wanted' posters were often painted on walls in public places. To my knowledge no such image of Baldaccio was ever done.

The cruel twist of fate that changed Florentine history also changed the life of Annalena. Rather than surrender to the 'maelstrom' around her and slip into the shadows, Annalena took control of the situation and as we will soon discover would go on to forge a new life and identity for herself. She would ultimately achieve great things in her own right.

Figure 1
The Hotel Annalena building, Via Romana, Florence

Figure 2
Sign outside the Hotel Annalena building

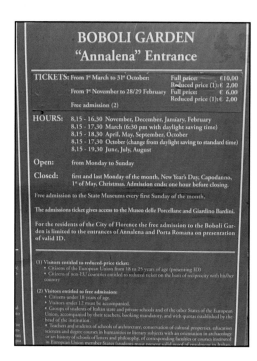

Figure 3
Sign depicting the 'Annalena'
entrance to the Boboli Gardens

Figure 4
Entrance to the Boboli Gardens,
opposite the Hotel Annalena building

Figure 5
The author at work in the
Biblioteca Nazionale Centrale
di Firenze

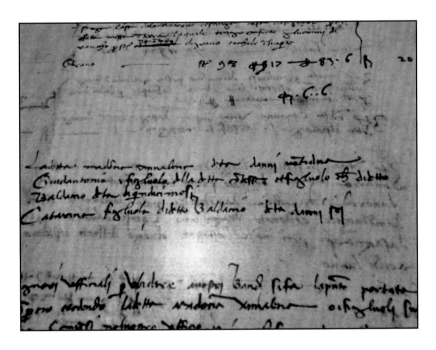

Figure 6
Excerpt from the 1442 catasto providing details of Annalena's age
and that of her son, as well as Baldaccio's daughter

Figure 7
The Mystic Marriage of St. Catherine (att. Maestro da Borgo alla Collina, 1423).
Church of San Donato, Borgo alla Collina

Figure 8
Detail from figure 7 showing inscription on the altarpiece depicting
The Mystic Marriage of St. Catherine (att. Maestro da Borgo alla Collina, 1423).
Church of San Donato, Borgo alla Collina

Figure 9
Panoramic view of the city of Florence, dominated by the cathedral
of Santa Maria del Fiore

COSIMO PATER PATRIAE

Figure 10
Statue of Cosimo de' Medici,
Uffizi portico, Florence

Figure 11
The frontage of the house that originally
belonged to Annalena and Baldaccio
in Via Romana, Florence. It formed the
nucleus of Annalena's convent

Figure 12
The Palazzo Vecchio in Florence

Figure 13
The tombstone of the descendents of
Baldaccio d'Anghiari, cloister of Santo
Spirito, Florence

Figure 14
Façade of Santa Maria
Novella church, Florence.
Leon Battista Alberti

Figure 15
Statue of St. Antoninus,
Uffizi portico, Florence

Figure 16
Adoration of the Christ child with St. Joseph, SS. Jerome, Magdalen and Hilarion
(Annalena Nativity), Filippo Lippi, (c. 1454), Uffizi museum, Florence

Figure 17
Detail from Figure 16 showing portrait
believed to be Annalena's brother

Figure 18
Crucifixion with St. Mary Magdalene,
Luca Signorelli, (c. 1490-1498), Uffizi,
Florence

Figure 19
Pala di Annalena, known as the Annalena altarpiece,
Fra Angelico, (c. 1435), San Marco, Florence

Figure 20
Mary Magdalene statue, Desiderio da Settignano and Giovanni d'Andrea di
Domenico, Spini chapel, Santa Trinita church, Florence

Figure 21
The penitent St.Jerome in the desert, Bartolomeo di Giovanni, (1485-1490). Museo del Cenacolo, Andrea del Sarto e San Salvi, Florence

Figure 22
Examining the painting of Busto del Salvatore, Museo del Cenacolo, Andrea del Sarto e San Salvi, Florence

Figure 23
Bronze bust defined as Ginevra Cavalcanti/Annalena Malatesta,
Museum of the Bargello, Florence

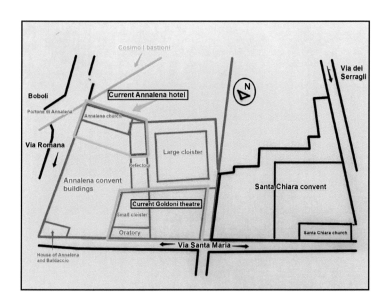

Figure 24
Estimated layout (not to scale) of the original Annalena convent (marked in red),
the modern day Hotel Annalena and Goldoni theatre (marked in green).
The adjacent Santa Chiara convent is also shown

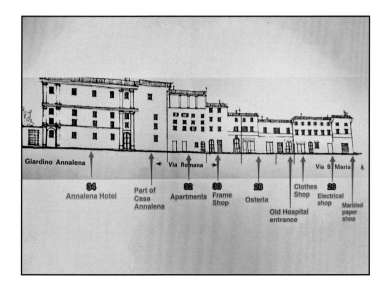

Figure 25
Selected modern day buildings and street numbers relative to the
Hotel Annalena on the Via Romana, Florence

Figure 26
Remains of an ancient column that
would probably have formed part of
the original Annalena convent

Figure 27
The rear of the Hotel Annalena building today,
showing traces of the original convent

Figure 28
Detail showing the original Annalena convent windows on the rear
of the present day Hotel Annalena (second floor)

Figure 29
Remains of an original
fifteenth century column
with worn capital, that
probably formed part of the
Annalena convent complex
(in present day artisan's
workshop, Via Santa Maria,
Florence)

Figure 30
The former refectory of the Annalena convent
(now Gurrieri associates, architects, Florence)

Figure 31
Fresco depicting St.Thomas and St.Dominic, probably sixteenth century.
Located in the 'sala riunione', possibly the former chapter house of the
Annalena convent (now Gurrieri associates, architects, Florence)

BOOK 2

CHAPTER 13:

A new life and the birth of a convent

'God hath taken back the child whom he hath given to us for but a short time on this earth. God only knows the pain and the deep sorrow that fills my heart at this time. My heart is so full of sorrow and emptiness I pray God will bring me through. God has found kindness in his heart and has comforted me greatly since it is his will, and he has prepared a good place amongst the angels for our dearest son. May he intercede with God for me. In return, I beseech our dear Lord to help strengthen my soul so that I might help others. I now know that the Lord is in need of me as much as I am in need of him. God protect me and guide my soul.'

Following the murder of her husband, Annalena is said to have resolved herself to abandoning the world and dedicating herself to God and the care of her son Guidantonio and possibly even Baldaccio's illegitimate daughter. Bearing in mind that Annalena was only twenty-one years old when she became a widow I have always thought that this was a huge decision for someone of such young years to make. However, such a choice in itself was not entirely novel during this period, since Annalena was following a long succession of similar-minded widows.

It has been noted that one celebrated widow in particular may possibly have influenced Annalena in her choices in the years following the death of her husband. This was Rita da Cascia who was a nun in the Monastery of St. Mary Magdalene in Cascia. This woman had suffered a very similar background to Annalena; she had endured a troubled marriage, her husband had been murdered and she had also lost children. Rita da Cascia received the stigmata on Holy Friday in 1442 and news of her life would almost certainly have been known to people at the time including Annalena. Rita da Cascia was beatified in 1626 and canonised in 1900 and even to this day she is greatly venerated.

The years between 1441 shortly after Annalena became a widow and 1449 proved to be yet one further intensely difficult period in her life. All of Baldaccio's possessions with the exception of those that had been taken by force were confiscated by the Florentine government. Annalena had to appeal to the Florentine government to win back what was rightfully hers and she found herself embroiled in legal cases. It was during this period too that Annalena had to endure the death of perhaps her father and certainly her elderly relative and mentor Contessa Elisabetta da Battifolle.

As a widow Annalena would have enjoyed a greater sense of freedom since widows generally had more financial resources and could engage in the ownership of property. Ironically she would have been in a more favourable position to shape and change her world, which indeed she did. However, because she was still living in what was essentially a 'man's world' it remained the case that she still had to conduct her life through men. For this reason it is pertinent to give particular mention to the male figures who played a vital role in facilitating Annalena's objective of founding her convent during these early years.

It was Annalena's brother Uberto who rushed to her side following the murder of her husband. Uberto was to play a crucial role in supporting his sister throughout the difficult ordeal of helping her to win back what was rightfully hers. It is interesting that she didn't appear to seek help from Cosimo de' Medici or even his son Giovanni de' Medici who was seen as a potential political successor to Cosimo at this stage. A recent publication shows that another Medici kinswoman, Piera de' Medici, who became abbess of the Santa Veridiana convent in Florence, had sought the help of Giovanni de' Medici to secure an inheritance deemed to be rightfully hers. This suggests that Annalena may not have trusted her godfather Cosimo, or anyone linked to the Medici or Florentine Government, at this particular time.

In the years following the execution of her husband, Uberto served as a 'mundualdus' or male legal guardian for his sister since Florentine women were obliged by statute to have some adult male associated with them in their legal transactions. The *mundualdus* could be a brother as in Annalena's case, or a father, husband or son or any male, in fact, aged eighteen or above. As I have already mentioned in an earlier chapter it is not known if Uberto also grew up in Florence, however, it is known that he was in Venice following the murder of Annalena's husband. Firstly, Uberto tried to persuade his sister to remarry and had even lined up a Venetian aristocrat as a suitable husband for her. To modern sensibilities, the fact that her brother had done this might appear that he was being rather insensitive to his sister's plight. However, in doing such a thing he was simply following the social expectations of the time. It would have been considered quite normal for families to reclaim their dowries so that they could marry off a young widow, particularly of Annalena's noble status, as quickly as possible to create a new alliance. Young and beautiful widows such as Annalena were regarded as dangerous in society since they were considered to be a potential threat to the honour of their family. It is worth mentioning that, although the circumstances in which Annalena had been catapulted into widowhood were quite unique, Annalena would not have been alone in being widowed at a young age. There were in fact a great many young noblewomen who were widows in Florence during the fifteenth century due to the age difference in marriage partners. Indeed, the Florentine *catasto* of 1427 indicates that widows made up an incredible 25% of the general population. In Florence at least 10% of women were widowed by the age of forty.

Annalena could easily have accepted the possibility of remarriage and fled from the city that had betrayed her. However, as I have already mentioned it appears that she had already made up her mind to retreat from the secular world and to devote herself to the care of her child and to serving God. In making such a choice Annalena once again demonstrated her strong personality. It has even been said that she obstinately refused to remarry. I thought of Uberto having to break the news to the gentleman whom he had arranged to be her new husband. How awkward the situation must have been for him. At the same time Uberto's own religious feelings as I will discuss in due course, must have enabled him to empathise with his sister's calling and so he naturally felt that he had to support her. It is worth pointing out that if Annalena had chosen to remarry, her situation might have proven difficult since her young son would have been required to remain with her dead husband's family, since he was his father's heir. If she had left her child to remarry and regain her dowry she would have been considered to be a 'cruel mother' (in contrast to a 'good mother' who chose to remain with her children, thus keeping their patrimony). Christiane Klapisch-Zuber provides a strong description of 'cruel mothers' who were forced to be cruel by their former in-laws, which makes interesting reading.

As a consequence of the confiscation of her husband's properties and goods Annalena and her child (children) found themselves having to leave their home in the Parish of San Felice in Piazza in Florence. It has been noted from the *catasto* of 1442 that Annalena was renting a property from the nuns of San Felice in Florence, and that she had apparently asked for a tax exemption, which she seems to have been granted. From the same *catasto* we learn that Annalena was living with her fifteen-month-old son Guidantonio and also caring for Baldaccio's six-year-old daughter Catarina (believed to be illegitimate) at this time. It is not known at which point Catarina entered the household; quite possibly this was following the death of Baldaccio. We do not know what became of her but most likely Annalena would have continued to look after her within the convent she would later establish, since generally illegitimate girls were less likely to marry as easily as legitimate ones and usually ended up in convents.

Annalena and her brother could never have imagined how difficult their task would be since this was no ordinary case. Their journey would be a long and arduous one. Not only did they have to appeal to the Florentine government but they also had to contend with individuals who believed that they had a right to claim ownership of goods and properties that had belonged to Baldaccio. As an example of this a certain Tommaso da Verrazzano had tried to get possession of Baldaccio's house so that he could live there. Annalena even became entangled in a long and dangerous quarrel with an individual called Vico di Vico Pichi who, following the assassination of Baldaccio, had made himself the owner of the castle of Sorci. It must have felt like Annalena was 'up against the world'. Fortunately, she had her brother by her side and he would be her rock throughout these difficult times.

On a more positive note, Annalena was able to obtain the castle at Ranco and many goods which had belonged to her husband without any trouble and she was able to sell these to invest in some buildings in Florence (she sold

Ranco for 300 *fiorini d'oro* to Messer Brandiglio di Francesco Brandiglio and to Francesco Viviano di' Goro d'Arezzo with permission from her brother on December 13th 1443). Clearly, since she was residing in rental property herself she must have been holding out for the return of Baldaccio's house in San Felice otherwise she would have used the proceeds of the sales to purchase somewhere for herself to live.

It would however be much later, with the protection of her godfather Cosimo de' Medici, that she would be given back all of Baldaccio's possessions with the exception of those that he had acquired by force. A provision dated February 27th 1445 documents the annulment of confiscated goods and their return to Annalena. It was only at this time, four years after her husband's murder, that she finally was able to gain possession of her home that had belonged to her husband in the parish of San Felice in Piazza, and which would eventually form the nucleus of her convent. By this date it would seem that the Florentines were beginning to see Annalena and her situation in a more positive light and they would appear to be in admiration of the religious nature of her intentions. It is tempting to speculate as others have done that the restitution of Baldaccio's goods to Annalena by the Florentine government during these years was a means of washing away the stains of their crime, knowing that she would be using the money for the building of her convent. This is indeed an intriguing thought.

In 1448 the city of Florence was struck by plague and any plans Annalena may have had for building her convent seem to have been put on hold. It is possible that she helped to attend to the sick in the city. This would be another '*annus horribilis*' for Annalena since this would also be the year that Contessa Elisabetta died on September 1st at the grand old age of eighty-one. This would indeed have been a great loss for Annalena since evidence exists to suggest that Contessa Elisabetta had continued to support her following her marriage and the death of Baldaccio. Contessa Elisabetta most likely served as a wise counsel during these years when Annalena was planning her convent.

As discussed in an earlier chapter, religion and piety had played an enormous part in the life of Contessa Elisabetta. We have already seen how she had lived among the nuns in the monastery of Santa Felicita in Florence and later in her life she was a patron of churches and other religious establishments. Sadly, she would never live to see the convent her young ward would later establish. Following the death of Contessa Elisabetta the

Florentine government carried out a reassessment of her goods to determine matters relating to Annalena's dowry since it must be remembered that it had been Contessa Elisabetta who had given the dowry. It was not unusual for dowry payments to continue to be made a number of years after a marriage. A document drawn up in September 1448 cites that in March 1441 Contessa Elisabetta da Battifolle had sold furniture and given up the Rocca at Borgo alla Collina to Annalena's husband Baldaccio, although the jurisdiction of her subjects remained in the hands of the Florentines. It was also noted that in 1442 Contessa Elisabetta's palazzo and Rocca in Borgo alla Collina were sold and payable to Annalena as payment of her dowry. It would seem that even in 1448 there were still matters surrounding Annalena's dowry that had to be resolved. Although not the same, anyone who has endured the complicated process of achieving probate in our modern legal system will appreciate the time, effort and sheer energy that is required to gain back what legally should belong to them. Fortunately, Annalena had youth, energy and drive on her side and this would help steer her through these complex and demanding times.

Despite Uberto's immense involvement in the life of his sister, sadly very little is actually known about his life. It is said that he was a *Cavaliere dell'Ordine Gerosolimitane* (Knight of the Gerusalemite Order) a military religious order in Venice. It may have been the case that Uberto had been raised from childhood in Venice by another member of the Malatesta family but I have been unable to confirm this. Certainly, the fact that he did come to help his sister suggests that both Annalena and he must have been in contact even after Annalena's father left her to be raised in Florence. Litta records that Uberto was respected by the Florentines and that he played an ambassadorial role in the Venetian Republic. It is also known that Uberto ultimately withdrew from the world and saw out his days at a hermitage at Vitterbo. Although, there is scant surviving information about Uberto we may possibly have some idea of what he looked like since a portrait believed to be of him is included in a painting which I will discuss in a later chapter. Annalena seems also to have been connected to a military order, that of the Cavalieri Gaudenti, probably because she was of aristocratic birth. This was a noble corporation dedicated to peacemaking and charity.

It was during this early period too that Annalena, full of faith in God, had gathered around her a following of solitary widows and unfortunates like herself, which quickly grew to become a small community of twelve women and several homeless children. It is important to point out that at this time Annalena had not yet founded her convent; this was merely a group of like-minded women who weren't nuns and were not bound by any vows; they were united simply by piety. In adopting such a way of life Annalena was following in the ancient tradition of domestic convents established by aristocratic women, whereby she and her companions would devote themselves to religious study, fasting, chastity and wearing austere dress. Interestingly, though, Annalena and her fellow companions were looked upon as nuns at this early date as can be seen by an entry in a register of deaths under the date August 14th 1449: *Una suora della Donna di Baldaccio, popolo San Felice riposta in decta* (A nun died in the convent of Baldaccio, Parish of San Felice). It is noteworthy that this early record also refers to Annalena's house as being 'the convent of Baldaccio'.

The year 1450 would be an important date in the life of Annalena and it was also an important date in the Catholic calendar since this was the year of the famous Jubilee or the 'Golden Year' as it was known. Many thousands of pilgrims from all walks of life and from all over Europe flocked to Rome, the 'eternal city', to seek indulgences. This Jubilee year would also be tinged with great sadness, however, since the plague struck during the month of May and many people died. Hospitals and churches were full of the sick and the dying and it is recorded that people apparently were to be seen in the infected streets 'falling down like dogs'. Apparently, the plague was so bad that even the Pope took leave of the city during the summer months. In December of that year further tragedy struck when hundreds of people died in a panic-stricken crush on the Castel Sant'Angelo Bridge.

Annalena was amongst those pilgrims who travelled to Rome that year to seek indulgences but she also had a far more important objective since she desired to seek formal permission from the Pope to open up her house to like-minded women who wished to join her in devoting themselves to God. The very fact that Annalena as a young woman would have travelled to Rome to meet with the Pope and seek his permission is again testament of her confidence, determination and piety. It is believed that the thirty-year-old Annalena travelled to Rome under the protection of Cosimo de' Medici and with the encouragement and support of Florence's Archbishop Antonino Pierozzi. It is known that the archbishop of Florence guided his pilgrims from his diocese to the city and it was he who had dubbed the Jubilee of 1450 '*L'Anno d'Oro*' or the 'Golden Year'. The 250km journey to Rome in Annalena's day would probably have taken at least eight days on horseback. In travelling there for that Jubilee year, Annalena would be following in the footsteps of the person she perhaps had looked up to as an example: Rita da Cascia, who had visited the city in 1446.

Another wealthy noblewoman Maria (Marietta) degli Albizzi also travelled to Rome that year in the company of her brother Luca (who had been a witness at the marriage of Annalena and Baldaccio) together with Giovanni de' Medici the son of Cosimo de' Medici. Lucrezia and Piero de' Medici also travelled to Rome at this time. Most likely they plus Annalena all formed part of the same group. In a similar way to Annalena, Maria (Marietta) also sought permission from the Pope to found a convent. That convent would be called the convent of Santa Chiara and coincidentally this would actually be built adjacent to the one Annalena founded.

Annalena must have felt an incredible sense of happiness and satisfaction in meeting with the Pope and realising her objective. Sadly, such happiness would be short-lived, however, since tragedy would strike Annalena's life once more. On her return trip home from the 'eternal city' her nine-year-old son Guidantonio fell victim to the plague and died. Unfortunately, in Renaissance times the loss of a child either at birth, from disease, or from being hurt in an accident was commonplace. The mortality of children was, as might be expected, especially high during plague years. People were aware of the fragility of childhood and there was even a commonly held belief that one's children were merely 'borrowed from God'. This, however, must not serve in any way to undermine the hurt and sorrow that parents must have felt whenever they did experience the loss of a child. The fact that Guidantonio had reached the age of nine must have led Annalena to believe that hopefully he had escaped the worst in his young years. How wrong could she have been. She had been a good mother to her young son. Like all mothers in Renaissance Italy she had been her child's first teacher and had instructed him well in religion and morality. Undoubtedly, he would have grown up to be a fine boy if only given the chance. Little Guidantonio died at the family home in the Parish of San Felice in Piazza and his death is recorded on September 16th 1450. Interestingly, there seems to have been an error on behalf of the registrar who recorded the death since the word 'fanciulla' has been written, which refers to a female child. Guidantonio was buried in his father's tomb in the cloister of the church of Santo Spirito in Florence. It is likely that Baldaccio's daughter Catarina, who would have been fourteen years of age by this date, was still being cared for by Annalena. Annalena was naturally greatly pained by the loss of her son and in reality any link to her past and her role as Baldaccio's wife and mother of their only child had been brutally severed. Ironically, she now had complete freedom to totally devote herself to God and abandon the dangers of the world. From this point onwards Annalena would have felt even more determined to focus completely on the foundation of her convent. On December 12th 1450 Annalena received permission from Pope Nicholas V enabling her to officially receive and keep in cloistered life in her own house honest young girls and widows who wished to separate themselves from the world and to profess the vows of the third order.

We tend to think of determined, motivational, enterprising young women as a feature of our own modern age. However, during the early 1450s whilst Annalena was still only in her early thirties and before she had officially received the cloth, she appears to have been engaged in buying up land and properties to realise her objective of establishing her convent. She transformed her home (her late husband's palace in Via Romana in the parish of San Felice in Piazza) into the nucleus of her convent and she would add further surrounding properties to this as her community grew. A document exists to show that a Florentine notary called Pierozzo Cerbini notarised various land transactions for her during this time. In Cerbini's documents, Annalena's brother Uberto occasionally acts as her representative. On June 12th 1453 Annalena bought two houses with the use of a 'stufa' (probably meaning a building that once formed part of a public baths). These were in the present-day Via Santa Maria and she united these with her original house. Annalena and her companions moved into these premises, which would later incorporate the Oratory of the convent. On August 4th 1453 Annalena and twelve companions officially received the habit of the third order of the penitents of St. Dominic in a formal ceremony in the great Dominican church of Santa Maria Novella in Florence (see **Figure 14**). Fra Stefano Benincasa was prior of Santa Maria Novella church at that time.

I should like to recount a rather amusing story. I had been explaining to my husband about Annalena becoming a third order nun or tertiary as it is also known and he appeared somewhat puzzled and asked 'but how could she become a nun if she had been married and had a child?' I explained to him that Annalena and her companions would only have taken simple vows and not the full vows of a professed nun. I added that tertiaries were affiliated to established orders and followed modified versions of their rules, which were generally more flexible than those pertaining to fully professed nuns. Tertiaries lived in communities rather like convents but in contrast to professed nuns they were usually able to enjoy some degree of freedom of movement that allowed them to liaise with the secular world. From the fifteenth until the mid-sixteenth century the third order became an acceptable way for laywomen to participate in organised communal devotion albeit with the presence and control of male authority figures, which I will later discuss. 'Oh I see, a "wannabe" nun then!'

Moving swiftly on, at this point I should like to consider in more detail the role of the aforementioned Dominican Antonino Pierozzi (1389–1459) who was the other important male figure in Annalena's life. Archbishop Antonino was a preacher, reformer, friend and critic of the Medici family. He became archbishop of Florence in 1446 and he was later known as St. Antoninus when he was made a saint in 1523. In his role as archbishop of Florence, which was a very powerful position, he was in charge of the religious life in the city. It is probably true to say that without Archbishop Antonino's help Annalena might never have founded her convent since it was probably due to his encouragement that she decided to become a Dominican tertiary in the first place.

It had crossed my mind as to why Annalena hadn't just become a tertiary in an already established convent, which would have been so much easier for her. Perhaps, following the immediate aftermath of her husband's assassination, people including those in the convents of the city had distanced themselves from her. Or could it have been possible that Annalena considered this as being too easy? It may well have been (as sometimes happens following some traumatic event in someone's life) that she needed to channel all of her energies into doing something positive which would help lessen the pain of her loss. Of course it may simply have been that she was wealthy enough to found her own convent.

Archbishop Antonino had accompanied Annalena and her group of twelve noblewomen to the church of Santa Maria Novella on that August day in 1453. It was Archbishop Antonino who was Annalena's mentor and he provided spiritual guidance to both her and her community of women. Female religious communities had to receive spiritual guidance and direction from their male counterparts at this time. Archbishop Antonino was very close to Annalena, indeed he was like a father figure to her. This closeness is expressed in a spiritual tract called *La Nave Spirituale*, which he wrote for Annalena and her women around the time that Annalena established her convent and which was intended to provide guidance for them as they embarked upon convent life.

What thoughts must have been in Annalena's mind on that summer's day as she criss-crossed the city from her home (Baldaccio's house in Piazza San Felice) in the Oltrarno across the Ponte Santa Trinita to the church of Santa Maria Novella? This had been a day that she had long waited for. I always think about this very important episode in Annalena's life every time we arrive in or leave Florence since the church of Santa Maria Novella with its Gothic *campanile* is the first and last great monument that can be seen before reaching the train station of the same name. In Annalena's day the basilica would have looked quite different since it would not yet have been adorned with its magnificent classically inspired facade designed by the great Renaissance architect Leon Battista Alberti. Like most other churches in the city, including Santa Maria del Fiore (the cathedral), San Lorenzo and Santa Croce, the church of Santa Maria Novella would have had a bare facade. It would only be later, around 1458, that Alberti would begin the redesigning of the church's original incomplete facade to create the one we see today. Furthermore, the interior of the church of Santa Maria Novella would also have looked quite different, since what we see today is the result of extensive renovation work carried out in the sixteenth century.

It is said that Annalena and her companions received the habit of the third order at the tomb of St. Catherine. This tomb no longer exists today as a result of the aforementioned remodelling of the church in the sixteenth century. I had read however that a group of women (probably Dominican Tertiaries) in the fifteenth century had owned an altar dedicated to St. Catherine, and this may refer to this tomb. My understanding is that this original fifteenth century altar/tomb of St. Catherine may have been located closer to the inner facade of the church and had replaced a former altar of St. Magdalene. An altar of St. Catherine of Siena can be found today above the organ near the door which leads from the nave of the church into the *Chiostro Verde* or Green Cloister, but it must be noted that this is of a later date. It is also possible, however, that the solemn ceremony of Annalena receiving the habit may have taken place in what is today known as the Spanish Chapel (called the *Sala Capitolare*, the chapter house in the past). I have visited the Spanish Chapel on many occasions and like many visitors to this place I have marvelled at the magnificent fourteenth-century frescoes painted by Andrea di Bonaiuto, better known as Andrea da Firenze, which adorn its walls. The frescoes depict the *Church Militant* and the *Church Triumphant* and amongst the plethora of figures represented is that of Villana delle Botti who is dressed in the black and white habit of the Dominican tertiaries much in the same way as Annalena and her fellow pious companions would have been on that very special day. I have thought many times of our dear Annalena and her companions entering that sacred space, their hearts full of joyfulness and love in readiness to commit themselves to the service of God. This would be the beginning of quite literally a new chapter in her life. In her earlier years as a Countess, Annalena would have been accustomed to wearing fine gowns and precious jewels. Although she must have experienced a few years of living a more austere way of life, such luxuries and memories of her privileged past would now be totally relegated to the very depths of her mind. They would have little or no meaning for her in her new life and her commitment to God would be of far greater value to her. Indeed, this would be the day that would mark the beginning of something momentous for Annalena. Although the founding of her convent was very much linked with the tragic end of her husband Baldaccio, Annalena through her sheer drive, determination and piety would transform her house of sorrow into one of the most beautiful, important and well-respected female convents in Florence. From something so tragic, something so glorious would be born.

The date when Annalena's convent was actually established is usually given as August 4th 1454, but it had clearly been in the making for at least five years. On June 9th 1455 Annalena received permission from Pope Callisto III to erect in her own house a public Oratory and to celebrate Mass and the Divine Office and have the use of a bell. The Archbishop Antonino is declared in the Papal bull as executor. It is interesting since clearly, once again, this wasn't as easy a process as Annalena may have hoped for. She met with objections from the nearby Camaldolese parish priests at San Felice in Piazza who opposed her intentions since they didn't wish to have another monastery close by. It was only thanks to the intervention by Archbishop Antonino that the monks relented and Annalena was allowed to have the Oratory built. At this point I have an image of the archbishop coming swooping to Annalena's rescue like some superhero! Documents survive which show that the Annalena women were required to donate three pounds of wax for candles each January to the monks in return. The new Oratory was blessed by the Archbishop Antonino and was dedicated to *S. Stefano Protomartire and S. Vincenzo Ferrerio* (St. Stephen Martyr and St. Vincent Ferrer).

Today, the mummified body of St. Antoninus lies encased within a glass casket within a special chapel called the chapel of St. Antoninus in the Dominican church of San Marco in Florence. The chapel can be found in the church that Antoninus had himself founded and which was paid for by Cosimo. The walls of the chapel of St. Antoninus are decorated with frescoes dating from the sixteenth and seventeenth centuries which depict stories from his life. So revered was St. Antoninus that there is also a cycle of frescoes dedicated to his life within the cloister, which is called the cloister of St. Antoninus. Although these frescoes were painted in the late sixteenth and seventeenth centuries, the lunette fresco depicting Antoninus's Ministrations during the plague of 1448–49 is of interest. Many citizens fled Florence at this time but their archbishop had refused to follow them and had instead worked tirelessly to help those who remained in the city. As previously mentioned it is believed that Annalena also assisted the citizens during this crisis.

To a non-Catholic eye the sight of a mummified saint doesn't rest easy, however, I forced myself to look at the shrivelled-up body of St. Antoninus dressed in his archbishop's robes. I had read that Antoninus (little Anthony) was so called because of his diminutive stature. However, from what I could determine he appeared (although I didn't really want to linger too long over this observation) to be of normal size. He may have been physically small in life but he certainly was mighty when it came to spiritual matters.

Once more I had the good fortune to feel a step closer to Annalena. In life, this man would have met, consoled, advised, encouraged and supported her. He would have felt the warmth of her heart, and would have been privy to her weaknesses as well as her strength of character. The latter he most certainly did since Archbishop Antonino had quarrelled with Annalena when he tried to transform her convent into an enclosed nunnery. The subject of enclosure of convents would be one which would surface time and time again throughout the *quattrocento*. Over the years in which Annalena's convent operated, Annalena would experience pressure from Archbishop Antonino, Pope Eugenius IV and Savonarola who all pushed hard for a more rigorous separation between the convent and the secular world. Annalena and her women successfully stood their ground against all of these men, further testament if needed of how strong-willed Annalena and her followers must have been. Annalena had many connections with elite members of Florentine society and she managed to maintain independence for her convent with the help of a powerful lay patron Lorenzo di Pierfrancesco de' Medici who used his influence with the Papacy to favour Annalena's religious community. The fact that Annalena fought so hard against enclosure suggests that her connection with the secular world was very important to her. It must be assumed that Annalena and her 'sisters' were engaged in charitable and good works within the community. The Annalena community flourished through Medici benefaction and was to remain unenclosed until 1586, long after Annalena's death, when Pius III ordered all tertiaries to take solemn vows or leave their communities.

As an expression of my gratitude for the support that Archbishop Antonino afforded to the subject of my book I feel it only polite that I should mention just some of the many other memorials that can be found in the city of Florence erected in his honour. In addition to the aforementioned chapel and cloister with their associated frescoes, any admirer of Florence's beloved archbishop saint should make a beeline for the tower-palace where, according to tradition, he was born. The so-called 'Casa di Sant' Antoninus' is located in Via dello Studio very close to the cathedral. A terracotta bust of the saint with an inscription can be found above its doorway. One can also see the cell that belonged to Antonino in the convent of San Marco, and on the exterior of Florence cathedral itself there is a marble statue of him in a niche. Several busts of the archbishop saint can be found dotted around the city including a terracotta bust which was based on a death mask within the church of Santa Maria Novella; his actual death mask itself exists today in San Marco. Indeed, the archbishop saint was held in such high esteem that a statue of him also stands alongside the likes of Michelangelo, Leonardo, Dante and Petrarch in the portico of the Uffizi (see **Figure 15**), the only ecclesiastic among literary and artistic giants. It was Antonino too who founded the beautiful little Oratorio di San Martino (Oratory of San Martino) right in the heart of the city, for the Buonomini Company which supported poor people of high social rank who were ashamed to be poor. Archbishop Antonino was so important to the Florentines that there is even a street named after him: Via Antoninus, which runs just across from the church of Santa Maria Novella leading eventually to where the present-day market of San Lorenzo is located. The archbishop saint is further remembered on his feast day every year, which is observed on May 10th.

CHAPTER 14:

Evolution of the convent

The convent that Annalena founded was just one of the many convents that were established in Florence in the second half of the fifteenth century. Indeed, from this time there appears to have been an explosion of convent building, and convents formed an important part of the urban landscape until their suppression at the beginning of the nineteenth century. Interestingly, during the fifteenth century convents were actually regarded as town or city attractions and were commented upon as such by contemporary chroniclers. Indeed, the chronicler Benedetto Dei included convents amongst the glories of Florence.

Within a short space of time the convent that Annalena founded developed into one of the grandest and most famous convents in the city. Francesco Albertini, author of the *Memoriale*, which is the earliest guidebook of the city of Florence, commented that the convent of 'San Vincenzo called Annalena' was a '*monasterio dignissimo*' (very dignified convent) and that it was built '*La maoir, parte della casa de' Medici*' (the greater part of the convent had been constructed by the Medici family). Indeed, exemplary adjectives abound in relation to any account of the convent Annalena founded. Richa describes it as one of the most 'distinguished' convents in Florence. It has also been described as one of the most 'remarkable' and one of the most 'desirable' convents in Florence. Certainly, when Richa visited in the eighteenth century he also observed that the Medici family had left their mark there and he wrote that Annalena's convent might well have been called the 'Monastery of the Medici' since their arms could be found in every corner of the convent. It might be pertinent here to add that although Annalena had chosen to remove herself from the world she seemed to have maintained her network of family and friends in high places and probably used them to promote and support her convent. In turn, by promoting themselves in convents such as the Annalena, the Medici helped to strengthen their position in the city.

Convents were generally located near the city walls and gates and the convent of Annalena was no exception. It was located near the city gate called San Pier Gattolino (the present-day Porta Romana, which only became known as this in the nineteenth century). Being located near to the city walls was important to convents since they offered protection. In return nuns would give protection to the city since they were often called upon to pray for the city when it was threatened with invasion, plague or famine. The area of the *Oltrarno* in which the convent of Annalena was located was historically one of the poorest in the city and it was largely composed of the labouring classes with a few patrician palaces belonging to some of the most prominent Florentine families. These included the Capponi, Frescobaldi, Soderini and the Ridolfi families, names which Annalena would have known well. Streets were largely unpaved in this part of the city and despite steps to improve public hygiene living conditions were still pretty awful. The great stone quarries of the Boboli Hill lay close by and it was from these that the *pietra forte*, the stone of Florence, was obtained and used to build the great palaces of the city including the Pitti Palace, the largest palace in the city. The Pitti Palace was built on the site of the Boboli Hill for the Florentine merchant Luca Pitti. Building was begun in the middle of the fifteenth century, roughly at the same time as Annalena was establishing her convent. I tried not to think of the mud and filth that must have filled the unpaved streets during its construction.

In the area surrounding the city walls fields of clay soil could be found, resulting in an industry based upon the production of roof tiles and bricks. Many of the roads that were close to the Annalena convent still bear the names alluding to these industries for example Via delle Fornace was so called because of its furnaces. Originally, as already mentioned, Annalena's convent was called *La Casa di Baldaccio* since the terrible fate of her husband was still fresh in people's memories and the house which formed the nucleus of her convent had originally belonged to him. It has been written that the house was also sometimes known as the *Casa dei Bini* after the Bini family who were believed to be the former owners of the property. This must refer to one of the other two properties bought by Annalena that had once belonged to the Bini family. Annalena's convent has been known under a variety of names since its conception including *Monastero di San Vincenzo* after one of the convent's titular saints, *Monastero di Annalena, Monastero di San Vincenzo d'Annalena, Monastero di San Vincenzo (detto Annalena)* and *San Vincenzo* (more commonly known as the Annalena). I will use these interchangeably throughout the text.

Annalena's convent grew organically and since sadly it does not survive today, we have to use such information that we have at our disposal to feasibly recreate what it may have looked like. Once more we are hugely indebted to Richa who was able to visit one of the earliest buildings of the convent and that was the Oratory, which still existed in the eighteenth century. This was built as somewhere for Annalena and her women to pray in and to celebrate Divine Office. A bell would have called the Annalena women to prayer. Richa informs us that the main entrance to the Oratory was in a narrow street (the present-day Via Santa Maria) and he also described the Oratory as being 'rich with pictures', which is supported by evidence written in the already mentioned convent memoirs. This manuscript also records that the Oratory had many reliquaries and that the pictures were donated by various devoted people. Sadly, no inventory survives today which gives a listing of the appearance of these pictures. We also know that the Oratory had a neighbouring garden since this detail is documented in a provision dated 1456.

Within two years of its foundation the Annalena convent had already achieved great prestige in the city of Florence since according to the communal provision of 1456 many Florentine citizens placed their young daughters with the Dominican tertiaries of San Vincenzo (more commonly known as the Annalena) to expose them to the 'good morals and devotion' of those religious women. At this date the entrance to Annalena's house was on Via Santa Maria and there were already twenty-five members of the community. We learn also from the same provision that revellers of a nearby tavern were impeding the Divine Office with their clamour and had been leering at the women over the wall of their garden. The situation must have been considered to be of significant concern since a law was drawn up in this same year which actually blocked the establishment of inns and taverns near the Annalena convent thus reflecting the respectability and spirituality of her establishment.

Annalena continued to add to her property portfolio and to the construction of her convent since a document dated June 12th 1458 records that she acquired three houses adjoining her own from Stefano di Nello di Ser Bartolomeo di Ser Nello. In subsequent years Annalena's convent grew rapidly in size. As her convent continued to evolve Annalena met with further complications since the Dominican order tried to bring it under their control. Annalena resisted such attempts and sought to retain the sole protection of the Archbishopric. This privilege seems to have been awarded to her and is stated in a bull of Pius II dated 1461. She must have been 'on a roll' at this time since she also appears to have had thoughts to establish a further two convents and even gained permission to do so by Pope Pius II. This indeed is further proof of how ambitious she was. However, she doesn't seem to have pursued such plans since she chose instead to focus all of her energy into expanding her existing convent with the addition of cloisters, dormitories and workshops. This expansion took place with sponsorship from the Florentine Comune, the Medici family and other powerful Florentine families. Undoubtedly, Annalena must have used her influence and connections to achieve this.

We are fortunate to have a city map of Florence dated *c.*1469 made by Piero del Massaio (from *Cosmographia di Tolomeo*) which, although schematic, shows the city walls and gates and some of the major buildings that existed at this time. Incredibly it includes both the Annalena convent and the adjacent Santa Chiara convent. The very fact that the Annalena convent is included in this very early map shows its importance in the fifteenth century. This is the earliest representation of her convent and as you can imagine I was 'over the moon' when I discovered it. The Annalena convent appears to be represented as not having a roof, whilst other buildings in the city including other convents and churches seem to be of a more complete construction. Could this possibly have indicated that the Annalena convent was shown as being in the process of expansion at this date? In 1474, only twenty years after the founding of her convent, the Annalena nuns appear to have outgrown their small Oratory and there was a need to replace it with a new church. Richa informs us that their first Oratory was '*quanto angusto*' (too narrow) for ecclesiastical functions and its principal entrance was '*spiacevagli*' (disagreeable) since it was on a narrow street. At this date Annalena was engaged in buying pieces of ground and houses in Via Romana. She bought two on the piazza near the Boboli Gardens (the present-day Annalena Gate) from Stefano di Nello di Ser Bartolomeo from whom she had purchased before, and this is recorded in a contract dated 1474. The Annalena women also gained a spacious and comfortable garden from ground that was sold to them by Messer Matteo di Messer Ellero, rector of the nearby church of S. Piero in Gattolino for 100 golden *fiorini*. It was on this site that the new church was built. Richa mentions that the completion date was incised in stone in the architrave on the outside of the door to the church:

SACELLVM SANCTO VINCENTIO ORDINIS PRAEDICAT.
DICATVM ANNO SALVTIS MCCCCLXXV.

The church building of San Vincenzo d'Annalena, as its name suggests and as seen in the above inscription, was dedicated to St. Vincent Ferrer. It was consecrated in a solemn ceremony on September 8th 1475, the year of its completion by Francesco Soderini, Bishop of Volterra, who was also at that time a cardinal. Indeed, the Soderini family contributed greatly to the building of the new church, especially Tommaso Soderini who was the father of Francesco. Tommaso was one of the most powerful men in the city and an ally of both Cosimo and Piero de' Medici. Tommaso's second wife had married into the Medici family; she was Piero's sister-in-law Dianora Tornabuoni, the sister of Lucrezia Tornabuoni. Both Dianora and Lucrezia appear to have been close to Annalena. Their closeness was probably due to the fact that Annalena was herself related to the Medici.

According to Richa an inscription could be found within the church itself, which stated that Annalena was the foundress of the convent and it also recorded Archbishop Antonino's role as executor. I will remind readers that he had helped Annalena obtain the papal bull from Calisto III. It also recorded that Francesco Soderini had consecrated the church:

D.O.M.
ECCLESIAM HANC
AB ANNALENA DE MALATESTIS

SANGVINE. MVNIFICENTIA. RELIGIONE
HEROINA TER ILLVSTRISSIMA
VNA CVM MONASTERIO SVB REGVLA
TERTII ORDINIS S.DOMINICI
CALLISTO III. P.M. APPROBANTE
S.ANTONINO ARCHIEP.FLORENT.
EXECVTORE APOSTOLICO
IN AVITIS AEDIBVS.A FVNDAMENT. EXTRVCTAM
FRANCISCVS SODERINVS EP.VOLATERR.
EXINDE AMPLISSIMVS S.R.E. CARD.
IN HONOREM SANCTORVM STEPHANI PROTHOM.
ET VINCENTII CONFESSORIS
DIE VIII. SEPT. MCCCCLXXV.
RITV SOLEMNI CONSECRAVIT.

The earliest surviving description of the church is a brief mention by Francesco Albertini, author of the *Memoriale*, which was written in 1510 only six years after Michelangelo's statue of David was placed in the Piazza della Signoria. Albertini informs us that the Annalena convent contained '*una tavola di Fra Filippo, et di altri pictori*' (an altarpiece by Fra Filippo Lippi and by other artists). I will discuss the artworks that could be found in the Annalena convent church in a later chapter. Although the Annalena women now had their brand new church it didn't mean that their old Oratory fell into disuse since it was later used as a burial ground for the nuns. The remains of 120 nuns were buried here before they were relocated in 1593. The Oratory also housed a miraculous image known as the *Madonna della Palla*, which is documented as still being there in the eighteenth century. I will also discuss this image more fully in a later chapter.

It is interesting to note that in the Piero del Massaio map of 1469, the Annalena convent is shown without its church since it hadn't been built by that date. However, in a map dated 1584 known as the Buonsignori map we can clearly see a representation of the Annalena church. This map is invaluable in any attempt to determine the original appearance of the Annalena convent church. However, it must be noted that this map is schematic albeit based on observation and any reference to it must be exercised with care. From what we can make out, the church is depicted without any ornamentation on its facade and the church is on three levels.

It is rather confusing, however, since on this map the Annalena convent church is shown turned on its side by ninety degrees. The facade of the church was actually facing on to the Via Romana.

Unfortunately, the architect of the fifteenth-century Annalena convent church is unknown and I will discuss this further in due course. Additionally, very little is known about the original form of the church. However, during the fifteenth century it is believed to have had a beautiful facade with marble and stone. A comparison with the adjacent Santa Chiara church shows the structure of the Annalena convent church to have been the more grandiose of the two. It is essential to point out that by the time Richa saw the Annalena convent church it had undergone significant alterations following damage as a result of some fortifications built close by in 1545, which I will discuss more fully in a later chapter. Nevertheless, Richa does include some important details which support the fact that the original convent church facade was once composed of decorative elements including stones, pilasters and columns. According to him the facade of the church collapsed as a result of these fortifications: 'tutto precipito con rottura delle pietre, de' pilastri and delle colonne'; 'everything crashed with the breakage of stones, pilasters and columns'.

We can build up a further idea of what the church may have looked like in Annalena's day from additional details provided by Richa. He tells us that the floor of the church once had marble slabs which had inscriptions of noble families who had links with the convent. However, sadly, once again these appear to have fallen victim to the destructive force of the work carried out for the fortifications, since these slabs appear to have been dug up by the orders of Duke Cosimo I to make way for the new bastions. By the time Richa saw the church there were very few remaining memorial slabs on the church floor. Interestingly, the church was restored in 1701, just a few decades before Richa visited it, and he acknowledges this restoration as being worthy of recommendation in itself. He also describes in some detail the church after it had been restored and modernised and said that the church interior had been renovated but the antique layout had survived. There would have been a high altar and a tribune at the head of the church.

It is documented that during the fifteenth century private individuals founded chapels in the church and members of Annalena's family, the Malatesta, were amongst those early patrons. My research has shown that as an example of a private patron (outside of the Malatesta family), a certain

Filippo d'Antonio di Segna Lenzi paid to be buried in a private chapel within the Annalena convent church. It is documented that in 1480 he founded two chapels in the church. He was buried here in 1490 and this would also be where other members of his family would be buried later. More is known about the names of several private individuals who founded chapels in the Annalena church from later centuries.

I was interested to read about a monumental stone altar frame in the V&A in London which may have been associated with the adjacent convent church of Santa Chiara and thought to be by the school of Giuliano da Sangallo at the end of the fifteenth century. This is pure speculation on my part but could this in fact have been executed for the Annalena convent church and perhaps linked with the tomb of the Lenzi family, rather than intended for the church of Santa Chiara? Of course this would be a dream for me should it ever prove to be the case. Even if not, then stylistically perhaps it may have been similar to those that could have been seen in the Annalena convent church. Such a thought leads me on to consider the structure of the Annalena convent church in relation to the church of Santa Chiara since more is known about the latter. The Santa Chiara church was a place of devotion for both nuns and the public, albeit separated from each other. There would have been a nuns' choir, which would have allowed the nuns to have been heard but not seen by the public. It must be assumed that although the Annalena convent church was of a different order it would have had a similar set-up. It is known that a new nun's choir was built in the Annalena church in the eighteenth century and therefore we must assume that this replaced an earlier one. It is also important to note that the Annalena Oratory was also referred to as the 'coro vecchio' or 'old choir'.

In the V&A there is also a reconstructed chancel chapel which once belonged to the convent church of Santa Chiara. This is useful since it can give us some idea of what the architectural space within the Annalena convent church might have looked like. As previously mentioned the convent of Santa Chiara was founded by the Florentine noblewoman Maria (Marietta) di Maso degli Albizzi, a contemporary of Annalena and sister of Luca degli Albizzi. The chapel was commissioned in the 1490s by a Florentine merchant as part of the rebuilding of Santa Chiara, which was begun in the 1480s, roughly the same time as when Annalena's convent church would have been built. During the nineteenth century the V&A bought the fifteenth-century high altar chapel of Santa Chiara and rebuilt it piece by piece in London. The reconstructed Santa Chiara convent chancel chapel is truly marvellous to behold. It is the only Italian Renaissance chapel outside Italy. It really is quite unbelievable that we should have this structure at all in London and for anyone interested in the subject of Italian Renaissance convents it is a 'must see'. I have of course seen the reconstructed Santa Chiara chapel in the V&A several times and I highly recommend using the available headset to listen to a recording of some beautiful, heavenly music called '*Jesu Corona Virginum*', a hymn dedicated to virgin martyrs, which is still sung in the Catholic Church. This recording allows the visitor to fully enjoy a truly immersive experience in this architectural space. One can easily imagine that one is listening to the Santa Chiara nuns in full refrain, or in my case the nuns of the San Vincenzo d'Annalena. I have to confess that I have often been moved to tears when listening to such celestial harmonies.

As with the Annalena convent complex, nothing really exists of the convent complex of Santa Chiara today; however, its church still remains although greatly altered. The part of the church on which the high altar chapel stood until 1860 is now a private house and garage. The chapel appears to have been a separate Oratory post-suppression of the Santa Chiara church in 1808. The original architecture of the Santa Chiara chapel has been attributed to Giuliano da Sangallo (*c.*1443–1516). It is possible that he may also have been the architect of the Annalena convent church. In a paper written by Giustina Scaglia there is a drawing which the author argues may reflect the original appearance or design proposal for the facade of the church of Annalena. Interestingly, this proposed design shows three tiers with statues on the top tier. The paper concludes that, 'It is highly probable that our drawing is related to the church completed for Annalena's monastery in 1475. The Statue of St. Vincent Ferrer is unqualified proof that it was an alternate proposal, if not the facade actually constructed'.

The buildings and gardens of both the Annalena convent together with the adjacent Santa Chiara convent complex are believed to have covered about 140,000 square feet of ground. The Annalena convent appears to have been the more important and larger of the two. The convent of Santa Chiara was apparently so close to the Annalena convent that there is said to have been a little door which led from one to the other, and a solemn visit took place between the two communities of nuns once a year. Later, however, there seemed to have been some discord between the two convents and the door was no longer opened.

I hope I have succeeded in constructing some idea of what the Annalena church might have looked like in the fifteenth century when Annalena was alive. I shall just summarise: the convent church facade overlooked the Via Romana and the church itself was probably on three levels. The facade possibly had decorative elements including sculptures. Its interior would have been based on a nave with side chapels patronised by private individuals. These chapels were adorned with altarpieces, some by very important Italian Renaissance artists. The floor of the church had marble tomb slabs with inscriptions of noble families who had patronised the church. There would have been a high altar and a tribune at the head of the church and also probably a nuns' choir.

After close examination and detailed research into the proposed original convent complex it is possible to determine that the present-day Hotel Annalena and part of the adjacent *vivaio* had actually been built on the site of what was formerly the Annalena convent church. It was also exciting to discover that the room which we normally stayed in, room number 9, the 'writers' room', must have formed part of the Annalena convent church and the long corridors which lead off to the other guest rooms would have led into the convent dormitory, perhaps even allowing access into the nuns' choir of the church. At the rear of the present-day Hotel Annalena building there are details which probably relate to the original fifteenth-century Annalena convent complex and I will explore these in a later chapter.

A very interesting account of the Annalena convent complex can be gained from a nun who was in the convent in the eighteenth century, Maria Vittoria Rosselli del Turco, who described it as being 'most comfortable and very beautiful, especially the superb cloister in which there could be found the sculpted arms of the Florentine Republic'. Rosselli also notes that these had been ordered by Annalena as a means of trying to re-establish the honour of her dead husband. The scholar Anabel Thomas has proposed that this could be seen as being strategic on behalf of Annalena since in offering her respect, allegiance and prayers to the Florentine government she would enjoy their protection in return. This may appear at first glance to be rather at odds with the fact that it had been the Florentine government who had declared Annalena's husband a traitor and ultimately murdered him. But of course as already mentioned it was the duty of a nun to pray for the city and since Annalena had dedicated herself to God she must have found it in her heart to forgive those who had committed the crime. She undoubtedly also wished that her dead husband would have been recognised in a more positive light, which in turn would have meant that she no longer would be seen as the widow of a disgraced citizen but recognised for her spiritual leadership. Additionally, maintaining close links with the Florentine Republic assured their continued support as benefactors of her convent. It must be remembered that Rosselli was writing in the eighteenth century and it could also have been the case that the sculpted Florentine arms that she saw in the cloister may have been added in the sixteenth century when the Annalena convent was largely rebuilt following a fire (which I will discuss in a later chapter).

CHAPTER 15:

Entering cloistered life

'My heart overfloweth with joy to behold "my daughters" within this great convent of ours. As servants of God we toil the soil to nourish our bodies and to feed our souls we seek his guidance. Listen well my dearest "daughters" so that you might learn and help steer others in the right direction. May God protect you.'

In modern times our perception of convents is that they are essentially religious sanctuaries for professed nuns and that they are totally enclosed spaces separate from everyday life. However, it is essential for the modern reader to be aware that in contrast to today, when only a small percentage of women in society enter convent life, during the Renaissance it was usual for women to enter convents at various times in their lives and not solely with the objective of becoming a professed nun. In the fifteenth century around one in eight Florentine women lived in convents. From the late 1450s, which was around the time the convent of Annalena was founded, the numbers of females entering convents was sharply on the rise and it is true to say that convents during this period were becoming very important and popular. Regardless of whether a girl was destined to become a 'bride of Christ' or a secular bride, convents including tertiary religious establishments such as that founded by Annalena could support a girl at various times throughout her life. It is interesting to note that during the time that Annalena was prioress many members of her own family had chosen to enter her convent. These included several of her nieces including Annalena, Camilla and Maria. Maria would later succeed her Aunt in becoming prioress of the convent. It was commonplace for members of the same family, sisters, aunts, nieces and sometimes even mothers, to be in the same convent. Additionally the class system of society was also mirrored within convent establishments. Convents played a crucial role in society since they served both social and religious purposes for laywomen. I shall now examine some examples of the different purposes that convents played in Renaissance society.

It has been said that convents were essentially 'dumping grounds' for girls and certainly many girls who were deemed unmarriageable, perhaps because of a physical deformity or illegitimacy, did end up in convents. It was also the case that some girls chose to enter the convent over being married against their will. Many girls also ended up in convents due to soaring dowry prices which occurred during the fifteenth century. Many fathers struggled to provide a dowry for their daughters, including those from elite families. Convent dowries were considerably lower than marriage dowries; a convent dowry was only about one-tenth of a wedding dowry and thus was more affordable. The receipt of monastic dowries contributed to the maintenance of conventual buildings, convent artistic projects and other requirements convents may have had. Indeed, in many cases monastic dowries were the lifeblood of a convent.

Families regularly sent their girls to board in convents at different points in their life as well as to be educated there. Convents provided a safe external environment for girls to be educated and most entered convents aged seven to nine years old. However, the majority of girls would return to their homes and it would only be a very small number who would actually choose to become a 'bride of Christ'. Most girls would return into society and become secular brides. All of these girls, however, would still have been exposed to the rhythms and rituals of convent life. Although there were no female religious orders specifically aimed towards teaching during the fifteenth century, Annalena's convent was one of those which had attained a fine reputation for learning. It is known that later, in the sixteenth century, the Annalena convent was the site of a well-known convent school. It has been noted that the convent of San Vincenzo d'Annalena was the convent of choice for wealthy Florentines. Reading and sometimes writing was taught in convents, however, the main focus was usually to impart moral and behavioural standards. Known as the teaching of 'the virtues', girls would learn reading, moral virtues and practical skills such as sewing. Indeed, convents played an important role in the socialisation of girls, teaching them good conduct and behaviour in preparation for either life within the convent or in preparation for their roles as wives and mothers in society. They served essentially as a sort of boarding house/finishing school. I have already mentioned that from as early as 1456 the Annalena convent was held in high regard by the Florentine government for their teaching of good morals and devotion. Such praise supports the crucial role played by convents in this aspect of society and how highly regarded the Annalena convent was in this matter, even from its conception.

One of the girls who entered Annalena's convent and who was educated there under the affectionate guidance of Annalena was Albiera degli Albizzi (b. 1457) one of the twelve daughters of Maso di Luca degli Albizzi. Annalena knew the Albizzi family well and was particularly fond of Albiera. It is probable that Albiera's sister Giovanna also acquired reading proficiency in Italian and (church) Latin from Annalena. Annalena is mentioned a couple of times in Maso di Luca's account book of 1480–1511. Albiera was a great beauty and she was admired by everyone in Florence. She was betrothed to Sigismondo della Stufa who was a politician and friend of Lorenzo de Medici. Sadly, in 1473 Albiera died of a fever when she was only fifteen years old and her death was to shock the whole of Florence. Following her untimely death there was a great outpouring of literary grief with many eulogies and prose written in her honour. One of those who wrote a tribute was the poet and humanist Angelo Poliziano. His works were collected in an elaborate codice and within this Albiera's fiancé Sigismondo Stufa included a dedication to Annalena. The codice was sent to Annalena and appears to have remained in her convent for some time even after her death. It is now in the *Biblioteca dell'Accademia delle Scienze* in Turin. The dedication page addressed to Annalena tells her, 'I send you all of these in the hope that they have the same power, since that I know that you too need comforters, and I am well aware of the affection you bore for Albiera'. A marble portrait bust of Albiera, which sadly is now lost, may also have found its way into the hands of Annalena. Such evidence does give us an insight into the loving, caring nature of Annalena and that she obviously had a particular fondness for this young girl. It also reveals the cultural circles that Annalena moved in and the importance to her of intellectual thought. In a further elegy by Naldo

Naldi (1436–*c*.1513), a poet whose patrons were the Medici, he addresses Annalena and implores Annalena's prayers as one who loved Albiera as a daughter.

I return to the statement made by Stefanie Solum that Annalena was the city's 'most important living female spiritual role model'. This indeed is quite an accolade and evidence supports such a claim when we consider that Archbishop Antonino had cited Annalena and her nuns as being religious models in a spiritual tract he wrote for Lucrezia Tornabuoni de' Medici (1427–1482), wife of Piero de' Medici, and contemporary and relative of Annalena. This spiritual guidebook was entitled '*Opera a ben vivere*' ('A work to live well by'), which basically was a handbook providing instructions for how his female reader could protect her soul from vice and thus 'live well'. Lucrezia held the Annalena convent in such high esteem that she looked to the rigorous practices adopted there as a model for her own religious life. Archbishop Antonino had originally given a copy of this spiritual tract to her sister Dianora. Lucrezia who was renowned for her piety and support of the church was a great benefactress of Annalena's convent and enjoyed a close relationship with Annalena. Their closeness is expressed by Archbishop Antonino who suggested that if Lucrezia so wished she could borrow '*La Nave Spirituale*', a spiritual tract which he had written for Annalena and 'her daughters of Christ'. We are fortunate to be able to obtain some idea of what Lucrezia looked like from some surviving portraits of her and in particular from frescoes painted by the fifteenth-century artist Domenico Ghirlandaio for the Tornabuoni family chapel in the church of Santa Maria Novella. It is believed that both Lucrezia and her sister Dianora may possibly appear together as the older females to the far left in the foreground of the scene depicting the *Birth of the Virgin*. A possible portrait of Lucrezia also appears in the scene of the *Birth of St. John the Baptist*, the third woman on the right that precedes the girl carrying fruit in a basket. Lucrezia's son Lorenzo de' Medici would continue his mother's connections with the Annalena convent and links with the Medici would extend into the following centuries and I will discuss these later.

Another function of convents was as a refuge for widows and other vulnerable women in society. Indeed, it must be remembered that Annalena's convent essentially began its life as a shelter for vulnerable women and children. However, even noblewomen when widowed often sought refuge in convents and even had their own cells. As an example of this I have already mentioned that Annalena's guardian Contessa Elisabetta chose to spend some time in a convent. One celebrated example of a widow entering the convent of Annalena during the years when Annalena was prioress was the Renaissance playwright Antonia Pulci (1452–1501). She became a third order sister in Annalena's convent where she lived for a few years after she was widowed. Pulci's work was circulated widely in Florentine convents, although most of it was written outside the convent before she entered religious life as a widow. Another of Antonia's relatives may have also been at the Annalena convent. Although Annalena's convent initially welcomed vulnerable women and children, it soon became the convent of choice for daughters of elite families. As we have already seen from its earliest days her convent was favoured by the Medici family, and this association would endure long after her death.

A further fascinating role that convents played in society was their important contribution to the economic life of the city. Convents for example provided a labour force for the silk industry during the fifteenth century; nuns would reel and spin the thread to be sent to weavers. They also engaged in sophisticated embroidery work. It is uncertain as to whether the Annalena nuns played a role in this industry during the fifteenth century but it is documented that they were engaged in sewing projects in the sixteenth century. By the end of the fifteenth century convents, including the Annalena convent, also began to run commercial pharmacies and the one at the Annalena would flourish during the sixteenth century and I will touch upon this later. Related to their commercial and entrepreneurial ventures, convents were also among the major landlords in the city and were greatly involved with the management of rental property.

It is well to remember that since so many convents existed in Florence during this period such establishments had to attract benefactors, patrons and clientele. In this way they functioned very much like businesses. We have already seen how Annalena with her social network attracted the support of prestigious patrons and benefactors.

CHAPTER 16:

Living by the rules

After months of researching, imagine my delight when I managed to track down a major surviving primary source that had belonged to the San Vincenzo Annalena convent during the years when Annalena was prioress and just following her death (Annalena died in 1491). This document just happened to be the Constitutions, or the rules of the convent, which is dated between 1475 and 1499. I have to admit that the discovery of the existence of this manuscript just had to be one of the highlights of my research. This document is immensely valuable since it allows us to gain an insight into the world of Annalena and her convent. No other contemporary sources exist to furnish us with such details. It is worth remembering that Richa's description of the Annalena convent was of a much later date. Additionally, Richa was only really able to gain a visual account of the convent and not all of it at that. Quite understandably, he would not have been able to experience the quotidian workings of the establishment.

Amazingly, this historical manuscript, which consists of seventeen leaves of parchment bound in vellum, is in the possession of the Kislak Center for Special Collections, Rare Books and Manuscripts at the University of Pennsylvania. Fortunately, it has been digitised in recent times and I was able to read it online. Thanks to the 'wizardry' of modern technology, I was able to digest the contents of the manuscript in the comforts of my own home. It really was quite incredible to think that I had the means quite literally at my fingertips to see and read this precious document, which is written in beautiful Gothic Rotunda script. As I read it I began to well up with tears. I just couldn't believe that I was reading something that would have been written out by the hand of one of the nuns in Annalena's convent, possibly even by Annalena herself, and such an important document at that. Most convents usually had their own Constitutions and these would generally have been drawn up by female members of the community or external male clerics. Annalena's spiritual mentor Archbishop Antonino may have had a hand in the formulation of the Constitutions for her convent since its tone bears some similarity to his previously discussed spiritual tract called 'La Nave Spirituale'. In both works Annalena's women are addressed directly as 'figliuole mie' ('my daughters'). Abbesses or prioresses also addressed their fellow nuns as 'daughters'.

I thought to myself, if this was my reaction on reading a digitised version of the manuscript then what would I have been like if I had been able to hold it in my hands! It is indeed a miracle that it has survived at all since, as I have already mentioned, virtually all the documents from the Annalena convent perished either in the fire that virtually destroyed the convent in 1511 or in other natural disasters such as floods. The manuscript containing the Constitutions may have been kept in Annalena's own chamber and must have been saved from the fire. The manuscript was possibly taken into safekeeping only to return to the convent at a later date, where it would remain until the suppression of the convent at the beginning of the nineteenth century. After this time it found its way on to the open market and it is known that it ultimately became part of the collection of Prince Petri Ginori Conti (an Italian politician and antiques collector) before it entered Pennsylvania University in 1963. The provenance of this work alone makes for fascinating reading and it has to be said that, on this occasion, I am pleased that the manuscript did find its way into private hands. It was a blessing in disguise since if it had not done so it possibly would have ended up in the original State archives in Florence and may have fallen victim to the floods of 1966 and been irretrievably damaged forever.

I have already defined what is meant by the term 'tertiary' and since tertiaries were not bound by the complete enclosure rulings that the first and second order convents had to adhere to, Annalena and her 'sisters' were able to enjoy a certain degree of freedom in their liaison with the secular world. However, from the Annalena Constitutions it is clear that they, like their second order sisters, were not completely free to come and go as they pleased. In its earliest years, that is during the time of Annalena, her convent seemed to have occupied a position between the second and third order. Physically, however, like the stricter convents, the Annalena convent was enclosed within a high wall and like those other convents, it essentially functioned as a microcosm within the city.

From another source it has been noted that the tertiaries from the Annalena convent would go into the city 'two by two', dressed in their black and white habits in the manner of Catherine of Siena and all tertiaries. On what occasions might the Annalena women leave the confines of their convent? They might attend Mass in the city and they would have carried out care work within the community, for example assisting the poor and the sick. A highly illuminating detail related to the Annalena women going outside their convent exists in a further important surviving document associated with Annalena. In a payment ledger drawn up by her notary, Pierozzo Cerbini, it is recorded that Annalena purchased a pair of shoes for two lire 'for going out'. This little detail is just the type of thing that scholars rejoice in discovering since it serves to breathe life into any research and allows the researcher to become much closer to the subject they are studying.

Even although the Annalena women were officially a third order community, like any other religious community who lived together there was a need for rules to give structure to their daily activities. This essentially was what the Constitutions defined. From these we learn once more that the Annalena women appear to have adopted some of the rules that were more akin to their enclosed sisters from the Second Order. Matters such as where and when to observe silence and a hierarchy of '*colpe*' (faults) with their associated punishments (albeit it in a somewhat reduced form) are included in the Constitutions.

I printed out each digitised page of the manuscript so I could read its contents at my leisure. Perhaps 'leisure' is the wrong word since my attempt to decipher it was no mean task. I pored long and hard over it for hours, days, weeks and even months, returning to it often so I could unravel its contents. In the manner of Sherlock Holmes, once more I had to rely upon my trusty friend the magnifying glass in order to examine the script more carefully. It took some time for me to adapt to the way the letters and words were written, for example I had to train my brain to read the letter 'z' to represent the letter 'r' and 'f' as 's'. I also had to get used to the frequent occurrence of two words written as one word for example 'dellofficio' meaning 'of the office'. Reading through the Constitutions also enabled me to gain a true insight into the physical spaces of the convent and how the convent itself actually functioned. As was customary in all female religious establishments at this time, there was a hierarchy of positions held in the Annalena convent. We know that Archbishop Antonino was the spiritual director of the convent and there is mention throughout the Constitutions of a 'prelata' (prelate), a 'priora' (prioress) and a 'soppriora' (subprioress). My thoughts turned to Annalena and her role as prioress of the convent; I imagined her to have been kind, maternal, considerate and supportive. She is known to have been an excellent role model for her female followers.

The principal duty of the Annalena women like all nuns was to pray and act as intercessors for individuals or the city. However, they also undertook jobs within the convent itself on a daily basis since idleness was perceived as a route to temporal thoughts. Like other nuns the Annalena sisters would probably have worked as scribes, pharmacists, teachers, kitchen staff, etc. The architectural spaces of the Annalena convent appear to have been similar to others of the period and included a church, chapter house, choir, refectory, dormitories, cells, infirmary, gardens, workhouse, kitchen, cloister, 'parlatorio' (parlour) and 'ruoto' (wheel). We know also from a later source that Annalena had her own chamber. The Annalena convent 'orto' (garden) was one of the biggest in Florence. The Annalena women would have grown their own fresh fruit, vegetables, herbs and flowers. We also learn that there was a shared language of bells within the convent, for example a bell would ring in the refectory for compline (evening prayer) whilst another called the sisters to church for the recitation of the Divine Office (the collective name given to the eight offices in the monastic day). The more I read, the more the words before me morphed into the sounds of the convent: 'Omni potens dominus benedicat... In nomme patris e fili e spiritus Sancti and Amen.'

According to the rules, the Annalena women were required to wear a simple unfussy white tonache (tunic), black mantello (cloak) made of coarse cloth and a simple veil worn over the head. They were expected to wear their habit at all times, even including in bed. A whole section within the Constitutions is devoted to how the Annalena sisters should behave in the dormitory (more about this in due course) and includes a rather lovely description of beds with straw mattresses, pillows of both straw and feather and covers of wool and soft cotton.

On a lighter note, I should like to share with the reader a rather amusing error I made related to the translation of the Constitutions and in particular to the details concerning the items of clothing that comprised the habit worn by the Annalena women. One phrase in particular completely threw me and this was: '*Et niuna tengha ciliccio alle cane o'altra cosa penitentiale sense licentia della prelate...*' Initially I understood part of this to mean that 'no one should have eyelashes like a dog' since I thought I had been clever in believing that the word '*ciliccio*' had something to do with eyelashes or eyebrows. In actual fact the word for eyelashes in Italian is '*ciglia*' and the word for eyebrows is '*sopracciglia*'. The translation of the word '*cane*' does indeed mean 'dog'. Did this mean that a rule had to be put in place because some of the Annalena women must have had a penchant for long, thick eyelashes? Almost immediately my mind filled with images of rebel nuns modestly dressed in their black and white habits fluttering their long eyelashes! Surely this had to be a mistake since I was certain that nuns would not have been so vain. Furthermore, eye make-up was never really used by women in Renaissance Italy and indeed, treatises on beauty from the period warned that too thick and dark eyelashes gave the face a sort of frightening appearance! Of course I had to reconsider my translation of the phrase and attempt to obtain the exact meaning of it in such a context. As it transpired not only had I mistranslated the word '*ciliccio*' but I had also failed to notice that the scribe appeared to have made an error. She/he had written the word '*cane*' meaning 'dog' instead of '*carne*'. On closer inspection of the script I noticed that the scribe had actually added a squiggle above the word '*cane*' to highlight that they had omitted the letter 'r'. It should have read '*ciliccio alle carne*'. I discovered that the word '*ciliccio*' had the meaning of 'sackcloth' and it was only later when I looked up the *Vocabulario della Crusca* (from one of the world's leading institutions in the field of research in the Italian language) that I found the phrase '*che porti lo ciliccio alle carne*' meaning 'repentance of sins'. Obviously, the word '*carne*' in this context doesn't translate as the usual meaning of 'meat'! Thus the entry within the Annalena convent Constitutions should be translated as '... no one should repent of their sin or any other penitential thing without permission from the Prelates'. As you can imagine I was hugely relieved to have corrected my rather amusing error.

A significant part of the contents of the Constitutions are devoted to how the Annalena women were to behave within the different spaces of the convent. The less serious *'colpe'* or 'faults' required the Annalena women to recite penitential psalms or for those sisters unable to read ('... *et quella che non sa leggiere...'*) they should say 200 Ave Marias (Hail Marys). Most likely this refers to the servant nuns who were not taught to read. Other punishments for small *'colpe'* included fasting on bread and water and heavier punishments were meted out for the more serious *'colpe'*.

The *'parlatorio'* and *'ruoto'* were spaces which enabled the Annalena women to have access to the outside world. It was in the *'parlatorio'* seated before grilled windows and most likely under the watchful gaze of an image of the archangel Gabriel (a common image in such a space because of its symbolic meaning of communication) that the Annalena women could meet with family members and friends. The *'ruoto'*, sometimes called *'gratta'*, was a rotating barrel-shaped device which was used for bringing items in and out of the convent. One of the Annalena women would have held the position of *'ruotarie'* deeming her in charge of the *'ruota'*. Such spaces were considered problematic, even dangerous, since quite literally they represented a portal between the sacred world of the convent and that of the secular world outside. We learn that these areas were carefully controlled since clearly there was the concern that the sisters might meet with temptation and be enticed back into the outside world. They had to obtain permission from the *'prelata'* or highest convent officer to talk at these convent spaces and if they didn't it was considered a very serious *'colpa'* and they would be punished. Furthermore, all visits to the convent to meet a sister would have been carefully vetted by the *'portinaia'* (concierge in charge of access to the convent) beforehand. On hearing that they had a visitor the sisters had to make their way to the *'parlatorio'* with lowered eyes and adopt a submissive voice speaking only with words of good virtue.

A further area within the convent that appears to have been carefully monitored was the dormitory. The prioress would carry out nightly rounds to check that all sisters were in the dormitory and then lock up an exit so that no one could enter or leave without her permission. Silence had to be observed in various parts of the convent and at certain times, since silence fostered contemplation and full dedication to God. Silence had to be observed for example in the refectory whilst eating, doing the laundry, making bread, weeding in the garden and during Mass. Silence also had to be observed from compline (evening prayer) until first Mass the next morning. Interestingly, as was commonplace in other female convents at this time the refectory was also a space where sisters would be publicly punished before their peers. If the rule of silence was broken then the punishment of '*mangiare in terra*' meaning to 'eat off the floor' would have been meted out. This meant that the sisters would be deprived of the 'luxury' of eating at a bench and table within the refectory. The refectory was where the Annalena sisters would eat communally and it was also a space that held great symbolic value since their eating together was also a re-enactment of the Last Supper of Christ. The Annalena women would have been seated at two long tables with their backs to the wall in view of an image of the *Cenacolo* (Last Supper). They could contemplate this whilst eating. The Constitutions tell us that the sisters were to eat using knives only The '*sala capitolare*' (chapter house) is an interesting space since this was where the sisters would meet to discuss their affairs, which would include a wide assortment of matters from important issues to the more mundane, for example they may have had discussions about the financing of the convent or whether they should plant more vegetables in their '*orto*'. This platform offered one of the rare opportunities whereby women in the Renaissance period were able to make decisions which would have been otherwise denied to them outside the convent. The chapter house functioned rather like a boardroom today. Within the Annalena convent chapters were made every Friday throughout the year and it would appear that punishments were also meted out in this space.

The Constitutions made for fascinating reading and the more I read the more I felt I was becoming enveloped into the world of Annalena's convent.

CHAPTER 17:

Artistic commissions for the Annalena convent

Convents were important artistic sites in Renaissance Italy and many artists at this time were commissioned to execute a variety of works for these establishments. It is known that rich and aristocratic convents, such as the Annalena, benefitted from donations from the families of the girls who boarded there and from rich patrons who had links with the convent. As we have seen, Annalena's own family the Malatesta appear to have patronised side chapels in her convent church and it has been written that the Malatesta coat of arms could be found in each one of these. Her relatives the Medici were also huge supporters of her convent, as were the Soderini family. It is important to point out that most works of art from Renaissance Italy were made and commissioned by men. Only rulers, consorts, nuns and widows were able to break through the barriers in operation to commission works of art. Thus as foundress and prioress of her convent Annalena would have been in a position to commission artworks and if she did then she would be an important example of a female patron during the period. Several important Renaissance artists including Fra Angelico, Fra Filippo Lippi and Luca Signorelli executed works for the Annalena convent.

In this chapter I will focus on the surviving artworks that were commissioned for Annalena's convent during, or as close as possible to, the period that she was prioress. I will also include works of art that were known to have existed during Annalena's time but sadly are now lost. I shall remind readers, however, that a terrible fire virtually destroyed the whole of the Annalena convent in 1511, some twenty or so years after the death of our foundress. Tragically, we will never know how many works of art may have perished as a result. It is known that her convent was rebuilt following the fire and an extensive artistic programme involving many great artists was put in place in the early sixteenth century, the first of many later refurbishment programmes. I will give a brief mention to some of these in a later chapter.

Since the Annalena convent no longer physically exists today, unfortunately we are unable to see any of the surviving artworks 'in situ' with the exception of some traces of frescoes believed to be of the sixteenth century. Many artworks, archival material and other artefacts relating to convents including those that would have belonged to the Annalena were removed during the Napoleonic suppression in the early nineteenth century. It is known that many art treasures ended up in France around this time. Additionally, some from the Annalena convent initially went into the museum of San Marco in Florence, before being transferred into other museums in the city.

It really is quite incredible that one of the earliest and most important works commissioned for Annalena's convent has survived. This is the *Adoration of the Christ Child with St. Joseph, SS. Jerome, Magdalene, and Hilarion* painted by Fra Filippo Lippi (see **Figure 16**). The altarpiece is sometimes called the *Annalena Nativity* and is housed in the Uffizi Gallery in Florence today. It was apparently among the paintings that were removed from Annalena's convent during the Napoleonic Suppression. Although this panel by Fra Filippo Lippi is undocumented during the fifteenth century, there is enough evidence to suggest that it was originally produced to adorn the community's Oratory (the first church of the Annalena convent). It was then moved from here and placed in one of the side chapels of the new Annalena church, which was completed in 1475. The Fra Filippo Lippi altarpiece is widely accepted by modern scholars to have been painted in the 1450s and therefore it is possible that it was commissioned around the founding date of Annalena's convent in 1454, or in the following year when Annalena and her companions were granted Papal permission to build the Oratory. Lippi's panel and works by other painters are recorded by Francesco

Albertini. The altarpiece was still in the convent church in the eighteenth century at the time when Richa visited.

At my first opportunity I headed to the Uffizi gallery to seek out this art treasure. As the crowds made a beeline for the Sandro Botticelli gallery to view his great Renaissance masterpieces the *Primavera* and the *Birth of Venus*, I excitedly sought out the Fra Filippo Lippi room. On entering, I was thrilled when I caught sight of the painting I had come to see. I instantly noted that it was fairly small in size. Such an observation is important since its relatively small size (137cm x 134cm) would seem to support the hypothesis that the altarpiece was originally painted for the Annalena Oratory. I have already alluded to the fact that the Oratory must have been fairly small in size since within twenty years Annalena's community had outgrown it and a new church had been built. The altarpiece is recorded as being in the chapel of the Nativity within the new convent church and its subject is apt for such a setting. Significantly, this painting is the first version of a composition invented by Lippi, in which the iconography of the Nativity is merged with that of the adoration of the Christ child in the presence of saints. Even if I hadn't been aware of the altarpiece's association with the Annalena convent this artwork is a veritable gem. The fact that it did belong to her convent was a reminder, if ever there was need of one, that paintings from the Renaissance period were not intended to be viewed through twenty-first-century eyes, that is, as a work of art intended to be hung in a museum or gallery. Paintings, sculptures and other artistic works from this period all had a life before they entered these establishments.

At this moment in time I also gave a thought to the artist who created this altarpiece. Fra Filippo Lippi was both a painter and a monk and his name will always be associated with scandal since he abducted a beautiful Florentine nun called Lucrezia Buti from a convent in the nearby city of Prato. Lucrezia bore Lippi a son and a daughter. The son, who was called Filippino, also went on to become a painter himself. Scandal, abduction of nuns... a cautionary reminder that the commissioning of a work of art, or indeed the execution of any work intended for a female monastic establishment, came with its problems. Abbesses, prioresses and nuns would have to liaise with male artists, architects and builders generally through a male intermediary or via the protective barrier of the convent grille.

In the gallery alongside Lippi's *Annalena Nativity* there is a painting of the *Adoration of the Christ Child with the young St. John the Baptist and*

*Saints c.*1463, also by him. This is the same size as his *Annalena Nativity* and it was commissioned by Piero de' Medici for the family cell in the convent of Camaldoli. Lippi was one of the Medici family's favourite artists. The small size of this altarpiece and the fact that it was commissioned for a small cell further supports the theory that the Annalena Lippi panel was located in the original small Oratory. As a relative of the Medici, Annalena's choice of an artist greatly favoured by them may have played a part in her choice of the artist Filippo Lippi. It has been suggested that the Lippi altarpiece may have been commissioned by her relative Filippo Malatesta.

Returning to Lippi's *Annalena Nativity*, as I stood before it I had to pinch myself as this would once have been the pride and joy of Annalena's convent. I tried to imagine the excitement and delight that Annalena and her companions must have felt when they first set eyes upon their newly painted altarpiece. I visualised the women in their black and white habits kneeling before it in their little Oratory. It must have looked really quite magnificent with the beautiful colours of the pigments illuminated by the flickering of candlelight. At this point I momentarily broke from my reverie and glanced around the gallery. I was all alone; call me crazy, but I suddenly felt the urge to kneel before the panel. For a few precious moments I was able to view this work in a more reverential manner than is customary in a museum setting. I gazed upon the holy family adoring the Christ child and it was as though I myself had become one of those who had made the journey to behold the newborn King. For Annalena and her followers the iconography of this painting would have had even more significance. Each and every element within its composition would have had a heightened meaning lost to our more modern eyes. The inclusion of the penitential Saints Hilarion, Jerome and the Magdalene is interesting. This theme of penitence would be further developed by Lippi in his subsequent paintings of the Nativity under continuing Medici patronage.

I was particularly struck by the inclusion of a figure that is believed to be a portrait of Annalena's brother Uberto in the guise of St. Hilarion (see **Figure 17**). We will remember that in the early years he had worked tirelessly with his sister to achieve her objective of establishing her convent and it seems fitting that his portrait (if indeed it is him) should appear in the altarpiece. Perhaps Annalena and her community of women wished to commemorate his early involvement in the foundation of their community. Uberto is believed to have aided his sister with the establishment of her convent even as late as 1456. It could have been the case that they may have requested that his portrait should be included even if it had been commissioned by Filippo Malatesta. It has also been referenced that it was her brother who actually commissioned the painting. I looked long and hard at this portrait, which appeared to represent a man aged in his thirties. The rendering of this figure appeared so vivid and natural that I found him to be quite arresting, to say the least. I studied his strangely handsome face with its dark eyebrows, slim, elongated nose and in modern parlance, 'designer stubble'. Indeed I was quite surprised that his face actually did have quite a modern look to it. I wondered how the women of the Annalena convent might originally have perceived him. Perhaps some of them had actually met him. A rather wicked thought entered my mind: had any of them surrendered their thoughts to ones other than sacred, I wondered? The figure is shown wearing a brown cloak and hood with the words 'SAN HILARION' inscribed upon his shoulder. It is said that Annalena's brother eventually withdrew from the world and saw out his days in a hermitage. This may explain why he might have chosen to be represented in the guise of St. Hilarion who had followed such an ascetic-like existence. Legend has it that Annalena was very beautiful and judging from the appearance of the figure thought to represent her brother, I could certainly believe it. With a huge stretch of my imagination I thought I could detect some resemblance in the face of the Madonna with that believed to be Annalena's brother. I gazed upon the beautiful face of the Madonna with her loose, blonde curls just visible beneath her veil. I would love to think that she might have been modelled upon Annalena but it is probably more likely that it was Lucrezia Buti.

On the right side of the painting, the upturned eyes of the figure of Mary Magdalene in the guise of a penitential hermit secluded in the wilderness caught my attention. The figure of this penitential saint would have held particular significance for Annalena, since the Magdalene was greatly promoted by the Mendicant orders and especially by Annalena's spiritual protector Archbishop Antonino. I shall discuss Annalena's affinity with the Magdalene figure more fully later on.

Indeed, in this altarpiece Lippi has drawn upon imagery that would have been important to Annalena and her women and includes references to the three monastic vows of Poverty, Chastity and Obedience. The plant which winds its way up the Magdalene's arm for example has been identified as being Butcher's Broom, an attribute of poverty. Possibly Annalena's mentor Archbishop Antonino had helped to devise such imagery. Behind the Magdalene there is a tower and it has been suggested that this may be a possible reference to the semi-enclosed status of the women of Annalena's convent. It is, however, impossible to know if the buildings depicted in the altarpiece recall those of the Annalena complex. It is known that the Oratory did have a neighbouring garden and perhaps the wilderness depicted in the painting reflects this. Interestingly, Lippi also painted an altarpiece for Le Murate convent which depicts a garden and this is shown closed: an allusion to the Virgin's purity and to the enclosure of the nuns within the walls. So there may indeed be some significance attached to this detail in the *Annalena Nativity* painted by him.

The Uffizi gallery is home to one further work that is known to have had a connection with the convent of Annalena. It is an altarpiece entitled *Crucifixion with St. Mary Magdalene* and is attributed to Luca Signorelli, an artist from Cortona (see **Figure 18**). Stylistically this painting can be dated to the 1490s, around the time of the death of Annalena. The altarpiece is significant in size, measuring 249cm x 166cm. It is unusual since it is painted on canvas and canvas altarpieces were rare in central Italy at this time. The fact that it is painted on canvas has given rise to the suggestion by some art historians that it was originally painted as a processional banner. However, it is also believed that it may have been placed near or possibly even hung over Annalena's tomb, which was located in the convent church. Certainly there are various allusions to death within the altarpiece and these may support this theory. With this in mind the altarpiece may have been commemorative. In support of the altarpiece perhaps having been close to the tomb of Annalena, the artist Lorenzo di Credi had painted an image of Mary Magdalene which hung near the tomb of Maria (Marietta) degli Albizzi, foundress of the nearby Santa Chiara monastery. If it did not serve such a purpose then Signorelli's altarpiece may have been placed in the dormitory or elsewhere in the Annalena convent. I pause for a moment to reflect on the notion that the Signorelli altarpiece may have once been near Annalena's tomb. In this work Signorelli has depicted Mary Magdalene as youthful and beautiful. She is shown dressed in contemporary clothes with long, flowing blonde hair. The inclusion of the Magdalene figure may be because she was Annalena's namesake saint, the compound of her name being 'Anna' and 'Maddalena'. By the time the altarpiece was thought to have been painted, the Annalena convent was experiencing a period of change. The Annalena community had come under the order of Savonarola's preachers albeit for a short time. It is worth bearing this in mind when considering this work. Signorelli's *Crucifixion with St. Mary Magdalene* reflects the importance of the cross in the sisters' devotions, which was probably fuelled by Savonarola's sermons and writings. A fascinating footnote to the history of this painting is that it was one of the art treasures that was taken by the Nazis in 1944 and hidden in Alto Adige in Northern Italy before being recovered by the 'Monuments Men' (a team assigned to protect and recover Europe's artistic treasures from the Nazis).

The next stop on my itinerary found me heading for the convent museum of San Marco. If I ever had to choose my favourite place in Florence then it would have to be here. Indeed, there is nothing more satisfying than to visit this most spiritual of places. A morning spent wandering through what were once the monks' cells in this former Dominican monastery instantly calms the soul and is time well spent. Around the time Annalena married Baldaccio, this building was in a state of ruin and was in the process of just being rebuilt. The area must have been a veritable building site and in contrast with today it would have been as far removed from a sense of peace and calm imaginable. Cosimo, Annalena's godfather, had appointed his favourite architect Michelozzo to undertake the project. Cosimo would even have his own cell here as did the Archbishop Antonino and Savonarola.

The friar/painter Fra Angelico or the '*Beata*' ('Blessed') Angelico, as he is known, lived in the convent of San Marco and was essentially the 'painter in residence' there for several years. Indeed, this former convent houses the largest collection in the world of his works, which include the world-famous frescoes in the former monks' dormitory cells and the altarpiece known as the *Pala d'Annalena* (also known as the *Annalena Altarpiece,* see **Figure 19**), which I had specifically come to see. It was truly a delight to walk through the silent cloister en route to the *Sala dell'Ospizio* (pilgrim's hall) where the *Annalena Altarpiece* and several other paintings by the friar painter are located. As I walked, I noted the cloister layout with its rows of columns crowned with capitals.

The *Annalena Altarpiece* is one of Fra Angelico's most important works and is considered to be a significant work in the evolution of Italian Renaissance art since it counts amongst the earliest examples of the popular Renaissance '*sacra conversazione*' type (depiction of the Virgin and Child amidst a group of saints in a relatively informal grouping). The date given to the altarpiece, which depicts the Virgin and child enthroned with Saints Peter Martyr, Cosmas, Damian, John the Evangelist, Lawrence and Francis, has been greatly debated over the years. It is believed to have been painted *c.*1435 and it has been suggested that since it includes Saints Cosmas and Damian the altarpiece was originally a Medici commission. The word '*Medici*' in Italian means 'doctors' and in the fifteenth century the saintly doctors Cosmas and Damian were identified with the Medici. It was believed to have been intended for the transept chapel adjacent to the old sacristy of San Lorenzo (the Medici church in Florence), which was originally dedicated to these saints. Around 1452 the chapel at San Lorenzo became the repository of relics that belonged to the Medici family. Recent thought is that the altarpiece was transferred to the Annalena convent shortly before the installation of a tabernacle of *Corpus Domini* by Desiderio da Settignano in 1461.

Upon entering the *Sala dell'Ospizio* it was as though I had died and gone to heaven, since I was surrounded by many of Fra Angelico's greatest masterpieces. I gasped audibly with ecstasy and joy at the sight of such visions of sheer loveliness. As much as I could have turned to look at any of those paintings and been more than happy, a shaft of early morning sunlight, like some divine beacon, uncannily guided me towards the painting I had come to look at. I felt so privileged to stand before this beautiful altarpiece and to enjoy it without the crowds that I knew would soon descend upon the place. We are indeed fortunate that this altarpiece survives and remains in Florence since this was one of the art treasures that was taken to Paris after the suppression of the Annalena convent.

One is always guaranteed a visual feast with Fra Angelico and indeed, the *Annalena Altarpiece* doesn't disappoint. He was indeed a 'sweet and angelic' painter. It is said that he would always pray before he started work on a painting, and when he painted crucifixions he did so with tears streaming down his face. Little wonder that his paintings and frescoes always appear imbued with the utmost holiness. Vasari described Fra Angelico as having a 'rare and perfect talent'; how true, I thought! I found myself totally enraptured by the breathtaking array of delicate hues so typical of this artist's palette and the sweet, small, rosy-cheeked face of his Madonna had me reeling with joy. This was certainly a most 'blessed' artist both in name and style and it really is true to say that his paintings could win over even the most non-religious of souls. He has depicted the Madonna seated upon a raised throne with the Christ child on her lap and beneath her gloriously painted blue mantle her body is just discernable. The rendering of the folds of drapery that fall over her knees is exquisite. The artist's hallmark painting of sweet rosy cheeks appear once more in the faces of the Christ child and some of the figures of the saints. The saints wear lovely flowing garments and some are shown barefoot standing either on a marble plinth or upon a grassy meadow. To the immediate right of the Madonna are the doctor saints Cosmas and Damian. Both wear red/magenta cloaks fastened at the neck and one can be seen with a shoulder uncovered to expose a blue tunic trimmed with fur and red stockings underneath. The sight of their cute red and white fur-trimmed hats make me smile as I instantly think of Santa Claus! With his right hand, the semi-leaning/standing Christ child delicately reaches out to touch his mother's inner veil, whilst holding a pomegranate, the traditional symbol of the Passion, in the other. The intricately patterned gold cloth stretched behind the Madonna with its visible hooks and set against a fictive marble loggia provides further 'eye candy' for the viewer. Indeed, this is an altarpiece that could delight both the senses and the soul for many hours but sadly, I must leave it since I have other art treasures to pursue.

I leave, however, with one small thought in my mind: quite astonishingly, Richa doesn't appear to mention the Fra Angelico altarpiece, which may perhaps suggest that it could have been located in a part of the Annalena convent that he didn't see or was unable to see. Possibly, it was housed in Annalena's own chamber or in the 'ward of the ill', as Richa describes it, which he was unable to visit. If intended for the former then it would be satisfying to think that if it had been commissioned by Annalena's relatives the Medici and it had entered her convent roughly at the time it was founded, then its inclusion of the two doctor saints and their allusion to healing may have served to help heal the soul of Annalena following the murder of her husband. If, on the other hand, it was once in the convent infirmary then yet again the allusion to doctors and healing would be relevant. Crucifixes and other images associated with healing could be found in hospital wards.

One of the most interesting and mysterious artistic commissions related to Annalena, and indeed the only known surviving documentation to support her involvement with an artistic commission, is found in the records of her notary Ser Pierozzo Cerbini. He had notarised various land transactions for her particularly during the years 1456–59 when she was actively buying up land and properties. Fortunately for our purposes, he kept a small separate ledger recording her expenditures for various ecclesiastical items. The entries related to sculptures by Desiderio da Settignano and especially a polychrome wooden statue of the *Mary Magdalene* is of particular interest. Desiderio was one of the most admired Florentine sculptors of the *quattrocento*. I have to confess that I have not seen this particular ledger but I have examined or rather attempted to examine some of the documents that belonged to Cerbini. These are kept in the ASF and survive as a huge collection of loose papers. I say 'attempted to examine' since regrettably I had to abandon trying to read them. In typical notarial fashion most of the records are written in Latin and the script is so incredibly miniscule to the point of being virtually illegible. I tried with all of my might to decipher their contents but to no avail; it was impossible. Thankfully, other scholars including Victor Coonin and Louis Waldman have laboured over his papers and I have taken the liberty to rely upon their findings regarding the aforementioned artistic commission. All was not lost, however, since the very fact that I was unable to undertake this task myself allowed me to pay considerable attention to the actual physical document itself. It really is quite impossible to describe what it feels like to see and come into contact with manuscripts and documents that were written almost 600 years ago. I can only compare it with the chill running down the spine that one may feel on rare occasions when listening to a piece of music. I admired the cover of *carta pecora* (parchment) with leather straps, binding and clasp. I even made a quick drawing in my notebook of the criss-cross stitching found on the clasps over the parchment cover. I felt the paper on which the script was written; it was thick and very cellulose-like, obviously handmade (regulations today regarding the handling of manuscripts seem to alternate between the wearing of gloves and not). Holding the paper between my fingers somehow brought me closer to Cerbini as I thought of his pen scratching upon its surface. I was pleased that I had inadvertently been given this opportunity to appreciate the more personal aspects of reading an ancient manuscript, something which is so often lost when one is engrossed in the actual task of reading and understanding the contents themselves.

From the separate ledger concerning Annalena's expenditures regarding the statue by Desiderio da Settignano, it is clear that Annalena was involved in the commission of the *Mary Magdalene*. However, it remains uncertain as to whether or not she was the original patron of the work. Significantly, the statue never ended up in her convent, rather it finally came to rest on her notary's altar in the church of Santa Trinita in Florence. It certainly was the case that Annalena paid for the materials and labour for the statue and it is recorded in the ledger kept by Cerbini that he himself had met Annalena in church on October 23rd 1458 where she gave him two florins to pay for wood for a 'Santa Maria Magdalena'. Desiderio received four florins in total for the sculpture. The sculpture of Mary Magdalene was Desiderio's last work and it would remain unfinished at his death in 1464. Until fairly recent years it was believed that the sculpture had been completed by Benedetto da Maiano. However, some recently discovered new documents related to the commission indicate that the statue was completed by a little known Florentine artist called Giovanni d'Andrea di Domenico who had served as an apprentice in the workshop of the more famous Andrea del Verrocchio. The statue had been left incomplete for some thirty-one years and these newly discovered contracts indicate that Ser Pierozzo Cerbini was the patron of the statue and that he had made an initial payment for its completion by Giovanni d'Andrea di Domenico. Cerbini probably intended the statue for his altar in the church of Santa Trinita from the outset and it may have been installed on the Cerbini altar in that church as early as 1499 when it was completed. Francesco Albertini recorded that he saw the Magdalene statue in the church of Santa Trinita in 1510 and he was the first to claim that Desiderio had left it unfinished at his death in 1464. Indeed, sixteenth century sources all locate the statue as being in the church of Santa Trinita. A seventeenth-century source specified the statue as being located at an altar on the interior facade of the church and identified this altar as belonging to the Cerbini family. Today the sculpture of the Magdalene can be found set within a niche in the Spini chapel in the left nave of the church (see **Figure 20**).

The question as to whether Annalena may have originally commissioned the statue is still open, since it is possible that she may have lost interest in the statue after Desiderio's death in 1464 and then gave the unfinished statue to her notary Cerbini who then hired Giovanni to complete it. It is notable that the commissioning of the statue took place soon after she had founded her convent and most likely Annalena was accumulating altarpieces and furnishings for her establishment. If she did originally commission the statue then this would have served as an excellent example of female patronage during the period. This artistic commission is indeed extremely interesting since it seems to have involved Annalena, Cerbini and the sculptor in an almost symbiotic relationship. It has been noted that Annalena may possibly have made payments for the Magdalene statue to Desiderio on behalf of her notary who received the statue in lieu of payment for his services. Such a method of payment, using one's debtors as a bank, appeared to have been commonplace in Renaissance Florence. Based on this assumption Annalena's involvement with this very important artistic commission still remains of interest, since it provides us with further insight into how such a transaction could be applied in the commissioning of artistic works. It is also possible that Annalena may have had a personal connection with Desiderio da Settignano.

Why might Annalena have been interested in this commission of a Mary Magdalene statue? The Mendicant religious orders, the Franciscans and the Dominicans, had promoted Saint Mary Magdalene and this saint became a favourite subject for sculptors and artists in fifteenth-century Florence. In his writings, Annalena's mentor, the Dominican Antonino Pierozzi, had promoted the iconography of the saint as a hermit who expiates her sins through penance, and called upon women to follow the example of Mary Magdalene. As a wealthy, pious convert the figure of Mary Magdalene appealed to affluent women such as Annalena. Perhaps she considered herself to have followed the Magdalene's example when she renounced all her earthly possessions following the death of her husband and in dedicating herself to God she had been redeemed.

The *Mary Magdalene* statue by Desiderio is represented as a fusion of two episodes in the saint's life: the Penitent Magdalene and when she was a young sinner redeemed through her love of Christ. It is noteworthy that Desiderio's representation of the saint is unusual and never seems to have been repeated. With this in mind, could Annalena possibly have had a hand in the unusual design of the statue if indeed she had been its original patron? I will remind the reader that Mary Magdalene is prominently featured in the aforementioned Filippo Lippi altarpiece and also appears in the altarpiece by Signorelli; it would seem that Annalena may have had a personal devotion to this saint.

I chose to make a pilgrimage to see for myself the actual Magdalene statue in the old Vallombrosan church of Santa Trinita. As I stepped into the silent, dark interior of the church I welcomed the shafts of sunlight that illuminated the right-hand side of the building, albeit only momentarily.

This offered me just enough light to gain a sense of the space of the church in its entirety. Most visitors to the church of Santa Trinita come to see the wonderful fresco cycle by Domenico Ghirlandaio in the Sassetti chapel, which depicts scenes from the life of St. Francis (1483–85). The Sassetti family were just one of the many wealthy families who patronised side chapels in the church of Santa Trinita during the fifteenth century. In the scene depicting the *Resurrection of the Notary's Son* it is possible to see what the area and the church of Santa Trinita looked like in Annalena's day and portraits of Florentines whom she must have known. This is valuable since the Santa Trinita bridge of Annalena's day was destroyed by floods and later replaced with the present-day one and the facade of the Santa Trinita church was remodelled in the sixteenth century. Fortunately, we are still able to see the remains of the early romanesque building in the inner wall of the church facade.

I headed over towards the Spini chapel on the left-hand side of the high altar and there she was, standing within the safe haven of her niche. I looked up at the almost life-sized haggard figure of the repentant saint with her long, bedraggled hair. I was instantly reminded of the more famous statue of *Mary Magdalene* by Donatello. This is not surprising since Desiderio had been greatly influenced by Donatello's statue. At the same time Desiderio includes features that are quite different, for example the more elegant pose which is said to recall a now lost Mary Magdalene by Filippo Brunelleschi. I marvelled at how the Magdalene's tresses of hair appeared to meld into her ragged clothes. In her left hand the saint firmly holds her attribute of the ointment jar since she is believed to have anointed the feet of Christ with ointment. Her small right finger is delicately crooked, as though she were politely holding a drinking glass.

I transported myself back in time to that autumnal day in October 1458 when Annalena had met with her notary, Cerbini. We do not know for certain which church they met in, however, since the Annalena convent church had not yet been built and the convent Oratory would probably have been in use by the Annalena women themselves, it is possible that they may even have met within the church of Santa Trinita, the very church I was now standing in. I imagined Annalena leaving the confines of her recently established convent, perhaps in the company of a fellow nun, and making her way along the Via Romana, passing by the church of San Felice and into the Via Maggio lined with its many wool shops. It must have felt good for her to embrace the autumnal air and to greet the outside world if only for a short time. I thought of her perhaps pausing to look at the muddy river Arno from the Santa Trinita bridge before stealing into the church of the same name. Annalena would, as I had done, have experienced the gloominess of the interior of this church, even more so in the darker autumnal months when daylight is sparse. Somewhere in the shadows the youthful Cerbini would have been waiting to greet her, perhaps in the company of the artist Desiderio himself. Annalena would have been accustomed to dealing with her notary by this date. I had visions of her retrieving a small, worn leather purse from her person. She carefully undoes the piece of cord that keeps it secure and removes two florins from the purse and hands them to her notary. He records their meeting and transaction. Indeed, there must have been an exchange of words between the two, but sadly my imagination stops short as to what these might have been.

Included on the bottom page of Cerbini's ledger dedicated to Annalena there is also a reference to a beautiful terracotta head of Christ by Desiderio. The entry seems to imply that Cerbini purchased the bust 'ready-made' and certainly Desiderio's studio produced many busts of women and children. It is believed that the terracotta bust probably represented the holy figure as a child. However, once more it is unclear whether the patron of this work had been Cerbini or Annalena. My belief is that it had probably been commissioned by Annalena since such busts of Christ would have been used for private meditation and probably kept in a nun's own room or cell. There is also an additional record of payments being made to a scribe named Torello for providing a missal. A reminder, indeed, that Annalena's convent had a variety of fine artistic works.

In pursuit of art commissions associated with Annalena and her convent I found myself heading next to the Museo del Cenacolo Andrea del Sarto e San Salvi, which I'm horrified to admit I had never been to before. This small museum is home to many art treasures including a very important painting of the *Last Supper* by the artist Andrea del Sarto. Interestingly, it also has some paintings by the great sixteenth century female artist Plautilla Nelli who herself had been a nun in the convent of Santa Caterina in Florence. I had always meant to visit this museum but I had never actually got round to it; what better reason than now! It was just by chance when searching through the internet that I had discovered that the San Salvi museum held a couple of paintings that had once been in the Annalena convent.

Unfortunately, only one of these was on public view. I had contacted the curator to arrange a possible viewing of this as well as the other painting, which was kept in storage. The museum, although not in the centre of Florence, can be easily reached by public transport. My appointment with the curator was scheduled for 10.00am. Since we had never visited this part of Florence before and we were unsure about the location of the museum we took the bus from the centre of Florence to San Salvi at about 8.30am. Unfortunately this was still '*ora di punta*' or 'rush hour'. Firstly, we had to fight with the crowds to get on to the bus, which was already full with standing room only. We stood crammed in like sardines for the duration of the journey, which much to both our surprise and relief was only short since it only took about ten minutes to reach our destination. It was enough time, however, to experience the melee of noisy traffic, irate bus drivers and rude passengers that must be typical of this early hour.

Of course we arrived well in advance of my appointment but fortunately, the museum was already open and we were able to enjoy a quick look around. Unsurprisingly, we were the only visitors at this early hour. On hearing that someone was in the gallery, a member of the museum staff appeared from an office and greeted us. As we wandered through the gallery I looked out for the painting that I had come to see. It was a painting of *The Penitent St. Jerome in the Desert*, dated 1485–1490, by Bartolomeo di Giovanni (see **Figure 21**), an important artist who had worked in the workshop of Domenico Ghirlandaio. The painting was possibly commissioned during the last years of Annalena's life or soon afterwards. This was yet one further painting that had been taken from the Annalena convent after its suppression. It had been transferred firstly to the *Accademia di Belle Arti* in Florence and then to its current home. Three panels depicting stories from the life of Saint Jerome, which are now in the Walters Art Museum in Baltimore, are believed to have formed the predella or base of this altarpiece.

I soon spotted the painting of Saint Jerome, who was one of the four Latin church fathers, renowned for both his learning and piety. I stared hard at the penitent bearded saint shown kneeling before a crucifix with a skull in the foreground. I could make out a lion, the saint's companion in the wilderness, lurking in the shadows. There were many other details alluding to the saint's life including a red hat which identifies the saint as a cardinal and books denoting Jerome's role as a Father of the church and the translator of the Bible into Latin. An owl sits upon a branch, which sprouts from the rocks of a cave; its presence, because of its nocturnal habits, may represent evil. Next to the owl a dove takes flight and the dove may signify good. My attention was drawn to a small church in the background on the right-hand side of the painting and a fleeting thought entered my mind: could this possibly have been based on the Oratory that Annalena had built for her convent? I rather hoped it was the case.

We had a quick look at the other paintings in the museum including the famous *Cenacolo* (Last Supper) by Andrea del Sarto. Suddenly, the woman who had greeted us earlier joined us in the gallery. I casually mentioned that I was awaiting an appointment with the curator. On hearing this she introduced herself as Barbara Pini, the curator of the museum, and she would be happy to see me straightaway if I wished. She then led us to her office where she had already sought out some information about the St. Jerome painting we had just looked at. She handed me an inventory file dated 1890 with details relating to it. Evidently, it had been attributed to several different artists over the years including Andrea del Castagno, Filippo Lippi, Filippino Lippi and the school of Ghirlandaio. The eminent art connoisseur Bernard Berenson had been the first to attribute the painting to Bartolomeo di Giovanni, an artist who was active in Florence in the later decades of the fifteenth century. Sadly, there was no mention of who had specifically commissioned the painting. However, more recent scholarship states that it was originally in the Annalena convent church and it was probably commissioned by the Minerbetti, an elite Florentine family. A scholar had noted that it might have been commissioned by Andrea Minerbetti and his wife Maria who had close family connections at the Annalena convent. It was Maria's family (the Bini) who had sold the property to Annalena and Baldaccio and which later formed part of her convent. The couple possibly commissioned the picture around the time they were married in 1492 or at the time they nominated the Annalena nuns to be godmothers of their daughter in the following year. The connection with Maria Bini is interesting since Bartolomeo di Giovanni is documented to have worked with the famous Renaissance artist Sandro Botticelli for the Bini family during the 1480s.

Barbara then led me over to her desk where the other painting that I had requested to see had already been brought in from the museum storeroom. This painting dates from the years just following the death of Annalena and was probably commissioned at the time that her niece Maria Malatesta would have been prioress of the convent. The painting was resting upon a thick layer of bubble wrap for protection. It wasn't incredibly large in size only measuring 63cm x 51cm and it was entitled *Busto del Salvatore* (Bust of the Saviour), and was painted in oil on canvas (see **Figure 22**). The only details listed about the painting were that the subject was a *Redentore* and that it was a copy of Allori. It had also been attributed to the school of Fra Bartolomeo. It was really exciting for us to see the painting 'up close and personal' as it were, and it was definitely another highlight of my research. I stooped over the desk to examine the painting carefully. It represented the profile of the bust of a young, bearded Christ wearing a heavy mantle. I observed that the artist had given careful attention to the rendering of Christ's wispy hair and beard. In my humble opinion, the painting did not however appear to be a work of the very finest calibre, but it was fascinating nevertheless. The canvas showed signs of damage on the upper part of its surface, particularly on Christ's hair. Barbara turned the painting over and it was even more of a thrill for us to see that a couple of labels had been stuck on the inside frame. One was an inventory label from the Uffizi gallery and dated 1881 whilst the other, which was more interesting, appeared older. The writing looked as though it could be dated to the sixteenth century and it was in a damaged state showing the appearance of water damage and/or flame damage. It gave a number and stated that it had been extracted from the Annalena convent in Florence.

Barbara looked through the inventory of works held '*in deposito*' (in storage) at the museum and found one further artwork that had come from the Annalena convent. This was a painting of a Madonna with child, of the Florentine School; however this was of less interest to me since it was dated to the eighteenth century, well after the time of our foundress. I left the San Salvi museum that morning feeling suitably satisfied that I had been able to locate and see for myself these artistic commissions which had once been in the Annalena convent.

Before returning to the city centre we stopped at a nearby cafe to 'refuel'. Thankfully, the bus ride back was more civilised. On reaching our destination I quickly looked at my watch; yes, there would be just enough time to visit the Horne Museum in Via dei Benci, the location of one further art treasure that had once belonged to the Annalena convent. The Horne Museum has a magnificent collection of paintings, sculptures and furnishings which were left to the Italian government by the English architect and art historian Herbert Horne upon his death in 1916. Included amongst its fine collection are works by Giotto and Simone Martini. The artwork I had come to see was neither a painting nor a fresco but a '*desco da parto*' or birth tray. I climbed up to the third floor of the palazzo and on entering the gallery space I was immediately greeted by the magnificent painted birth salver. The large twelve-sided birth tray is dated to around 1457, roughly when Annalena had established her convent. A scene of the Last Judgment features on the front of the tray and a winged cupid with pipes and a coat of arms representing the Albizzi and Soderini families can be seen on the reverse. It was a revelation for me to discover that the '*desco da parto*' had possibly belonged to Albiera degli Albizzi whom as I have already discussed was educated at the convent of Annalena. Indeed, several girls from the Albizzi family had entered Annalena's convent. The birth tray was possibly commissioned as a wedding gift for Albiera's mother and then was handed down to Albiera to mark her marriage and the hope for future children. Following the premature death of Albiera the '*desco da parto*' was given to the Annalena convent. A further work linked with Albiera and ultimately Annalena is a manuscript illustrated by Francesco Rosselli, a miniaturist, engraver, cartographer and half brother of the more famous painter Cosimo Rosselli, which was commissioned by Albiera's fiancé Sigismondo della Stufa. It now survives in the Vatican library.

Sadly, I had exhausted all the known surviving artworks in Florence that were commissioned for the convent at the time of Annalena. There was only one final painting I had to see and this found me returning home to the UK. At the time of writing, this painting, which is attributed to the Florentine artist Francesco Botticini, had been relegated to the storerooms of the Courtauld Gallery in London. Frequent visitors to the Sainsbury Wing of the National Gallery in London may remember the large painting of the *Assumption of the Virgin* also by Francesco Botticini, which used to greet visitors as they climbed the great staircase leading to the galleries.

The Courtauld painting by Botticini entitled *Crucifixion with Saints Vincent Ferrer, Peter Martyr, Stephen, Catherine of Siena and the Blessed Antoninus at the Foot of the Cross* was possibly commissioned in 1474 and had made its way into San Marco in Florence probably from a Dominican church or convent, most likely from the convent of Annalena. It was then bought by an art collector and dealer during the nineteenth century before entering the Courtauld collection in 1966. I had arranged in advance to view the painting and on arrival at the Courtauld I was escorted by a Dr Garrett to the small storeroom where it was kept under lock and key. After clearing security procedures we stepped into what I imagined to resemble a bank vault. The space was full of stacked racks containing paintings. I stood and watched as Dr Garrett deftly steered the racks open using hand movements on a wheel; she reminded me of a sailor at the helm of a ship. All at once rows and rows of carefully stacked paintings were revealed including the painting I had come to see. I had only ever seen a black and white reproduction of it before and I was surprised to discover that it was much smaller than I had expected. The painting was lunette-shaped and set within a gold frame, which was of a later date. The panel depicts St. Antoninus kneeling before a crucifix flanked by two pairs of saints: Saints Vincent Ferrer, Peter Martyr, Stephen and Catherine of Siena. It is painted in tempera on panel and its lunette shape is interesting and has prompted suggestions that it may once have been set over a door. However, on seeing the painting at first hand it would seem to be too small for such a location. I was interested to read later that this proposal had in fact been dismissed, based on this very point. I had also read that it could possibly have formed part of the top of a small altarpiece or piece of liturgical furniture, perhaps a wooden tabernacle, which to my mind seemed plausible.

In order for me to examine the painting more closely I was allowed to stand very carefully between the racks. The small size of the painting would have called for it to be originally viewed close up (albeit not as close as I was looking at it) in order to see the details. The panel clearly had a Dominican message with its inclusion of the Archbishop of Florence Antonino (Annalena's spiritual mentor) shown dressed in his archbishop's attire and in the company of Dominican saints. This panel is one of the earliest representations of Archbishop Antonino after his death and there seems to be a strong iconographic link between this panel and a painted standard which hung over Antoninus's first tomb in San Marco and which still exists. The inclusion of St. Catherine, who was a female Dominican tertiary saint, and St. Stephen and St. Vincent would have been especially appropriate for the Annalena convent church which Archbishop Antonino had consecrated in the names of Saints Stephen and Vincent Ferrer. The artist had depicted the outstretched Christ on the cross with copious amounts of blood pouring from his body. This detail appeared to be more Northern European in its influence than Italian. Dr Garrett held a torch to the panel so that I could observe its details more clearly. At such close quarters I was able to determine that St. Catherine was depicted trampling upon a hairy demon. I was also able to observe the faces and attributes of the other saints as well as the condition of the surface of the wooden panel. I look forward to the day when this work can be firmly documented as being derived from the San Vincenzo di Annalena convent.

I should now like to discuss those artworks that were associated with the convent around the time of Annalena, but which have now sadly been lost. These only exist in the form of documentation since no physical trace of these works has been found to date. An example of such are two figures believed to have been painted (frescoed) for the cloister or facade of the Annalena convent by the great Renaissance artist Paolo Uccello, famed for his love and mastery of perspective. Giorgio Vasari in his *Lives of the Artists* mentions that Uccello painted two figures for the Annalena convent but does not specify whereabouts in the convent these were painted or what they represented. To this day, it is written in the Hotel Annalena brochure that there is a lost work by Uccello which they believe is still hidden there. A really interesting reference to Paolo Uccello and his association with the Annalena convent can be found in a pamphlet published in 1886 by a journalist called Angiolo de Witt. It concerns the discovery of a *Pieta* painted in a niche in a room within a privately owned house that originally belonged to Annalena and Baldaccio. This was the house of course that became the nucleus of Annalena's convent. This indeed is a great story; how fabulous would it be to uncover a great artistic treasure within your own home? The author proposed that the *Pieta* had been painted by Paolo Uccello. He even postulated that this image of Christ rising from the tomb may possibly have been the Christ that Baldaccio had turned to and asked pardon of his sins before going to the Palazzo della Signoria where he was assassinated. Intriguingly, de Witt's publication was essentially ignored by those interested in the 'oeuvre' of Paolo Uccello since stylistically the *Pieta*, which can be seen illustrated in a sepia photograph provided by de Witt, didn't seem to be close to even the earliest works attributed to this famous artist. De Witt's pamphlet does, however, provide some useful information for the dating of Uccello's aforementioned two figures that he did for the Annalena convent, as well as giving dates related to when the convent was founded. De Witt mentions that the house located in the aforementioned site had been acquired by the Comune for Baldaccio not long before his marriage to Annalena in 1439 and that it was cited as part of a guarantee of Annalena's dowry. According to de Witt's research, following Baldaccio's death the property was inherited by Annalena's son and after the son's death from the plague in 1450, it passed to Annalena who transformed the house into an order of Dominican nuns in 1454. It has been pointed out by a scholar that both the *Pieta* and the aforementioned two figures by Uccello may have predated the Annalena convent.

One further artistic work that can also be ranked amongst those that are now considered to be lost is a miraculous image known as the *Madonna Della Palla* (Madonna of the Ball). Fortunately, a book written in the eighteenth century exists which is completely dedicated to this particular image. The author Domenico Manni informs us that the image was made of polychrome terracotta and it was originally placed in a tabernacle in a street outside the Annalena convent. This street was probably the Via Santa Maria and this appears to have been why the street got its name. The author describes how the sculpture came to be known as the 'Madonna of the Ball': one day a young boy was playing in the street and he hurled a ball at the tabernacle; the Madonna supposedly caught it in her right hand while the Christ child in her arms recoiled in fear. After the miracle on the street the *Madonna della Palla* was transferred into the Oratory, the first church of the Annalena convent. The first known date that the author gives for the venerable image to have been in the Annalena convent is 1461–1462, only a few years after the convent was founded. The Annalena convent supposedly received a terracotta Madonna and child reportedly sculpted by Donatello (the ball was gilded much later) from San Marco and this is recorded in the convent archives. A rather lovely additional note states that on Saturdays the nuns sang '*La Salve*' in the Oratory, and other religious prayers, at an open window close to the image. This window looked out on the Via Santa Maria so that the inhabitants of the houses opposite (according to ancient custom) accompanied the orations inside. The earliest surviving record of the *Madonna Della Palla* appears in the 1527 Annalena archives. It is recorded that following the death of a nun from the plague the prioress prostrated herself in humility before the Madonna vowing to replace the dead sister with a young girl with no dowry. Manni also informs us that there was a magnificent altar for this image which had been erected before 1563. Notably, in the seventeenth century the Danish scientist Nicolas Steno (1638-1686) had often prayed before the *Madonna Della Palla* and sent fifty *scudi* to have a pair of silver candlesticks made for the altar of this image. When Richa visited the Annalena convent he saw the Oratory and specifically noted a devotional *Virgin in Relief with a Child*, which in his day was still greatly venerated by the nuns. He adds that oil lamps and wax candles were lit before this precious image, which undoubtedly must have been the *Madonna Della Palla*. The Annalena convent was also a great repository for reliquaries and as noted in an earlier chapter there were also crucifixes including the one believed to have belonged to Annalena's husband Baldaccio. This crucifix was seen by Richa but is lost today. There is also a record of another crucifix which was once in the church of San Vincenzo d'Annalena; this was sculpted in wood and painted later to look like bronze but this also appears to now be lost. A further artwork (now presumed lost) and also believed to have once been in the Annalena convent church is an altarpiece depicting the Virgin presenting the girdle to St. Thomas and saints. This was attributed to Fra Paolino da Pistoia (1490–1547), a Dominican friar who painted in a style similar to Fra Bartolomeo. It is recorded as being placed in the first altar on the right on entering the San Vincenzo d'Annalena church. Mention is also made of a connection between the commission of this painting and Cosimo de' Medici, which is interesting.

As I have illustrated, the Annalena convent was indeed an extremely important artistic site and we have seen that a plethora of important Italian Renaissance artists executed works there. My search continues for further artistic commissions linked with her convent, at or close to the time when Annalena was prioress. Hopefully over the course of time other artistic treasures will emerge from obscurity to throw further light on our understanding of Annalena and her religious establishment.

CHAPTER 18:

Annalena and her legacy

At this point dear reader forgive me if I should depart slightly from my usual format and substitute the voice of dear Annalena with that of one of her spiritual 'daughters'.

'The day hath come when it pleaseth God to grant our dear "mother" her final rest. On hearing that our dear foundress has indeed departed from this earth and passed to the glory of heaven our hearts overfloweth with sadness but also gratitude. We have indeed been blessed to have had such a kind, charitable and great servant of God as our guide. We will endeavour to carry forth the good name of our beloved foundress and that of her great convent in this fine city of ours. God bless our dear foundress and grant us fortitude. May God guide us and protect us always and may he make us worthy of seeing her in his glory.'

On March 3rd 1491 a dark day descended upon the convent of San Vincenzo d'Annalena and indeed, upon the city of Florence itself. Since it was on this day that the subject of this book, our dear foundress Annalena Malatesta, departed from this earth. Annalena was seventy-one years old when she died, a good age considering that fewer than 5% of the population lived more than sixty-five years at that time. Annalena died from apoplexy, what today we might call a stroke. The term apoplexy is derived from a Greek word signifying a stroke or blow. It must be assumed that she was struck with a fatal apoplectic fit which even the convent infirmary nurses couldn't save her from. It is tempting to weave into the narrative that this was perhaps God's way of letting others know that she had, indeed, served him well on earth and it was now time for her to take up the place that he with his great mercy had reserved for her amongst his angels. A more realistic notion of the truth is supplied by Richa who tells us that exhaustion and fasting over the years finally took their toll.

Even at the end of her days Annalena would have been surrounded by her spiritual family of 'daughters' who would have paid their last respects to their dear foundress. Amongst them were women from some of Florence's leading families including the Soderini, Albizzi, Capponi, Frescobaldi and Gambacorta, all families whom Annalena would have known well. Included amongst them was the daughter of Attilio de' Medici, Annalena's relative. All would have been greatly saddened to hear of Annalena's death. Additionally, several of Annalena's own nieces would have been present including two who would eventually succeed her in becoming prioresses of the convent. Richa wrote that Annalena received all the sacraments and ended her days 'santamente' or devoutly. Annalena must have died content and at peace with the world. She would not have feared going to God. She must have died satisfied in the knowledge that the convent that she had founded had become one of the finest and most highly esteemed convents in Florence. At the time of her death there were over one hundred nuns in her convent. Most likely the convent bell would have tolled the news of her death and the church bells of the city would have echoed solemnly in unison. Local criers and messengers would also have spread the word further. Soon the whole populace of Florence must have mourned the loss of one of their most beloved and illustrious citizens and it is possible that Annalena would have been granted a public funeral.

Annalena had lived an exemplary life, one that was full of good works. She had played a pivotal role in the spiritual life of Florence and indeed she must surely have been regarded as a living saint. Whilst her husband Baldaccio had become famous through his bravery, cruelty and ultimately his assassination, Annalena had achieved her greatness through her piety and charity. Never could there have been two more contrasting characters. When Annalena was buried in her convent church it must have resonated with the utmost holiness. The church would have been full of flickering candles, the heavy scent of incense filling the air and the chanting of psalms by both priests and nuns. Her body was buried in a casket in the tribune of her convent church at the top of the steps which led from the sacristy. This was the area where the priests would prepare for Mass.

Once more we are indebted to Richa since he informs us that the inscription on her tomb read:

D.O.M.
ANNALENAE MALATESTAE
QVAE COENOBIVM HOC
FVNDITVS EXCITAVIT
ALIARVMQ. AB ILLA ANTISTITVM SEPVLC.
MCCCCLXXXX.

This included the year of her death. Anniversary Masses would have taken place following her death and long afterwards. Her name and her life story would have been inscribed in the now lost convent necrology. Interestingly, Richa claims that shortly before Annalena's death she declared Lorenzo the Magnificent and all of his descendants to be 'participants in all the convent's meritorious works'. It is more than likely that Lorenzo the Magnificent was a major benefactor at the Annalena convent since his mother Lucrezia had been before him. Curiously, later Richa seems to confuse Lorenzo with his younger cousin Lorenzo di Pierfrancesco de' Medici. He also had associations with the Annalena convent and I will elaborate upon this in due course. Touchingly, in her will Annalena had showed gratitude towards her husband's homeland Anghiari. In memory of him and of his land, Annalena left instructions that children or widows from Anghiari from the most noble families could enter her convent without dowries. Based on this, Annalena must have loved her husband and believed him to be innocent of any treason. Annalena's convent had been born as a result of the tragic circumstances of the death of her husband, which had involved the Florentine government. She had then battled against the government to realise her objective, which as we have already seen was no easy task. In this she had shown great fortitude and had emerged as a formidable force in her own right. This was one of the characteristics that had made Annalena and her convent unique over the many others that had been founded during the same period.

The convent which Annalena had founded would continue to flourish for centuries after her death and gain even greater prestige and would continue to be called the 'Annalena'. The year in which Annalena died marked the beginning of great change for the city of Florence and indeed the convent that she founded, since the Dominican friar Girolamo Savonarola was 'waiting in the wings' ready to rule the city from the pulpit. Crowds of people had flocked to hear his Advent sermons at San Marco in 1490. Even more crowds came to hear him speak in the city's cathedral when he spoke during Lent in 1491. His visions were apocalyptic and Florence would never be the same again. Savonarola called for a renewal of the church and of the *Signoria* (Florentine government). In its earliest days the convent of Annalena had fallen under the jurisdiction of the Archbishop of Florence Antonino, and the nuns at the convent of Annalena had managed to successfully resist Savonarola's repeated attempts to impose solemn vows on their community. But in the 1490s the friars of San Marco took control of their convent after the nuns requested that Savonarola minister to them.

I shall select some important episodes that shaped the subsequent history of the Annalena convent following the death of its foundress. By the end of the fifteenth century Florence was a city in turmoil as the power of the Medici was overthrown by this fiery monk and the Medici were expelled from the city in 1494. However, even when the main branch of the Medici family had gone into exile in the same year, the nuns at the convent of San Vincenzo d'Annalena continued to enjoy Medici protection under Lorenzo di Pierfrancesco, the cousin of Lorenzo de' Medici. Indeed the Annalena convent memoirs, dated 1466 but believed to have been written in the sixteenth century, cite that Lorenzo di Pierfrancesco was a principal supporter of the convent. Following the execution of Savonarola in 1498, Annalena's niece Maria who had become prioress of the convent soon after the death of her aunt petitioned the Pope for release from the jurisdiction of San Marco. The San Vincenzo d'Annalena sisters were released in 1500 by Alexander VI in a bull declaring the women exempt from any authority of the Dominican order. Oh how Annalena would have been satisfied if she had known this!

One celebrated episode in the history of the Annalena convent occurred in 1503 when Caterina Sforza (the illegitimate daughter of the Duke of Milan) hid her six-year-old son there during the second exile of the Medici. Caterina Sforza's third husband was Giovanni di Pierfrancesco de' Medici and their son was called Giovanni di Giovanni de' Medici (later called *Delle Bande Nere*). He was the nephew of the convent's chief benefactor Lorenzo di Pierfrancesco de' Medici and as an adult Giovanni became the father of Duke Cosimo I. The six-year-old Giovanni apparently was disguised as a girl and was taken care of by the Annalena nuns for eight months. It is said that the nuns kept the boy and his servants in the foundress's own rooms. In doing this it could be understood that the Annalena sisters were acting in response to the many favours they had received from the Medici. In turn the Medici would always be grateful to the nuns of the Annalena convent for saving Giovanni's life and the Annalena convent would continue to enjoy Medici favour thereafter.

A more tragic episode linked with the Annalena convent around this time was a terrible fire which happened on Sunday January 11th 1511 during the time that Annalena's niece Maria Malatesta was prioress. The disaster was recorded in the aforementioned (but now lost) *Memoriale del Monastero di S. Vincenzio* written in the sixteenth century by Suor Laudomina di Ludovico Antinori. According to her, the fire lasted all night and virtually destroyed the convent. It had apparently started in the bread room, which was on the ground floor. Flames could be seen from this room and from the vaults, which contained oil and wine. So great was the fire that the flames were seen to reach the summit of the roof. According to Suor Laudomina, Piero Soderini ordered guards from the Palazzo della Signoria to keep watch on the *porta* (entrance) of the Annalena monastery, which was kept open all of the night.

Fires were a constant hazard in both homes and convents during this period since people would have used oil lamps and braziers and in the case of convents a great many candles. Two serious fires are recorded at the convent of Le Murate, one in 1471 and another in 1498. The latter is believed to have been an act of arson associated with the days of turmoil surrounding the last days of Savonarola. According to Giustina Niccolini, a chronicler of Le Murate, at the time of the earlier fire even Lorenzo de' Medici helped to combat the flames and offered to pay for the whole restoration of the convent as an act of charity. Florence did have a fire service, which was known as *La Guardia del Fuoco*, and this had been established from the fourteenth century. They must have been called out on a continuous basis. Each quarter of the city had its own fire station workshop, which was always open day and night. I recently discovered a reproduction of a print by Ammanati, which is in the Uffizi, showing a very rudimentary fire-extinguishing machine that must have been similar to the one that would have been used to combat the fire at both the Le Murate and Annalena convents. Basically it comprised of a vat which would have been filled with water and this was connected to a manual pump.

I took a moment to think about that terrible day in the history of the Annalena convent. The commotion and sheer panic that the sisters would have experienced must have been horrendous. I could almost hear the screams of those poor women in their desperate attempts to escape from the all-consuming flames of the fire. Since the convent's historical documents are now lost (many having perished in the fire) we have no surviving original records to know the full details and if there were any human fatalities or injuries as a result. We can only hope that there were none. But certainly fires did cause loss of life and the gravity of the incident might suggest otherwise. I imagined how in their state of panic some of the Annalena women might have tried to save some of the treasures of their beloved convent. It is believed that they threw whatever they were able to from the windows of the convent. Certainly, there was major damage to the physical fabric of the convent itself and sadly, as I have already mentioned, it must have been the case that many artworks, furnishings and manuscripts also perished in the flames. For the purpose of research this has indeed been a significant loss.

However, we are fortunate that some artworks appear to have escaped the cruel fury of the fire, for example it is recorded that a choir reliquary, which was an image of the crucifix in relief, was not completely destroyed but did suffer some lasting scars from the inferno. Sadly, I have been unable to trace this work and I am unsure as to whether this may have been the crucifix I have already mentioned in my list of lost artworks.

The fact that the painting of the *Annalena Nativity* by Fra Filippo Lippi survived the fire suggests that the convent church must have escaped the fire or certainly the worst of the blaze and we must be thankful indeed for this. The other major work associated with the Annalena convent, the *Annalena Altarpiece* by Fra Angelico, also appears to have survived and perhaps suggests that it must have been in a part of the building untouched by the fire or indeed somewhere else. Our foundress Annalena would have been absolutely devastated if she had witnessed the tragic event. Everything that she had worked for and built up over the years was reduced to mere charred ruins. Her niece Maria, who as I have already mentioned was the prioress at the time, must have been traumatised but thankful that her aunt had been spared from such a terrible sight.

Such was the affection for Annalena's convent and the recognition of its importance that the rebuilding of it was begun almost immediately after the fire. Like a phoenix rising from the ashes, the convent that Annalena had founded had not only been reborn but it would attain even greater importance. The citizens of Florence together with the Florentine government and the Medici helped to restore the convent to its former glory and indeed it was made even more marvellous. The Medici of course made certain that their support would be made visible to all by placing their arms throughout the newly rebuilt convent. An extensive artistic programme was put in place, the first of many later refurbishment programmes of the convent. The rebuilding of the convent continued until 1515 with the architect Baccio d'Agnolo involved in its execution. Annalena's niece Maria who was still prioress of the convent at this time must have felt both relieved and happy that the convent her aunt had founded would live on. By 1515 it is noted that there were 110 nuns at the Annalena convent while the convent of Le Murate had 200 nuns. The total number of nuns in Florence and its surroundings at this time was 2,500.

My main objective of this book has naturally been to focus on the art commissions around the time of its foundress Annalena, however a great many more artistic works were also executed later. I will select only a few examples from this period for discussion. One of these was a fresco cycle of the *Rosa Mystica* or 'Mysteries of the Rosary' which was painted in the vaults of the new *Coro d'Estate* (summer choir) by the painter Giovanni Mannozzi (Giovanni di Ser Giovanni Mannozzi). This artist lived just opposite the Annalena convent in Via Romana and today a plaque marks the house where he lived. He painted many tabernacles in the city including one that is attributed to him on the Ponte Vecchio and which can still be seen today. Mannozzi was buried in the nearby church of San Pier Gattolino. In addition, the beautiful *Coro d'Estate* itself was designed by the architect Giulio Parigi and it was also decorated with an altarpiece of the *Coronation of the Virgin* by the design of Bronzino.

Included amongst the refurbishment of the convent was a most beautiful and excellent infirmary which was located in the palazzo that had belonged to Annalena and Baldaccio and which was where Annalena first lived with her small group of women. During the sixteenth century the Annalena nuns played an important role in the marketing of medicines. After the siege of Florence in 1529–30 the nuns set up a commercial pharmacy and opened its doors in 1535. Customers could buy medicines, syrups and other remedies from the convent pharmacy. According to Richa (translated), the Annalena nuns traded 'in every sort of medicament needed for any kind of illness' and were compounding 'every sort of medicine' in their workroom. The Annalena nuns cultivated herbs for medicinal use in their extensive gardens and harvested saffron on their farm-holdings.

Sadly, yet one further tragic episode would leave its mark upon the history of the Annalena convent and this was the previously mentioned damage to the Annalena convent church facade. This was the result of fortifications that had been erected during the long struggle for supremacy between Florence and Siena. The ruling Duke Cosimo I of Florence had a stretch of wall, ramparts and an underground passage that even today still connects the Boboli, Corsi and Torrigiani gardens erected as part of the fortifications. According to the diary of a contemporary, the first stone of the baluards was laid on May 16th 1545. Cosimo I himself threw a golden necklace into the *fosso* (ditch) with some medals. The portion of the fortifications near the Annalena church was begun on March 12th 1548. Richa provides us with the vital piece of information that the church facade overlooked Via Romana and that it was damaged and its entrance blocked principally due to the building of a *Portone*, which became known as the *Portone di Annalena*. This *Portone* or gateway was built into the fortifications and measured about fifteen feet in width, which was almost half the width of the street. From my detailed study of maps which show the line of the fortifications, the *Portone* indeed is shown to abut the facade of the Annalena church. This would explain why Richa commented that when he saw the church, its position was considered to be in a confined space, since although the fortification walls had been demolished by this time, the *Portone* was still in place. Sixty '*braccia*' (corresponding to approximately 115 feet) were cut from the Annalena convent garden, pulling down the outer walls and leaving the convent within an irregular-shaped garden which was described by a former nun of the Annalena convent as being 'mutilated from its former grandeur!' Yet again I was disappointed to find that no images appear to exist which show the *Portone di Annalena*, which was only demolished in 1843, and was an important landmark of the city. A *stemma* (coat of arms) representing the Santa Brigida convent, which was close to the Annalena convent, appeared on the *Portone*. A *stemma* representing the Annalena convent could be found on the Porta San Gattolino and it is likely that one was also on the *Portone di Annalena* considering its proximity to their establishment.

At the time of the building of the fortifications the area around the Annalena convent must have resembled a building site with mounds of rubble laced with broken marble columns, pilasters and fragments of stone, some with incised epigraphs, all tragically lost to the world forever. The Commemorative *lapide* (stone) above the door of the church may have been amongst these casualties. The horror and dismay that the Annalena sisters must have felt is quite unimaginable. How awful it must have been for them to watch their 'hallowed' church facade crumble as it surrendered to the forces of man-made destruction. Such an act must have seemed sacrilegious to them even although they knew that the purpose behind the construction of the fortifications was to provide protection for the city. It seems that in this instance at least, their prayers alone must have been considered far from adequate. The fortifications were in place until they were destroyed in 1571; thereafter, the area was left abandoned for many years.

During renovations of the convent church carried out in the sixteenth century Annalena's body plus those of her nieces Suor Maria Malatesta and Suor Clara degli Albizzi, who had succeeded her in becoming prioresses of the convent, were buried in the same tomb and reinterred in front of the high altar of the church. Stefano Rosselli in his *Sepoltuario Fiorentino* in 1657 describes the high altar as having no coats of arms or other insignia, only the marble slab marking the burial place of the convent's first three abbesses whose new tomb had been provided by Giovanna d'Austria in 1573.

Despite terrible setbacks in the history of the Annalena convent it was during the Medici Grand Duchy, also in the sixteenth century, that the convent continued to reach great heights, since it was particularly favoured as a centre for the education of the daughters of the elite Florentine families. It has been noted that the teaching of reading at the Annalena convent was especially suited to the requirements of the Medici Courts at this time. Indeed, it has been written that the Medici regarded the Annalena convent as a sort of 'retirement home' for its pensioner ladies-in-waiting and female servants. The Malatesta name lived on within the Annalena convent with Annalena's great niece Maria (the daughter of Conte Gabbiano Malatesti da Rimini) serving as prioress; she died in 1577.

On March 2nd 1621 the nuns of San Vincenzo d'Annalena acquired the hospital of San Pier Novello, which was located virtually adjacent to the house that had been the nucleus of the convent and which originally belonged to Annalena and her husband, together with the *orto* (garden) behind and at the side of the hospital up until Via Santa Maria. The hospital was suppressed on January 25th 1751 after 400 years of it serving as a hospital and it was conceded in whole to the nuns of the Annalena convent. Even up until the beginning of the nineteenth century it was still possible to gain access into the Annalena convent via a doorway of the *ex Spedale di San Pier Novello* (old hospital) at No. 64 Via Romana. This led into a cloistered *cortile* (courtyard).

During the seventeenth century the Annalena convent was especially favoured by the Grand Duchess Vittoria della Rovera who was a pious woman and a generous benefactor. The nuns at the Annalena convent are documented as being very much involved in the production of textiles and needlework for the Duchess.

At the beginning of the eighteenth century further restorations occurred within the convent including the second cloister and the church by A.M. Ferri. Many important artists were involved in the decoration of the Annalena church at this time including Pier Dandini, Antonio Domenico Gabbiani, Antonio Puglieschi and Rinaldo Botti. Each chapel was furnished with excellent altarpieces. In the first chapel on the left was a miraculous crucifix in relief which apparently remained intact following the destruction of the church facade in the middle of the sixteenth century implying that it might date to as early as the fifteenth century. The chapel next door housed Fra Filippo Lippi's *Annalena Nativity* altarpiece. The chapel opposite displayed a San Jerome praying at the foot of Christ by Bronzino, which was commissioned by the Malatesta. The next chapel displayed an Annunciation in a similar style to the San Jerome. Richa added that the patrons of the altars were the Dini in the Nativity chapel, the Landi in the Chapel of the Annunciation and the Geraldini in the chapel of the crucifix. A new nuns' choir was also built within the church. The Annalena convent became the model for two other convents: SS Trinity in Modigliana and the Degli Angiolini convent in Florence, which were built in the seventeenth century.

The Annalena convent remained active until 1786 when it was transformed into a *conservatorio* (educational establishment) for women. However, even in 1802 the convent was still called the *Monastero di Annalena* or Annalena's convent. In 1790 Marchese Tommaso Corsi bought land which included part of the Annalena gardens and it was transformed into a beautiful romantic garden. This was the first English garden in Florence and it was realised between 1801 and 1810. It was around this time also, in 1807, that the entrepreneur Luigi Gargani bought the land that had once been occupied by the Annalena convent and he transformed it in part into a theatre. Due to its proximity to the Palazzo Pitti, the theatre, which was known as the *Teatro Goldoni* and designed by Giuseppe Del Rosso, was patronised by Florentine nobles in the mid-nineteenth century. The Goldoni Theatre was linked to the Pitti Palace by means of underground passages. It is worth mentioning that in some later documents the theatre was even called the *Teatro di Annalena*. The main facade of the theatre was in Via Santa Maria 15, near the corner of Via delle Caldaie where it still is today. I was interested to discover that its architect was instructed to work economically and to use whatever existing materials were available on site such as tiles, fragments of stones, etc. including those from the old original Annalena convent Oratory. It was rather alarming to read that as a consequence of this it was a miracle that the theatre didn't collapse upon its audiences from the time of its inauguration in 1817 until it was restructured in 1979! Giuseppe del Rosso, who was the municipal architect of Florence at the time, was responsible for many building and restoration projects in Florence and just outside. Interestingly, he used some fir trusses/beams from the Annalena convent church in his restoration of the church of S. Alessandro in Fiesole. He also constructed the building known today as the '*Casa di Annalena*' on the Via Romana, which was inspired by neoclassicism, which was fashionable at that time. By 1820 the building known as the '*Casa di Annalena*' was purchased by General MacDonald of the French army who renovated it and extended its estate and then lived there with his wife Caroline Bonaparte, sister of Napoleon, in 1830. As part of the renovations of the palazzo, the old Annalena convent church was completely demolished and replaced with stables. Elsa Dawson in her curious booklet about Annalena and her convent wrote that workmen were haunted by the spirit of Annalena who interrupted their work. The author reported that it was said that Annalena often stood before the workmen with outstretched arms begging them to leave unharmed the consecrated ground to the beauty of peace and holiness. Even after the demolition of the Annalena convent the people continued to give the palazzo and the site the name 'Annalena'. Following a curious twist of fate, when General MacDonald died, the building was inherited by his son who sold it to the Religious Order of Sisters of the Sacred Heart. They founded a convent school to educate young noble Florentine women. Once again Annalena would have been pleased!

A further chapter in the life of the Annalena convent site occurred in 1919 when two floors of the palazzo were converted into a pensione by the Calastri–Rossoni family and it took the name of 'Pensione Annalena'. As I mentioned in the very first chapter of this book, the pensione soon became the favourite haunt of writers.

During the years of WWII the pensione was a haven for those seeking refuge during the German occupation in 1943. Thereafter, the building continued to enjoy life as a hotel again.

CHAPTER 19:

Annalena Malatesta, the veiled lady?

Throughout my research into the life of Annalena Malatesta, I had dreamt of one day stumbling across an image of her and finally being able to put a face to her name. Most certainly there would have been some representation of her within her convent whether it be in the form of a commemorative bust, or the inclusion of her image within an altarpiece or other artistic work. As foundress of the San Vincenzo d'Annalena convent she was obviously a very significant figure and any representation of a convent's foundress would have been important in the history of that establishment. Convents prided themselves upon the foundation and history of their communities. An example of a representation linked to a foundress of a Florentine convent at this time is that of Annalena's contemporary Maria (Marietta) degli Albizzi, foundress of the adjacent convent of Santa Chiara. A sculpted bas-relief exists which relates to her. This image was used by later chroniclers to explain the foundation and development of that community's history. With Annalena's aristocratic status and familial connections with the Medici it would be expected that she would have been commemorated in some way. Above all her contribution to the spiritual life of the city of Florence had been immense. Sadly, however, there would not seem to be any confirmed documented image of her to date.

Somewhere in the depths of my memory, I believe I saw a bronze bust of a woman dressed in nun's clothes on display in the Bargello Museum (*Museo Nazionale*) in Florence. I could picture the bronze bust and I knew that I had seen a photo of it in one of the books that I own. I frantically searched through the bookshelves in my study and finally found the book which I believed I had seen it in. It was an old book entitled *Women of Florence* by Isidoro del Lungo, published in 1907. I excitedly flicked through its yellowing pages crammed full of stories relating to some of the most important women from Florentine Renaissance history. As I searched through it a whiff of mustiness reached my olfactory senses and I was instantly transported back to the second-hand bookshop where I had bought it. Suddenly, I caught sight of the image I had hoped to see. Indeed, it was the same bronze bust that I thought I had seen in the Bargello Museum all those years ago. The black and white photograph served to illustrate the story of Albiera degli Albizzi whom we have already seen had a close connection with Annalena.

The caption to the photo read: *A BUST CALLED GINEVRA CAVALCANTI, BUT NOW GENERALLY SUPPOSED TO BE A PORTRAIT OF ANNALENA MALATESTA* (Florence Museo Nazionale). I noted that the image of the bust had been taken by Alinari photographers and the photograph still exists within their archives where it is recorded as *'Bronze bust of a woman (Ginevra Cavalcanti or Annalena Malatesta?)'*. It was photographed by Alinari at the Bargello c.1890. In the book by Isidoro del Lungo written in miniscule print beneath the photograph is the word 'Donatello' suggesting that it was a work from the fifteenth century.

The first identification of the sitter of the bust as being Annalena Malatesta would seem to have been proposed by the eminent art historian Jacob Burckhardt in 1884. He also attributed the author of the work to be Lorenzo Vecchietta, a Sienese artist. In 1901 the author Zippel also supported the identification of the sitter as being Annalena Malatesta. By the time that Isodoro del Lungo's book had been published in 1907, and as indicated in the caption to the photograph, clearly the author of the bust had changed. Fuelled by both curiosity and excitement I was interested to investigate further since it was clear that the attribution and the identity of the sitter had changed over the years.

Indeed several candidates have been proposed over time to be the sitter besides Annalena and Ginevra Cavalcanti and these include Contessina de' Bardi (the wife of Cosimo de' Medici) and Caterina Sforza. In more recent years there has even been an observation that there is a similarity between the female donor figure depicted in Masaccio's famous fresco of the *Holy Trinity* in the church of Santa Maria Novella with that of the female sitter of the bronze bust. Only a couple of details relating to the bronze bust seemed to have remained constant over the years and that is that the bust had been in the possession of the Medici and had been housed in the Medici Grand Ducal collection in the sixteenth century. Based on this it must have been of significant importance. Certainly, the fact that the bust was made of bronze, which is a costly medium, would serve to illustrate that this was a considered commission. Additionally, most scholars seemed to agree that the bust had been made from a death mask and it was probably intended to commemorate the subject. Such a detail is invaluable in the interpretation and dating of this work. Curiously, in the Medici collection in the eighteenth century there would appear to have still been some uncertainty about who the sitter of the bust was, since it was called '*Donna velata incognita*' ('Unknown Veiled Lady'), or '*Sacerdotessa Velata*' ('Veiled Priestess'). Lord Balcarres, in his book *Donatello*, 1903, points out that the Medici family records would have been unlikely to have called anyone of importance an '*incognita*'. He proposed that the bust represented Contessina de' Bardi (wife of Cosimo de' Medici) and if this was the case it couldn't have been sculpted by Donatello. He ruled out this possibility since Contessina de' Bardi didn't die till 1473: 'and as this bust is obviously made from a death-mask it is clear that Donatello could not be its author (Donatello died in 1466)'. I do agree that if the sitter had been an important female member of the Medici family then it would be unlikely that the bust would have been recorded as an '*incognita*'. In 1907, the same year that Isidoro del Lungo's book was published, another scholar (Gottschewski) had related the bust to an entry in one of the Medici inventories which he took to be an image of Caterina Sforza, the wife of Giovanni de' Medici. He based this identification on a portrait medal of her in the Bargello. However, once more this identification of the sitter remains problematic. Although Caterina Sforza had some connections with the Annalena convent she had stronger links with the convent of Le Murate where she had her own cell, and it was in this convent that she was buried following her death in 1509. Caterina died at the relatively young age of forty-six years old but the female sitter of the Bargello bust would appear to be older than this age. My head was spinning with all the permutations!

A major factor that serves to complicate any interpretation of the bronze bust is the type of clothes worn by the female sitter. On the surface it may appear easy to assume that since the individual appears to be wearing nuns' garments then the sitter must have been a nun. However, many noblewomen of the period, once widowed, often wore a veil (usually white) and some even chose to be portrayed wearing both a veil and sombre clothes, thus making it difficult to determine whether they were laywomen or nuns. Some of these noblewomen even chose to be buried in the habit of a tertiary. Caterina Sforza is invariably portrayed wearing the iconic widow's veil. An example showing her dressed in typical widows' apparel appears in a fresco by the artist Giorgio Vasari in the Palazzo Vecchio. Since the bust under discussion is made from bronze it is impossible to determine the actual colours of the garments worn, which would assist with determining whether these were the clothes of a particular order of nuns or simply widows' apparel. I am not convinced of the possibility that the female sitter of the Bargello bust could portray Caterina Sforza in widows' garb, since the robe worn by Caterina in both the medal and the fresco in the Palazzo Vecchio seems to be of a less modest design compared with that worn by the sitter of the bust. Additionally, it has been pointed out that the identification of the bust with the medallion is unconvincing because the shape of the nose differs in each. In the Museo di Casa Vasari (Giorgio Vasari's former home) in Arezzo there is a reference to some documents which contain a list of the names of the Medici family members and the places where their portraits are conserved. The list includes portraits of both Caterina Sforza and her third husband Giovanni di Pierfrancesco de' Medici having once been in the monastery of Annalena. It may have been the case that the aforementioned fresco painted by Vasari within the Palazzo Vecchio was based on the original held in the Annalena convent. Although it seems that any identification of the sitter of the bust as Caterina Sforza would be improbable, it had been a bonus that my research had actually flagged up possible further artworks associated with the Annalena convent.

The more recent observation, first noted by Professor James Beck, that there is a similarity between the Bargello bust and the female donor represented in Masaccio's famous fresco of the *Holy Trinity* in the church of Santa Maria Novella, is worthy of consideration. Indeed, the dress and features of the mature woman represented offer a valid comparison with the Bargello bust. However, yet again, there is no proof that the woman depicted in Masaccio's fresco was the sitter. The female donor figure in Masaccio's fresco may belong to either the Lenzi or Berti family but it is uncertain as to whether they would have been in a position financially to have been able to commission the costly bronze bust. Nor would identification with either of these families explain how such a piece would have ended up in the Medici collection.

This was all very well, I had delved deep into all of the research and now it was time for me to see the bust for myself and discover what the current views are about this important work of art. The imposing fortress-like palazzo of the Bargello is Florence's oldest civic building; its foundations were begun in the mid-thirteenth century. It was known as the Palagio del Podesta in Annalena's day when it was home to the chief criminal magistrate of Florence. This was once the site of gruesome executions including those of the Pazzi conspirators in 1478 and 1479, following the unsuccessful attempt to assassinate Lorenzo de' Medici during Mass in Florence cathedral. Today the Bargello is the city's national museum and it houses a vast collection of Renaissance sculpture and other artistic treasures. We searched high and low throughout the museum galleries but sadly, we were unable to find the bronze bust anywhere. I just had to assume that it had either been put into storage or it had now found a new home elsewhere. Unfortunately, it was a Sunday and there didn't appear to be any curatorial staff on hand to inform me of the present whereabouts of the bust. I left the museum feeling somewhat deflated to say the least. I would just have to return at some later date. That date would come about much later than I had hoped for, since it would be several months before we would return to Florence. The ensuing months were frustratingly difficult since I desperately wanted to see the bronze bust for myself and I couldn't wait until our return.

Finally, we arrived back in Florence and naturally the Bargello was on top of my 'to do' list. Once more I went in search of the elusive bust just in case we had missed it on our previous visit. Alas, there was still no sign of it. This time I was determined to obtain the contact details of someone who could help me. I managed to corner one of the front-of-house museum staff who told me that I needed to speak with Luisa Palli. At last I thought I might be getting somewhere, however, no sooner had I been told this than the woman's colleague quickly added that Luisa hadn't arrived yet; could I possibly return in about half an hour? I joined Richard at a nearby cafe before returning to the Bargello. I went directly to the lady who had given me the contact name and she phoned the office upstairs. Almost immediately she handed me the phone to speak to Luisa in person. At this point I was actually shaking like a leaf. In my best Italian I explained who I was and why I had come to the Bargello. Before long Luisa came to meet me accompanied by another person and they duly led me upstairs. They both appeared to be very friendly and helpful. Naturally, my first question was to determine whether the bust was indeed still in the Bargello. Luisa told me that it was, but that it was '*in deposito*' (in storage). I politely asked if I could possibly see the bust and she explained to me that sadly, I wouldn't be able to do so because photographers were currently at work in the storeroom. She did, however, seem keen to help me further and I waited patiently as she hunted through a cabinet full of ledgers. She quickly retrieved a couple of them for me to look at with her. The ledgers just happened to contain the 1879 inventory details of entries made into the Bargello Museum from the Medici *Guardaroba*. Sure enough there was an entry for a bronze bust 'number 26' listed under '*incognita*'; it was described as being a bust '*di buon lavoro*' (of good work). The *Guardaroba* was where the artistic collection belonging to the Medici family was stored. Also listed alongside the entry was the name 'Ginevra Cavalcanti wife of Lorenzo de' Medici' and this was documented in the original inventory of 1553. Clearly an error had been made in the recording of this detail since Ginevra Cavalcanti was not the wife of Lorenzo but the mother of Pierfrancesco il Vecchio de' Medici. Undoubtedly, if the sitter of the bust was Ginevra Cavalcanti then surely there would have been no uncertainty over its identification. Additional details noted in the inventory of 1879 were that the sitter's eyes were closed and that she was wearing a nun's veil that covered the shoulders. A further note described the bust as resting upon a quadrilateral base of wood tinted to look like bronze. The most interesting observation for me, however, was that the bust was recorded as appearing to have suffered from fire '... *che sembra aver sofferto dal fuoco*'. On reading this I became hugely excited since, just twenty years after Annalena's death, there had been that terrible fire at her convent in 1511, which almost completely destroyed everything. Could this at last be some definitive proof that the bust had been in the Annalena convent and represented our foundress? Perhaps it had been one of the furnishings and works of art that had been saved from the flames on that terrible day?

However, as I have already discussed, fires were commonplace in the city during the Renaissance, for example there had been the fires at Le

Murate convent in both 1471 and in 1495. Significantly, a disastrous fire had also occurred at the Palazzo Vecchio in 1690, which destroyed twenty-seven rooms including the *Guardaroba*. Many precious items from there were however saved, but a great many valuable objects had perished in the disaster. My mind switched into overdrive as I attempted to think through every possibility. Meanwhile, Luisa's assistant took the ledger over to the photocopier to make copies of the relevant inventory entry so that I might take them away. She also kindly gave me a photocopied image of the bust. On the back of this, Luisa scribbled down an email address of someone else in the Bargello who might be able to help me further with my research. That person, Ilaria Ciseri, just happened to be the director of the Bargello! Without hesitation when we returned to our apartment which was only a few minutes away from the Bargello, I immediately sent an email off to Ilaria to arrange an appointment to visit the storeroom to see the bronze bust. It was a long shot, as I explained in the email that we would be returning to the UK that weekend. If there was a possibility that I could see the bust before our return I would be most grateful. In reality since it was already Tuesday and late afternoon at that, I felt sure that I would have to wait until our next visit to Florence. Much to my surprise and delight, I received an email back later that day to say that I could indeed visit the storeroom that Thursday morning at 11.00am. I was over the moon, needless to say, and I immediately confirmed that I would indeed be there.

Thursday came and I was feeling both excited and apprehensive at the prospect of meeting with the director of the Bargello. It was early in the morning when Richard and I wound our way through the narrow streets and past the Palazzo Vecchio right in the heart of the city on our way to the Bargello. We had already enjoyed a morning coffee en route but it was still too early for my appointment. To while away some time I decided to visit the beautiful ancient Benedictine abbey known as the Badia which is virtually opposite the Bargello. The elegant, tall, slim *campanile* (bell tower) of the Badia is one of the great landmarks of Florence and soars upwards like a candle on a birthday cake. The Badia offers a true oasis of calm and it is another of my favourite places in the city. On many occasions I have slipped inside its doors to take refuge from the heat and attend either Vespers or Mass. I adore the silence of this place and its faint smell of incense that often fills the air. At this early hour, as expected, there were only a few visitors and a couple of worshippers inside. I sat down on the left-hand side just inside the entrance to the church and looked over at one of the Badia's greatest art treasures, the altarpiece showing the *Apparition of the Virgin to St. Bernard*, painted by Filippino Lippi in the fifteenth century. I smiled as I remembered that Filippino Lippi was the son of Filippo Lippi and Lucrezia Buti, the nun whom he had run off with.

I tried to meditate upon the stillness of the moment but no matter how hard I tried, it was impossible to do so. Thoughts of my impending meeting filled my mind. It was no use, I couldn't relax and I thought it best just to leave and go over to the museum early. On this occasion, since I did have a bit of time on my hands, I didn't mind joining the long queue of tourists that had already gathered outside the enormous wooden metal-studded doors of the Bargello. I patiently waited my turn to enter the museum. Once inside, the ticket lady whom I had seen two days before seemed to recognise me and she promptly phoned the office to say that I had arrived. As I awaited her response, once more I was caught off guard when she thrust the phone into my hands so that I could speak to Ilaria. I managed to collect myself enough to respond in Italian to her instructions. She told me that she would meet me in the main office and she gave me directions on how to find it. I could feel my heart racing as I crossed the historic courtyard with its many coats of arms emblazoned upon its walls and its ancient well at its centre. A fleeting thought reminded me of the gruesome history of this place since it was near this well that many noble Florentines had been beheaded. I stopped at a door which was cordoned off with a red rope. I felt terribly important as I lifted the rope and entered the space which was normally out of bounds to the public. I climbed up the stairs to the Superintendent's office where Ilaria was waiting to greet me. After some initial introductions she then led me to the storeroom. We entered into a large, bright, modern room which was a cross between a warehouse and a laboratory. It was crammed full of objects arranged on shelves marked with sheets of paper with images of the objects and their inventory numbers. I caught sight of Luisa's assistant who was dressed in a lab coat and already busy at work. I followed Ilaria over to where the bronze bust was located. There it was sitting quite high up on a shelf alongside two other busts. It was as though I were meeting with a real person and someone that I felt I knew very well. I couldn't contain my excitement and even exclaimed in the presence of Ilaria that seeing the bust was just like meeting with an 'old friend'! She very kindly gave me permission to photograph the bust (see **Figure 23**), although it has to be said this was no easy task. She told me that since the bronze bust was very heavy it could not be removed from the shelf, as it would have required a couple of men to lift it. Ilaria apologised saying that sadly, there was no one around who could assist us at this time. I assured her that this wasn't a problem and that I just felt privileged to have the opportunity to be there at all.

I was mindful that I should remember this experience in its entirety, since I would never be able to get that close to the bronze bust again. I took the time to really look at the bust with my own eyes before subjecting it to the photographic lens. First of all, it is worth recalling that since the bust had been cast in bronze, which is a costly medium, the sitter must have been important. The preferred medium for a religious bust at this time was wood and should this indeed be a depiction of a nun, the use of bronze would have been unique. I noted that the bust rested upon a bevelled wooden plinth. The sitter appeared to be a woman aged over fifty with rather thickset features and I must admit, not how I had imagined the features of a noblewoman to look. The sitter's face appeared serene and her smile was gentle and warm. It was such a joy to be able to be so close to the face that had lingered in my memory for so long. Even though her eyes were closed as they would have been in death, she appeared to be alive and it was as though she was aware of my presence and felt happy to see me. Indeed it was difficult to believe that it was a mere object that I was scrutinising since the sitter's presence was uncannily real. Her mouth was firmly closed and her lips were thin but she was most definitely smiling, particularly on her right side. I could also detect a dimple at the corner of her mouth, also on the right side. I also noted that the right side of her nose differed from the left side: it appeared to be a little less than perfect, slightly pinched or indented. The bust indeed appeared to be so incredibly lifelike and on close inspection I could just determine details such as eyelashes. Indeed, it has been noted that the bust's striking verism, together with its elderly subject matter and ecclesiastical clothes, is highly unusual. A plaster cast of the woman's death mask, her clothes and veil would have been made and the resulting bronze bust would be a direct imprint of this death mask. Generally the telltale signs that a death mask has been used are the sitter's sunken cheeks, dropped corners of the mouth and the still-closed eyes. It has been noted that the juxtaposition of a dead face with closed eyes in an upright portrait bust makes it appear uncanny. Usually the artist would have sculpted the piece with open eyes to give the impression of a living sitter. However, in this instance there appeared to be no desire on the part of the artist to revive the sitter.

Despite not being in the full flush of youth, the elderly woman's features still had an enviable fullness and smoothness to them. It was only on closer inspection that I could detect a few faint vertical lines on her forehead. It is probably the case that the mask was taken before 'rigor mortis' had set in. The reason that the sitter's features appear younger is probably due to the fact that during the process of taking the cast, the weight of the wet plaster would have caused any wrinkles to disappear.

I felt that this was the face of someone who had experienced no fear of death and had felt at peace with the world on her deathbed. I marvelled at how the veil covering her head fell in beautiful molten folds on to her shoulders. The sculptor had even taken the time to include some patterning on the veil. I observed the closely fitted wimple beneath the veil and the tunic with its button fastening. Although I wasn't certain, I could see that there were some areas on the surface of the bronze bust that were of a light brown colour, perhaps the result of fire damage. Ilaria prompted me to take a photograph of the back of the bust and I had to climb up on a ladder to do so. I have to say that this proved to be rather awkward as I tried to stretch my arm around the back of the bust without touching it. A quick glance at my camera image display however puzzled me, since it was totally blank. Imagine how stupid I felt when Ilaria pointed out to me that I had actually been pointing the camera lens towards the wall instead of the bust! In all my excitement I hadn't even thought about what I was doing. Still recovering from my embarrassment, I made one further attempt to photograph the back of the bust and this time I made sure that I was pointing the camera lens in the right direction. Unfortunately, it didn't make my task any easier and I was relieved when Ilaria very kindly offered to assist me. As she did so she observed and pointed out that there was a hole at the top of the head of the bust and she urged me to take a look. I had already noticed that there were two small holes at the front of the bust towards the lower part of the sitter's gown. Together, we looked up into the bust and noted that it was hollow inside. Such details are interesting since they prove useful for the understanding of the casting process involved in the making of the bust. Although I was unable to examine the back of the bust in its entirety, I was able to study photographs of it later and it must be noted that the reverse appeared to be as detailed as the front in its execution. This was a fine work indeed.

I was conscious that time was ticking on and I had no idea what Ilaria's schedule for the day was. I could have stayed in the storeroom forever but I was mindful that Ilaria was a busy person, after all, she did have the Bargello Museum to run! In consideration of this I told her that I had obtained everything that I needed. In reality, I found it very difficult to say goodbye to the bust, my 'old friend', and I only wished I could have spent more time in her company. I followed Ilaria back to her small office, which was crammed full of interesting books and papers. I quickly glanced around the room and admired a couple of beautifully painted terracotta Madonna and child panels adorning the walls. I told her that I was envious of her wonderful office and she responded with a smile and said that indeed it was truly marvellous. I asked her if there was any possibility that the bronze bust might be returned to the public galleries again in the near future; sadly she thought it probably unlikely. She then picked up a catalogue which was conveniently on hand and she handed me the publication to look at. It just happened to be a catalogue that had been published in 2015 which she had co-authored, to mark 150 years of the Bargello Museum. She opened it at a page which included a couple of sepia photographs. I looked closely at the photographs and spotted the bronze bust on public display in what was called the 'first room of bronzes'.

Although I had been unable to find out too much more about the bronze bust it certainly had been an extremely worthwhile visit. I thanked Ilaria for her kindness and support and I left the Bargello discreetly through a small door tucked round the back of the building which was not normally accessible to the public. I stepped out into the scorching midday sun and into the Via Proconsolo, which was buzzing with activity, a veritable melange of delivery vans, buses and tourists. I crossed over to the age-worn steps leading up to the Badia where I had arranged to meet Richard. Within a few minutes, I caught sight of him coming across the road, *gelato* in hand; he had obviously had a good morning too!

To conclude my research on the bust I needed to go to the BNCF to check out one further reference. I had pre-requested the book and it was ready for me to consult. The volumes (I hadn't quite realised that there was more than one book) were kept in a glass-fronted cabinet directly behind the collection desk in the rare books consultation room; such an awkward place to store books I thought. I watched on in amazement as the librarian and her colleagues manoeuvred themselves around awkwardly in order to gain access to the cabinet. Finally, I was handed three heavy volumes which I heaved over to the nearest available reading desk to look at. They were full of black and white photographs accompanied by only a few lines of information. I very quickly found the photograph and details of the Bargello bronze bust in one, and it took even less time to read its corresponding brief entry. The books had been written by K.Langedijk and published in 1981 and it was quite interesting since the author's own conclusion was that the identification of the sitter should rest on it being: 'a lady of the Medici family who died in the second half of the fifteenth century'. This was indeed a very generic claim by the author and appears to have been perpetuated by later scholars. In 2007 it was identified as being a funeral bust of a woman presumed to be of the Medici family, a work from the Florentine School and dated from the second half of the fifteenth century.

It has been noted that any identification with individuals belonging to the Medici family is purely based on the fact that the bust's provenance is the Grand Ducal collection. If one considers Langedijk's 'lady of the Medici' in its broadest sense, then I will remind the reader that since Annalena Malatesta was related to the Medici she must naturally be included in the proposed line-up of possible candidates for the bronze bust. With this in mind and to ensure that I had considered every possibility linked with the very generic proposal by Langedijk I needed to investigate three further Medici women to complete my research on the bust. These were Lucrezia Tornabuoni, Ginevra Alessandri de' Medici and Piera de' Medici. To my knowledge these Medici women had not previously been considered as possible candidates.

Lucrezia Tornabuoni de' Medici (1427–1482) was the wife of Piero de' Medici and mother of Lorenzo Il Magnifico. She was known as the 'first lady of Florence'. She was a very important member of the Medici family and an influential figure in Florentine politics, a benefactress and author of many important literary works including sacred narratives and lauds (hymns of praise). It could certainly be understandable that she may have wished to be portrayed as a religious figure, as in the Bargello bronze bust. However, since she was such a prominent member of the Medici family the words of Lord Balcarres ring true once again since it would seem unlikely that such an important person as Lucrezia Tornabuoni would be called '*Donna velata incognita*', or '*sacerdotessa velata*'.

Ginevra Alessandri de' Medici (d.1472) was the wife of Giovanni di Cosimo de' Medici and another relatively prominent member of the Medici family. Although she was not a nun she helped to support the convent of Santa Verdiana where the aforementioned Piera was abbess. Ginevra's connection with a religious establishment was, as we have already discovered, not unique amongst female members of the Medici family. In their patronage and support of convent building, the Medici women were simply undertaking appropriate acts of piety and charity whilst at the same time helping to strengthen the Medici regime. I do believe that if the bust represented Ginevra Alessandri de' Medici then as was also the case for Lucrezia Tornabuoni, Caterina Sforza or any immediate member of the Medici family, the bust would have had a confirmed identification. There would have been no mistake as to who the sitter was, since the intention would have been that the portrait bust would have been instantly recognisable and celebrated as a member of the Medici family.

Piera de' Medici (*c*.1400–1482) was, like Annalena, a relative of the Medici who had entered the convent of Santa Verdiana in Florence around 1406–1410. She basically worked her way up to become a powerful abbess of that convent. It is known that Piera used her Medici connections to further both the interests of her religious community as well as the Medici family themselves. It is also true to say that since the bronze bust was made from a death mask then it is possible that it could represent Piera since she was in her eighties when she died.

In my opinion, the sitter of the bust could only have been one of two women (who were both Medici kinswomen), either Piera de' Medici or Annalena Malatesta. Satisfied with the fact that I have analysed and weighed up all of the possibilities as far as I can, I feel happy to run with the hypothesis that the identity of the sitter of the bronze bust in the Bargello could be Annalena Malatesta. My conviction is based upon the fact that Annalena's name has been linked with the bronze bust since the latter decades of the nineteenth century and has even been referenced as such in 2009. The name of Piera de' Medici on the other hand has never been linked with the bronze bust in its history. As to who the author of the bronze bust was, the most recent attribution that I have been able to find is that it is a work of the Florentine school from the second half of the fifteenth century.

What we do know about the bust is that it did end up in the Medici *Guardaroba* in the sixteenth century before entering into the Bargello. What we do not know for certain is who commissioned it and where it was originally located. I believe, and I must stress that this is my own personal view (which is based on my own investigations and careful analysis of available sources), is that it may have been commissioned by the Medici family for their palace to commemorate their kinswoman Annalena Malatesta when she died in 1491. The Medici family as we have seen had long supported Annalena and her community. Annalena and her convent had served as a powerful exemplar for Lucrezia Tornabuoni de' Medici in particular. Alternatively, it is more likely that the Medici commissioned the bust to commemorate their kinswoman and intended it to be placed near Annalena's tomb in her convent church. I would of course be delighted if either of these proposals should ever be proven.

As we have seen, the bust has been documented as seeming to have suffered fire damage and this was possibly as a result of either having been in the Annalena convent fire in 1511 or the fire that had occurred at the Medici *Guardaroba* in 1690. If it was originally in the Annalena convent it might have been one of the convent treasures that had been saved and not completely destroyed by the fire before being removed for safekeeping and finally ending up in the Medici *Guardaroba*. If it had suffered damage in the *Guardaroba* fire in the seventeenth century then it must have been one of the works that was saved from that fire. Another possibility is that the bronze bust, if it had been placed near Annalena's tomb in the convent church by the Medici, may have been removed for safekeeping when the fortifications were built by Duke Cosimo I in 1545, which caused the damage to the church facade.

The above scenarios may explain why there was some uncertainty about the identity of the sitter of the bust in the Medici *Guardaroba* archives in later years. However, at a much later date someone must have had some reason to believe that there was a connection with Annalena Malatesta. Clearly, the bronze bust did have a life before it entered the Bargello Museum and I do hope with all my heart that the 'veiled lady' whom I had come to know so well will one day be firmly identified as Annalena Malatesta.

CHAPTER 20:

The Annalena convent buildings today

I have lost count of the number of times that we have walked around the area that was once occupied by the convent of San Vincenzo commonly known as Annalena. In order for the reader to gain an understanding of this site I shall describe the area and some of its major landmarks today.

Essentially both the Annalena convent and that of the adjacent Santa Chiara would have been encompassed by parts of Via Romana, Via Santa Maria and Via dei Serragli. The Annalena convent would have stretched from the site of the current Goldoni Theatre on Via Santa Maria towards and including Baldaccio and Annalena's house (which originally formed the nucleus of her convent) on the corner of Via Santa Maria and Via Romana. The convent then extended along the Via Romana southwards including the present-day Hotel Annalena building with the adjacent *vivaio*. The convent site would have incorporated the ground opposite the Hotel Annalena, which is now the entrance to the Boboli Gardens (*L'Ingresso d'Annalena*), extending towards the Grotto of Adam and Eve (sometimes called the 'Grotto of Annalena') within the grounds of the Boboli Gardens itself. The present-day Corsi Annalena garden was also once part of the Annalena convent grounds. I have attempted to estimate the layout of the original Annalena convent complex in relation to the present-day buildings and to where the original Santa Chiara convent was located (see **Figure 24**). I have also included an image to enable the reader to identify the position of the present-day buildings along the Via Romana (see **Figure 25**), which once formed part of the Annalena convent. Fascinatingly, using the technology of Google maps, it is possible to determine the vastness of the site that was once occupied by the Annalena convent.

If this were a modern-day game of monopoly we could imagine Annalena cheering with delight as she bought up properties and land in this whole area at each throw of the dice. Once the story of Baldaccio and Annalena is known it is easy to comprehend how this area of Florence became so entwined with her name.

Whilst we were staying at the Hotel Annalena we were lucky enough on a couple of occasions to be able to sneak into the grounds of the adjacent *vivaio*, which can be found just inside a wrought-iron gate next to the actual hotel itself. Sadly, nowadays the gate leading into the garden is nearly always closed to the public only allowing access to apartments for residents. This *vivaio* was until very recent times one of the few nurseries that could be found in the city of Florence.

Significantly for our purposes it was here upon this ground that some of the Annalena convent buildings were erected. Beyond the *vivaio*'s associations with the Annalena convent this garden had actually enjoyed a great horticultural heritage since it became famous in the early nineteenth century for the cultivation of rare bulbs and rare species of plants.

More times than often we had only been able to gain a bird's-eye view of the *vivaio* from our balcony in the hotel. From this vantage point the gardens always appeared to look quite miserable, tired and faded. Only the presence of some dilapidated greenhouses, a collection of withered plants in broken terracotta pots, lonely dead shrubs and a collection of redundant plastic hoses coiled like snakes lurking in dark corners could be seen. Some tall trees including a few umbrella palms, a sole magnolia and a pine of some sort provide a home to the bird life of the area. I have often interrupted my thoughts to gaze upon the birds that flock here, watching them as they swoop through the branches of the trees. In Annalena's day this part of the city would have appeared to be much more like the countryside since there would have been an abundance of greenery and wildlife, and the garden would have been resplendent with birdsong.

Modern apartment buildings now occupy part of the site where the cloisters of the Annalena convent once stood. When Richa visited the convent in the eighteenth century he saw two cloisters, one large and very grand and another smaller one. Indeed some of the columns which may have once formed the original fifteenth-century cloister have been incorporated, albeit much altered, within the structure of the modern-day buildings that can be seen today (see **Figure 26**). Interestingly, the composite capitals of these columns look very similar, albeit more weathered, than those that belong to the cloister that is known as the 'Brunelleschi cloister' at the church of Santa Croce. This was completed in 1453, roughly the same date as those of the Annalena convent. The large Annalena cloister would have measured approximately 40m x 40m. It is useful to note that it would have been slightly larger than the *Chiostro Verde* or Green Cloister at the church of Santa Maria Novella.

In a snatched moment when we had been lucky enough to stand within the *vivaio* upon that once sacred ground that had belonged to the Annalena convent, I observed that some creative resident had recycled a few decorative broken columns (more than likely from the original cloister) to use as planters. Oh what I would have given to be able to get my hands on one of those fragments!

At the rear of the present-day Hotel Annalena (see **Figure 27**) it is still possible to see a series of small blocked-up arched windows which run along its upper storey (see **Figure 28**). These were probably the cells of the convent and I will discuss these later. Incorporated within a much higher part of the building there are also the vestiges of a larger aperture, which is also now blocked up. Standing upon that once hallowed ground it was as though I had momentarily entered a portal to the past. In my mind I could hear the bell ringing to summon Annalena's women to recite Divine Office in their church and the sound of muffled footsteps in the cloisters. Such echoes of centuries past even extended to my olfactory senses as the soothing scent of lavender and rosemary from the Annalena women's convent herb garden filled the air. As quickly as those images, sounds and smells from the world of Annalena entered my mind, sadly they were immediately erased on seeing a child's brightly coloured plastic playhouse that instantly brought me back to the present day. A reminder if one is ever needed that many changes have occurred here over the centuries, some good, some bad.

I have already mentioned the fortifications that were built by Duke Cosimo I in 1545 and the subsequent damage caused to the Annalena convent church facade. This was testament indeed that Annalena's convent had not been shaped merely by the ravages of time alone but that man and natural forces had also played their part in the history of the convent. When the fortification walls were dismantled in 1571, when there was no longer a need for them, the nuns received back the part of their garden that been destroyed and they used it for the planting of vines. A remnant of part of the wall that was built as these fortifications still stands today in the *vivaio*. It serves to separate the *vivaio* from the adjacent Corsi Annalena garden. This wall today is covered with a verdant mantle of vegetation. It appears tranquil and strangely beautiful. To the uninitiated it is but a wall, but to those who are 'in the know' it is an important facet in the history of the Annalena convent. It is fascinating to think that the land just beyond the wall was once the vegetable garden belonging to the Annalena sisters. This was known as the *Orto dei Mori*, since it is thought that this was part of the Annalena convent gardens where mulberry trees (*gelsi* or *mori* in Italian) once grew. With time this was the name given to Via dei Mori, which skirted the Annalena convent garden. I had read that some branches of this species of tree can still be found on this site today. Much later the old *orto* was left abandoned and an enormous mound of earth and bricks remained. Since the Corsi Annalena garden is now privately owned it can only be visited by appointment. Once a year in May, the garden is open to the public as part of the National Open Gardens scheme in Florence. It was on one such occasion that we were fortunate enough to be able to visit.

On the day of our visit the sun was shining as we waited excitedly alongside a small number of other people outside the gates to the garden. Before long the gates were opened up and everyone rushed inside to explore the garden's delights. We, however, stopped just within the entrance gate to study the 'infamous' wall. It stood firm and strong as it had done for centuries; what tales did it have to tell, I wondered? We then walked along a gravel path that loomed high above street level. The elevated aspect of this path is due to the fact that this formed part of a new wall that was later built to enclose the Annalena convent gardens so as to block the view of some factories nearby. This wall was later reduced in height during the nineteenth century. We looked down upon the people in the road below who were totally oblivious to our presence.

On the whole, visitors to the Corsi Annalena garden will understandably remain blissfully unaware of the disruption caused by the fortifications all those centuries ago, since no obvious visible scars can be seen. Rather, they are attracted to the beautiful ornamental features of the garden, which include the parterre with fountain and terracotta urns and pots full of geraniums. Of course such elements of the garden didn't escape our attention either. I paused to savour some enchanting roses that were in full bloom. The ground was littered with fallen rose petals and I stooped to collect a few to keep as a souvenir. The morning sun was growing quite intense and we sought out a bench so that we could rest awhile in the shade. This moment of repose allowed me to contemplate and listen mindfully to the sound of the birdsong which filled the air. I savoured the moment and fully embraced the warm sunshine as it caressed my face. However, my reverie was soon interrupted by the sight and sound of some lizards as they darted amongst gaps between the foliage of a nearby shrub. After a short while we had to tear ourselves away from this blissful paradise, and we did so feeling satisfied that we had been able to appreciate yet one further part of what had once been the Annalena convent grounds.

On leaving the Corsi Annalena garden and before entering into the aforementioned road called Via dei Mori, one passes by the side of the small church of San Pier Gattolino, which also fell victim to the fortifications built by Cosimo I. Indeed, it was totally demolished but rebuilt by a workman known as Umido. This street eventually leads into the longer street called Via dei Serragli, which was known as Via Fornace at the time of Annalena. Inserted into the wall at the corner of this street there is a modern terracotta relief of a Madonna with a child holding what appears to be a globe. This relief is of interest since it could possibly be related to the aforementioned (now lost) stone sculpture known as the *Madonna della Palla* (Madonna with a Ball). This ancient sculpture may have been in an outdoor location before ending up in the Oratory of the Annalena convent. I will remind the reader that this sculpture was considered to be a miraculous image and it was greatly venerated and it soon became the focus of a cult. Perhaps the modern-day terracotta relief, albeit modified, is the legacy of this former miraculous image. On the opposite side of Via dei Serragli on the side of the old Goldoni Cinema (originally the Goldoni Arena) we encounter what was once the location of the Santa Chiara convent. Today a B&B called the Casa Betania, which is coincidentally run by nuns, is located on part of the grounds that once belonged to this convent and borders that of the Annalena. Continuing further along Via dei Serragli at the corner with Via Santa Maria, the church of Santa Chiara whose chapel I have previously discussed can still be seen, albeit greatly modified. Turning into Via Santa Maria itself passing by the Goldoni Theatre and leading towards the corner with Via Romana we pass by the grounds upon which the original Oratory of the Annalena convent was built; an information panel proudly marks the spot.

We had the good fortune of having previously met with one of the area's long time residents, a local artisan whose workshop is located on or very close to what would have been the site of the former Annalena Oratory. The small, elderly, silver-haired artisan dressed in a fawn work coat splattered with brown varnish and paint had been more than happy to help me with my enquiries and had positively welcomed us into his tiny workshop. Stepping inside was like entering into an Aladdin's cave, since it was a veritable treasure chest of curiosities and crammed full of artworks both restored and awaiting restoration. Although I had explained to him that I was currently doing some research about the history of the area, and that I was especially keen to find out more about the ancient Annalena convent, the old man clearly felt he had other matters he wished to discuss with us. For a good ten minutes he seized the opportunity to tell us all about the demise of the Florentine artisan in modern times. Evidently, this was a subject that he felt strongly about and rightly so. He had animatedly told us in his very fast Italian that, unless the Florentine government took more measures to appreciate the importance of artisans and their skills, then their art would be lost forever. He had pointed out that he and his son were amongst the very few left who were engaged in such specialist craftsmanship of artworks. At this point in our conversation his son, who was also dressed in a fawn work coat, appeared from a bench in a back room. The old man introduced him to us and afterwards his son returned to the back room as quickly as he had appeared. The artisan then resumed his earlier conversation with us, which had steered off in a direction that appeared to involve the Mafia and money. We listened and pretended to understand but in all honesty it was quite impossible since he spoke at a rate of knots. We politely allowed him to vent his feelings before we at last touched upon the subject that I had wished to discuss. I remember he had a glint in his eyes as he enthusiastically told us about the history of his workshop. He mentioned a few details about the use of the building during the 1960s, which was fascinating but I had rather hoped that we have might travelled back a few more centuries in time! Things looked a bit more promising when he lured us into the hidden depths of his workshop, a space which was normally out of bounds to the casual visitor. In the semi-darkness of that tiny space he pointed up to some columns and proudly declared that they were once part of the old convent. I remember that we stood in utter amazement; we couldn't believe our eyes or our ears! Sure enough, wedged between some recesses containing an old wooden glass-fronted cabinet and shelves brimming with art books and a collection of boxes, we saw some ancient-looking columns. They had proudly supported the roof of the old gentleman's place of work for as long as he could remember, he told us. We asked him if we could take some photographs and once more his enthusiasm shone through. He called to his son to bring over some ladders and a torch so that we might study the columns at close hand. His son held a torch up at the capital of a column whilst Richard stood precariously on a rung of the ladder to photograph it (see **Figure 29**). I carefully noted its appearance as he did so. It had apparently been damaged during the restoration of the Goldoni Theatre that had been carried out during the 1960s. When we turned to leave the tiny confined space we observed a semi-circular recess behind us. Its unusual shape led me to think that it could possibly have originally been the location of an altar. Could this perhaps have been where the miraculous *Madonna della Palla* was once housed? I pondered awhile over the significance of the place and in particular I thought of the Annalena women as they sang their religious songs before the image. I could almost hear the voices of those holy women together with the echoes of those of their neighbours who chose to join them on Saturday nights. The artisan finally very kindly allowed us to take a photograph of himself behind his workbench. He stood proudly against a backdrop of old carpentry tools and restoration materials. These were quite literally the 'tools of his trade': an assortment of well-used old wooden planes, chisels and pliers juxtaposed with some keys, scribbled notes and photos tacked to an old shelf. The glint in his eyes was still clearly visible behind his miniscule spectacles and his work-worn hands were testament to decades of experience; these were the true tools of his success. Hanging above him were a variety of gold picture frames, some empty and one containing a photograph of himself and his son standing before a crucifix they had proudly restored. We took one final look around the workshop then bid our farewells. I had felt so incredibly grateful for the help that the elderly gentleman had given me and to convey this, as I shook his hand I placed the palm of my left hand warmly over his right in a seal of friendship. Within seconds of leaving the old man and his workshop and stepping out into Via Santa Maria, the sound of a hammer banging upon wood could be heard reverberating through the empty street. It was 'just another day at the office' for the artisan and his son but for me it had been an experience that I would never forget.

Interestingly, above the artisan's workshop are modern apartments which probably once formed part of the house that Annalena and Baldaccio had lived in. I later discovered that one of these apartments was available on the internet for holiday rental. Details of the apartment included a description of a most unusual elevated architectural feature, which had been cleverly incorporated into the structural layout of the premises. It is my guess, and I have to emphasise that it is only a guess since I have not been able to visit this apartment, that this may have been where the bell of the Annalena Oratory once was.

At the corner of Via Santa Maria and Via Romana the original house of Baldaccio and Annalena (which later formed the nucleus of her convent) can be found. It is so exciting to think that this is where all the magic happened, as it were. Looking at its exterior today it is difficult to imagine that when Annalena and her family lived there it was a splendid palace with rich furnishings inside. On the ground floor of this building facing Via Romana there is now an artisan's shop which specialises in handmade marbled paper and bookbinding. Indeed, if exquisite handcrafted notebooks and hand-marbled papers in a multitude of mesmerising, swirling patterns are your thing, then you will be in for a treat. Artisan workshops such as this one are a true delight to find in the city of Florence where ancient arts linger on in a modern-day world. The interior of the shop, although small, is quite deep and it has been restored quite sympathetically having an immaculate red-brick ceiling and whitewashed walls. Some of the building's original architectural features appear to have been retained including vaulted/arched ceilings. This space with its vaulted appearance was where distillations were conducted since it once formed part of the famed Annalena Infirmary and *Spezieria* (Pharmacy). I have a passionate interest in the history of perfume and medicine so I was thrilled when I discovered this. In place of the beautifully displayed sheets of marbled paper and leather-bound books, I visualised copper alembic flasks, herbs, roots and plant materials.

Next to the aforementioned premises is what once formed part of the San Pier Novello hospital. It has changed its aspect totally and the upstairs is now a rather charming B&B. A member of the family who owns the present-day B&B had very kindly shown us around the interior of the building since we had an interest in perhaps staying there at a future date. I was excited to learn that within this historical building some frescoes had been discovered and had recently been restored. The frescoes have been attributed to the school of Andrea Orcagna and date from the last two decades of the fourteenth century. I was even more excited to discover that the building actually included one of the rooms that had once been part of the house that had belonged to Baldaccio and Annalena. Naturally, this was one further experience that I would never forget. The entrance to the hospital is now a gallery/workshop and it still bears its ancient inscription and carving upon its architrave. It reads: *Hospitium Rodoliphorum Nobilis Familiae*, alluding to the patronage of the Ridolfi family who left money for the construction of a 'poor house'. This family was one of the principal families of the 'Ferza' quarter, the area in which Annalena lived in and established her convent. Their *stemma* (coat of arms) can be found widely in the area including one among the rooftops above the B&B. We had often passed by this gallery/workshop but unfortunately it had always been closed with its shutters firmly pulled down. On one occasion however we found it to be open. We caught sight of a gentleman just disappearing within its doors and we managed to catch his attention before he closed up the premises once more. I explained to him that I was doing some research on the ancient Annalena convent and I brazenly asked if I could possibly look around his art workshop. To my delight he was very accommodating and allowed both Richard and myself to enter into the extremely small space which he called his workshop. I remember that it was so tiny that you could barely 'swing a cat' inside. We only stayed for a few moments since quite frankly it would have been impossible to remain there for much longer. However in that short space of time I had been able to survey the small interior. I had also complimented the artist on his paintings, which were everywhere to be seen. Before we left, I observed that there was a narrow door on the back wall. Once again I was audacious enough to enquire about this and the gentleman led me over to it and opened the door. I could see that it led out to a very small courtyard, most certainly the vestiges of a former part of the Annalena convent.

Along the Via Romana in the direction of the Hotel Annalena several other small shops, apartments and a restaurant can be found, all of which would also have once been part of the former Annalena convent premises.

Of course it would have been rude for us not to patronise the restaurant, purely for research purposes of course! The *Osteria dell'Enoteca* oozed character and charm and the building had been subject to sympathetic restoration work. I noted the use of ancient red bricks, vaulted ceilings and features made of ancient doorways. Of course this is all particularly relevant when one is fully cognisant of the building's fascinating past. Another interesting element of the building was a glass-covered trench in the floor which exposed the deeper levels of the structure. There were even a few artefacts on view presumably unearthed during the restoration work but unfortunately, nothing that was of any real importance for my purposes. Oh how I wished to have been a 'fly on the wall' during the course of that restoration work though! Quite coincidentally, where the restaurant is today there would probably have been the kitchens and workshops of the Annalena convent. Interestingly, within the restaurant there remains evidence of some old terracotta water pipes. It is known that the Annalena convent was hooked up to the water supply of the nearby Boboli Gardens, which enabled the Annalena sisters to irrigate their *orti* (vegetable gardens). This was a privilege conceded to them courtesy of Ferdinando II (1610–1670).

Finally on reaching the entrance to the Hotel Annalena we arrive at the last part of the area that had encompassed the Annalena convent complex. Any walk around the block proves to be a useful exercise and serves to throw some light on the vastness of the site. There was, however, still one more part of the convent complex I had yet to explore and this just happened to be the part of the '*Casa di Annalena*' building that had once formed the refectory of the convent. I had discovered that today this part of the building is occupied by the architectural studio of Gurrieri Associates. I was fascinated to read on their website that their '*Sala Riunioni*' or meeting room was once the site of the old Annalena refectory and still has traces of sixteenth century frescoes. On our return home to the UK we arranged to visit the Gurrieri Associates studios on our next trip to Florence.

That next trip soon came round, and once more we stayed in the 'Writer's Room' at the Hotel Annalena. On the morning of our appointment we made our way through to the back of the hotel building to where the Gurrieri Associates studio can be found. As we approached the office a woman came out to welcome us. She led us into a spacious studio which was flooded with bright January sunshine. We introduced ourselves and told her that we had an appointment. She informed us that the '*Professore*' with whom we would be meeting had not yet arrived. She directed us over to a bench near the entrance door so that we could wait. Whilst we were seated I took the opportunity to survey the whole length of the room (see **Figure 30**). I noted the beautiful vaulted ceiling and lunettes. From where we were positioned looking down towards the opposite end of the former refectory we could just make out two lunettes with '*sinopie*' (underdrawings for frescoes). There would probably have been a *Cenacolo* or painting of the Last Supper below them and also a *lavabo* (wash basin), as was customary in refectory spaces.

A handful of architects were already diligently working at their desks and I envied their beautiful workplace. However, as was typical of my way of thinking, in my mind I had already replaced those architects with images of Annalena and her fellow sisters. They were dining at simple long wooden trestle tables on either side of the room with their backs to the walls, silent in their act of simple contemplation upon the *Cenacolo* beyond. I shuddered to think that it would have been in this space too that some of those sisters would have experienced the humility of being reprimanded before their peers. I quickly banished this thought from my mind and instead focused on the light which radiated from the large modern studio windows; aptly its brightness filled the room like some divine beacon.

Before too long an elderly gentleman wearing a winter coat and hat entered the studio. He came over to us and introduced himself: '*Buongiorno mi chiamo Francesco Gurrieri…*' He then led us through the studio to his office (possibly the former chapter house of the convent) where he invited us to sit down and we waited as he disappeared off into an adjacent room so that he could switch on some lights and remove his coat and hat. We sat at a long desk and whilst we were waiting, another gentleman joined us, introduced himself as Federico and sat down opposite us. I explained in Italian that I was particularly interested in the convent at the time of its foundress Annalena Malatesta. After a short time Francesco returned and I enquired about two frescoes that were clearly visible in the small room in which we were seated. He told us that some eminent Florentine art historians had already subjected the frescoes to scrutiny. He also told us that the frescoes depicted St. Thomas and St. Dominic (see **Figure 31**) and most likely there would also have been a depiction of a Deposition. The frescoes were in excellent condition; however, there were only traces remaining of the one depicting the Deposition. I sought Francesco's opinion about their date and authorship and he replied by saying that it was difficult to say with any certainty who the artist had been, but they had been painted in the sixteenth century. He added that they could have been painted by anyone from Andrea del Sarto's time, or probably later by the hand of Giovanni Mannozzi. I already knew that this artist had executed works for the Annalena convent so this was interesting.

I asked Francesco whether he knew of the whereabouts of any other artworks associated with the Annalena convent and he told us that he didn't but most likely they had ended up in museums or were sold on the open art market. Whilst he was speaking to us he got up from the table and crossed the room where he retrieved some old maps from somewhere. He sat back down again and spread them on to the surface of the table. We were already familiar with some of the maps, particularly the sixteenth-century 'Buonsignori' map of Florence and the eighteenth-century map by Ruggieri. He then invited us to look at the maps with him and we huddled around him with our heads bowed as though in prayer, which was quite apt considering where we were. With the aid of a magnifying glass we were soon able to locate the position of the refectory building within the Annalena complex depicted in the Buonsignori map. Federico, who had been seated silently with us the whole time, indicated that he had to leave since he had another appointment. He said goodbye and slipped out of the room leaving us to continue poring over the maps with Francesco.

Soon afterwards Francesco suggested that we should take a look at the architectural features outside the building. We excitedly followed him into the adjacent room where he had left his coat and hat and we waited as he took them from the coat rack and popped them back on again. When he was ready he then opened a door that led us out into the garden. We could see the line of columns with their capitals, which would have marked the structure of the cloister and as discussed earlier had been incorporated into the present-day buildings. From this vantage point we were able to gain a much better view of those important architectural elements that had once belonged to the Annalena convent. Francesco pointed to a lower part of the building next to us where some steps led below ground. He informed us this was probably a subterranean passage which led to the Boboli Gardens and was built at the time of Cosimo I's fortifications in the sixteenth century. It was also now possible to view at close quarters the stone *stemma* (coat of arms) which was placed above some modern doors. Until now we had only ever been able to partially see this from a height and from some distance from the corner of our balcony of the Hotel Annalena. I admired the *pietra serena* stone which it was carved from and noted its details of a shield with several small mounds separated in the middle by a broad diagonal band, which I knew to be the *stemma* of the Ridolfi family.

We followed Francesco over towards the main building of the former refectory and he pointed up to some dark traces on the exterior of the building which were the *finestrelle* or small windows that I discussed earlier. I welcomed this opportunity to gain a second more detailed look at these. I could clearly see a line of small windows which were interspersed with modern windows albeit half hidden amongst the peeling yellow stucco and exposed brickwork. The latter was most certainly from the original convent building too. Although these vestiges of the former cell windows looked dark in colour, closer inspection revealed that they had been built from grey *pietra serena* stone. At such a sight I found it quite impossible to contain my delight and I clasped my hands together and uttered an excitable '*Incredibile!*', which needs no translation. These *finestrelle* would have been similar to those of other convents of the period, for example at Sant' Apollonia and at the convent of San Marco in Florence.

I wished that we could have spent more time exploring the exterior of this building but we could sense that Francesco was keen to return to his office. We followed him back and once inside we took one more last look around the refectory space and asked his permission to take some photographs, which he kindly granted us. I was immensely grateful for his help and more particularly for the opportunity to look round the former refectory and chapter house of the San Vincenzo d'Annalena convent. Before parting, Francesco asked for my contact details and in return he presented me with a gift of a small book that he had written about the dome of Florence cathedral. He told us that this was his great passion before he signed the book for us.

CHAPTER 21:

Endnotes

Over the five years or so that I have been researching and writing this book I have to confess that as much as I love the city of Florence there have been times when I have just had to seek complete refuge from it. The numbers of tourists descending upon the city has increased to the point when sometimes even the peaceful oasis that the Hotel Annalena affords is not quite enough. Thus much in the same way as the group of young people in Boccaccio's Decameron had fled to the hills to escape the Black Death, we do the same to seek respite from the plague of tourists. It is here, up in the Florentine hills not far from the city centre, that one can find true calm and tranquillity. Our haven is the beautiful Pensione Bencista at Fiesole, a truly special place that will always be dear to our hearts. We have been privileged to stay at this delightful residence several times over the years. The name *Bencista* means a 'place where one feels good' and it would be difficult for anyone not to feel good here.

It is fitting that I should choose to complete this book within the confines of a pensione, much in the same way that my initial interest to write it was inspired by one. In this enchanting place it is possible to stand back from my labours and gain new insight and refresh my thought processes. Even if one doesn't have a myriad of thoughts occupying the mind, this is a place which offers serenity, calm and beauty that I believe cannot be surpassed anywhere else. Sitting on the terrace at the back of the Pensione Bencista the view over the city of Florence is tremendous. The cathedral of Santa Maria del Fiore topped with its magnificent cupola by Filippo Brunelleschi stands proud in the not-too-far distance. As I write this, the city has a hazy veil surmounting it but this does nothing to lessen its majesty. A sprinkling of guests sit on the terrace, lost in their own quiet thoughts and they too are equally mesmerised by the stunning view before them. Sitting up here high above the city there is no need to fight the crowds. Each and every one of us has renounced the lure of venturing into the magical city that stretches out before us. Staring out into the far distance I allow the warmth of the mid-October sunshine to restore my soul. I look over at the old wisteria standing guard on the terrace with its gnarled trunk firmly rooted in the ancient Fiesolan earth, a land that still pulsates with Etruscan energy. A gentle breeze causes the trees to sway with pleasure and I observe how it disturbs the yellowing leaves of the old wisteria causing them to fall upon the gravelled path below. I catch one of them in my hand and make a wish and as I do so my wish, of course, is that I could stay in this heavenly place forever. Although it is autumn, vestiges of the summer months linger on and I am instantly drawn to some pink and red roses which, although well past their prime, still exude memories of the month of June with their sprinkling of fresh petals amongst others that are brittle and tinged brown in colour. A few red and white geraniums jostle for survival in stone troughs and the summer verbena is now twixt flower and berry. Promise and hope are everywhere to be found here as I catch sight of some white azaleas, survivors from the previous spring. Protected in their rotund terracotta pots, chances are that they will make it through the cooler months into yet another year.

Such delights of seasons past are mere bedfellows, however, to the true stars of the autumn and winter months: the tree laden with cachi (a member of the persimmon family) with their beautiful bright fruit hanging like the golden apples of Hesperides and the ripe black fruit of the olive waiting in anticipation of their harvest in the colder months of November and December. Long shadows of autumnal sun stretch across the yellow-orange stuccoed walls of the pensione and the only sound is the strimming of vegetation in the distance. Thoughts come with such ease in this oasis of calm and I quickly transfer them into my notebook. No sooner have I done so than once more I am distracted by a further vision of loveliness. I allow my eyes to feast upon the scene before me: a basin of silvery-blue green olive trees, and beyond, a thin belt of umbrella pine trees and other tall trees the identity of which I am uncertain. The whole is punctuated by tall dark-green cypresses which stand like sentries guarding the gentle slopes. Villas dotted amongst the landscape form a thick girdle around the city. It is a view that is worth savouring forever. All at once a church bell tolls somewhere in the distance. Some butterflies dance playfully over some blue-lilac plumbago flowers and I watch them until they disappear out of sight. We revel in all the magnificence that this place affords until the sun retires for the day. At which point, as though in the theatre when the scenery is changed, we are rewarded with one further pleasure, the setting of the sun. We watch intently as the sun's warm, yellow glow sinks deep into the horizon. We are reminded that although the day has come to an end there is the promise of a new day ahead with all that it has to offer.

As I indulge in the glory of everything I have almost forgotten to add that this paradise on earth has actually a part to play in the story of Annalena, albeit small. The property once belonged to the ancient Florentine family of the Valori, the very same family that included Niccolo di Bartolomeo Valori who was present at the marriage of Annalena and Baldaccio. Indeed, perhaps it has been no mere coincidence after all that we should have fallen in love with this place.

For the 'umpteenth' time I am sitting writing at the patio table on the verandah of the 'Writer's Room' in the Hotel Annalena. I pause for a moment and close the book in which I have been scribbling and rest my pen upon its cover. I take time to survey my surroundings and to listen to the birdsong above me. I savour the cool air that circulates around and breathe it in deeply, filling my lungs so that I may retain forever a small part of this place that Annalena once breathed. Once again I marvel at the thought that this site has endured so much history and so many changes over the centuries. Of one thing I am sure, though: as certain as night follows day the centuries will forever march forward and onwards, and the 'Casa di Annalena' and the site on which Annalena's convent once stood will bear witness to further changes in the future. For this reason I rest content in the knowledge that I will have played some small part in recording for posterity the life of Annalena Malatesta and the convent that she founded. Building upon a sentiment that can be found in that quaint little book which was written in the 1950s by Elsa Dawson, I feel honoured to have been one of the 'chosen few' to whom Annalena has revealed her love and appreciation and it is with her blessing that I have told her story. It would be Annalena's name that would live on and ultimately leave an indelible mark upon the city of Florence whilst the names of other foundresses of convents would fade into obscurity.

The year 2020 was especially significant since it marked the 600th anniversary of Annalena's birth. Let me leave you dear reader with some prophetic words about Annalena written by Niccolo Machiavelli in his *Florentine Histories*: '... *La cui memoria, per il munistero creato e nominato da lei, come al presente vive, cosi vivera sempre...*' translated as '... the convent which she founded, and which was named after her, will preserve her memory forever...'

Postscript

Shortly before the completion and publication of this book, the Hotel Annalena came under new management. Perhaps somewhat sooner than I had ever imagined, but nevertheless it serves to remind us that, just as I alluded to in the paragraph above, 'time stands still for no man'.

The year 2019 marked the centenary of the Hotel Annalena and the beginning of a new chapter in the life of the hotel. The new managers have made improvements to the former interior appearance and condition of the hotel and revised some details of its historical background contained in their original brochure. Therefore, as a result, some descriptions that I have included in my narrative may have changed. With its new updated image, the current owners have worked hard to ensure that this immensely important, historical hotel in the city of Florence will endure well into the future and continue to attract guests from all over the world. Despite the move towards a more modern image I was pleased to see that the new managers had not erased the legacy of Annalena from their vision, far from it. On a recent visit to the hotel at the end of 2019, a new sign had just been hammered into place across the front of the hotel reception desk. The name 'Annalena Malatesta', written in old Italian script, was quite literally 'front of house' for everyone to see, and a reminder of the building's history. Notes about Annalena and personages from her time also pervade the corridors leaving the guest unable to escape her presence.

Continuity and change are strange bedfellows but bedfellows all the same. No matter what changes may occur, the story of Annalena and the convent that she founded, I am happy to say, will live on for always in this great city of Florence.

Selected bibliography

Albertini, F.: Memorial of many statues and paintings in the illustrious city of Florence (1510). Modern edition, Centro di Firenze, 2010

Berti, P.: Carta degli sponsali di Annalena Malatesta con Baldaccio d'Anghiari, Archivio Storico Italiano, Nuova Serie, Vol. 5, No.1 (9), Giornale Storico degli Archivi Toscani: Anno I. Dispensa Prima, pp.42–49, 1857

Brocchi, G.M.: Vite de' santi e beati fiorentini scritte dal dottor Giuseppe Brocchi. Parte Seconda. Gaetano Albizini, 1761

Buonsignori, S.: Gazeteer of sixteenth century Florence, 1584/94. http://cds.library.brown. edu/projects/florentine_gazetteer/

Catasto: 1427 and 1442. In the Archivio di Stato di Firenze (State Archives, Florence; ASF)

Cavalcanti, G.: Istorie Fiorentine, 1838/9

Ciaroni, A. and Avery, C.: Dai Medici al Bargello: I bronzi del Rinascimento, il Quattrocento, Volume Secondo, 2007

Ciseri, I. and Marini, M.: 150 Anni del Museo Nazionale del Bargello, 2015

Collegiata di' Orsanmichele, Acquisti Medici-Tornacini. In the Archivio di Stato di Firenze (State Archives, Florence; ASF)

Coonin, V.A.: New Documents concerning Desiderio da Settignano and Annalena Malatesta. The Burlington Magazine, CXXXVII, 1995, 792–799

Cosmographia di Tolomeo: Tolomeo map dated *c.*1469 made by Petro del Massaio (Cod.Vat. Lat. 5699)

Dawson, E.M.: The Story of the Palazzo Convent of Annalena. Printed by Giulio Giannini &

Son, 1958 and later edition

Della Robia, E.V.: Nei Monasteri Fiorentini, Sansoni, Firenze, 1946

Del Lungo, I.: Women of Florence (translated by Steegmann, M.G), 1907

D'Urso, G. (ed.): La nave spirituale di S. Antoninus Pierozzi domenicano arcivescovo di Firenze, 1998

De Witt, A.: La Pieta di Paolo Uccello affresco che trovasi nella casa di Baldaccio d'Anghiari e di Annalena Malatesta al num. 24 di Via Romana in Firenze. Oggi proprieta de Signor Barone Bartolomeo Guitera De Bozzi. 1886

Forti, G.: Annalena Malatesta, Storia Fiorentina Del Secolo XV, In Rassegna Nazionale, Vol.172, pp.404-418, 1910

Kent, D.: Cosimo de' Medici and the Florentine Renaissance: The Patron's Oeuvre, Yale University Press, 2000

Klapisch-Zuber, C.: Women, Family, and Ritual in Renaissance Italy. University of Chicago Press, 1985

Litta, P.: Famiglie celebri di Italia.1819–1883

Llewellyn, L.: PhD thesis, Courtauld Institute, London. Art, Community and Religious Women in the Oltrarno, Florence. The early visual culture of the convents of Santa Monica, Santa Chiara and the Annalena. 2016/17

Machiavelli, N.: Le Istorie Fiorentine, ed. Barbera, 1888

Machiavelli, N: History of Florence. Commentary by Hugo Albert Rennert Ph.D. 2006

Magnelli, F.: Pianta della città di Firenze, surveyed in 1783, engraved by C. Zocchi

Mallett, M.: Mercenaries and their masters: warfare in Renaissance Italy, Pen and Sword Military, 2009

Manescalchi, R.: Il Battesimo di Piero della Francesca dov'era collocato? Chi lo commissionò? La soluzione Manescalchi, Stilearte.it, September 12th, 2018

Manni, D.M.: Notizie della ven. immagine di Maria Vergine della palla che si conserva da lungo tempo nel monastero di Annalena di Firenze, 1763

Newbigin, N.: I Giornali di Ser Giusto Giusti d'Anghiari (1437–1482): Edition, Letteratura italiana antica, 2004

Passerini, L.: Baldaccio da Anghiari. Florence, 1866

Pensione Annalena: Brochure and leaflet

Reali, O. et al: Il Teatro Goldoni a Firenze. Bolletino degli Ingegneri, Vol 15, No.10, pp 3–17, 1967

Richa, G.: Notizie istoriche delle chiese fiorentine divise ne' suoi quartieri. Firenze: Viviani, 1754–1762. (Volume 10, Quartiere di S. Spirito. 1762)

Ruggieri, F.: Pianta Della Citta Di Firenze, 1847

Scaglia, G.: 'Three Renaissance Drawings of church facades' Art Bulletin, Vol 47, pp.173–185, 1965

Selected bibliography

Scott, L.: Echoes of Old Florence. Her Palaces and Those Who Have Lived in Them, 1894

Solum, S.: Attributing influence: The Problem of Female Patronage, in Fifteenth-Century Florence. The Art Bulletin, Vol.90, pp.76–100, 2008

Solum, S.: Women, Patronage, and Salvation in Renaissance Florence: Lucrezia Tornabuoni and the Chapel of the Medici Palace (Visual Culture in Early Modernity), 2015

Strocchia, S.T.: Learning the Virtues: Convent Schools and Female Culture in Renaissance Florence, Garland, 1999

Strocchia, S.T.: Nuns and Nunneries in Renaissance Florence, Johns Hopkins University Press, 2009

Strocchia, S.T.: The Nun Apothecaries of Renaissance Florence: Marketing Medicines in the Convent. Renaissance Studies, Vol.25, pp.627–647, 2011

Strocchia, S.T.: Abbess Piera de' Medici and her Kin: Gender, Gifts, and Patronage in Renaissance Florence. https://doi.org/10.1111/rest.12043, 2013

Taglieschi, L.: Reprinted from Memorie Historiche e Annali della Terra d'Anghiari. In Archivio del Convento dei Servi di Maria di Sansepolcro. 17th Century

Thomas, A.: Art and Piety in the Female Religious Communities of Renaissance Italy: Iconography, Space, and the Religious Woman's Perspective. Cambridge University Press, 2003

Thouar, P.: Racconti Storici, Firenze, 1888

Tonini, L.: Della Storia Civile e Sacra Riminese, III, Rimini, 1862

Trachtenberg, M.: Archaeology, Merriment, and Murder: The First Cortile of the Palazzo Vecchio and its Transformations in the Late Florentine Republic. The Art Bulletin Vol. 71, No. 4 (Dec. 1989), pp.565–609

Vivarelli-Colonna, L.: Annalena Malatesta, La Contessa d'Anguillara. Storia ai tempi della Repubblica di Firenze, 1877

Waldeman, L.A.: The Mary Magdalen in Santa Trinita by Desiderio da Settignano and Giovanni d'Andrea. Pantheon LVIII pp.13–18, 2000

Zippel, G.: Le Monache d'Annalena e il Savonarola, 1901

Index